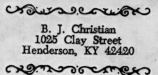

The JOY of Signing

Lottie L. Riekehof

•

The New
Illustrated Guide for Mastering
Sign Language and the Manual Alphabet

GPH

GOSPEL PUBLISHING HOUSE
Springfield, Missouri 65802

02-0518

ACKNOWLEDGMENTS

Without the assistance and encouragement of many persons, this book would not have become a reality. My deepest appreciation is here expressed to:

Pearl Goings, the artist who spent many evenings and Saturdays working with me drawing new pictures and updating those that had originally been prepared by Betty Stewart for *Talk to the Deaf.*

Sandy Flower, who devoted many hours to the final inking of the line drawings.

Linda Martin, who patiently served as sounding board, script reader, critiquer, and who suggested the present format which makes the book readable and clear.

Wayne Warner, book editor at the Gospel Publishing House, for guidance along the way; and **Nancy Stevens,** for the final editing.

David Johnston, publisher, who believed in the concept of a sign book in 1963 when no book with line drawings of signs had ever been published and who strongly encouraged the preparation of another volume.

My many deaf friends whose signing skills were an inspiration to me. Their knowledge of sign language, corrections of my signs, explanations, discussions of origins and most of all their acceptance of me as a hearing person brought about the original work and this revision.

Finally, to my many friends who were understanding of my periods of hibernation in order that "the book" could be completed.

© Copyright 1978 by the Gospel Publishing House, 1445 Boonville Avenue, Springfield, Missouri 65802

2nd Printing 1978

Library of Congress Cataloging in Publication Data

Riekehof, Lottie L
  The joy of signing.

  Published in 1963 under title: Talk to the deaf.
  Bibliography: p.
  Includes index.
  1. Sign language. 2. Deaf—Means of communication.
I. Title.
HV2474.R53 1978   001.56   77-83947
ISBN 0-88243-518-3

Printed in the United States of America

Contents

Introduction

The need for an updated manual of signs as used by the adult deaf population became apparent and *The Joy of Signing* was prepared with much of the basic material that appeared in the author's previous texts, *Talk to the Deaf* (1963) and *The American Sign Language* (1961). Vocabulary, pictures, and origins were added, revisions were made, and a new feature was added: usage of the sign in context.

The signs that have been added are not inventions of the author but are signs that were observed to be in use by deaf persons and by professional interpreters with whom the author associated not only at Gallaudet College and in the Washington, D.C. area but also in other parts of the country. Intended as a basic text for anyone wishing to communicate with deaf people, this manual also provides the basic vocabulary needed for persons entering interpreter training programs.

The sign language is a living, growing language and as is true with spoken languages, vocabulary will continue to be added. The adult deaf population is interested in an enlarged sign vocabulary but not in unnecessary innovations, initializations, and markers, particularly if the traditional basic sign provides sufficient clarity. The section of this manual covering word endings and word-form changes will explain this further and will point out markers that have been in use over the years as well as those now recommended for use in some educational settings.

The Joy of Signing does not attempt to include the many new signs developed in recent years for use with children, but is meant to provide the learner with knowledge of the basic traditional signs used by adult deaf persons today and with knowledge concerning the base from which new signs were developed. This knowledge will give the signer a means of judging whether some of the new signs are actually conceptually based or not. This is not to say that all "new" nonconceptually based signs are unacceptable, but it is important to know the basic signs that are acceptable to the deaf adult before venturing into newer signs and systems.

There have been varying reactions to some of the "new" signs appearing in various texts today, and the general consensus among deaf adults is that new signs that are conceptually based have a place, particularly for deaf children who should have as much language stimulation as possible in as precise a form as possible and in as many modes as possible in order to provide them with the language tools they will need for their educational development.

All of the signs listed in this manual are not used by all deaf people, just as all words in a dictionary are not in the everyday vocabulary of hearing people. The number of signs in one's vocabulary is not as important as the proper use of the signs one knows. A sign does not exist for every word in the English language but a good signer will know how to choose the most appropriate sign and the one that most nearly expresses the desired thought.

When a sign cannot be found to portray the exact meaning, fingerspelling is perfectly acceptable. Although beginners find this a chore, experienced signers frequently fingerspell even words that do have signs. Certain short words such as car, bus, and job are usually fingerspelled. It is not necessary to find or to invent signs for such short words since the fingerspelled configuration is read as a sign.

4

Signs in this manual have been grouped by chapter into natural categories but the search for an individual sign is best made by using the index which provides an alphabetical listing. If the word for which you are searching is not listed, look for the word closest in meaning and check the usage in that entry to see whether it would be an appropriate choice. This manual contains a number of synonyms for many of the entries but is by no means meant to be exhaustive. The group of words listed for an entry will give you a general idea of the words that are included in the concept being signed. Close observation of the ways deaf people use signs is the best way to improve your own skill.

Using the Manual

To learn signs accurately from this manual, it is important to study the complete entry. First, look at the picture to get a general idea of the sign (remembering that the front view presents a mirror image and is therefore pictured in reverse to the reader). Next, read the origin of the sign so you will understand the reason for a particular sign formation. Often the relationship between a sign and its meaning is quite obvious. When the origin is understood, a sign is more easily remembered.

An attempt has been made to not only present a clear drawing but also to provide a step-by-step description of the hand positions and movements. It is important to read the description to see whether you are making the sign properly. Now that you have learned how to make the sign, repeat it and say the word that goes with it. Make the sign several times, speaking the word each time so you become accustomed to signing and speaking simultaneously.

Read the sentences that show you the proper usage of the word. Simply listing a word alone does not provide the learner with sufficient information. Contextual phrases and sentences are included not only to provide meaning but also to give you practice material. Try signing the sentences and fingerspell the words for which you have not yet learned signs. Phrases and sentences for each entry in this manual have been prepared in straight English form. However, a good sign language teacher will be able to take these sentences, enlarge upon them, and demonstrate ways to change them into the ASL pattern (as explained in the section "The Language Pattern of Signs").

The order in which signs are learned is up to the signer or the teacher. It is suggested that signs having an obvious relationship to their meaning be learned first since the signer will feel more comfortable with such natural signs. Sports and foods are both categories in which natural motions are made and it is suggested that these be among the first to be studied.

Enjoy signing—it is more than a means of communication. Signing frees you to express yourself in a natural way. It is the author's pleasure to introduce you to *The Joy of Signing!*

History of Sign Language and Fingerspelling

The language of signs used by deaf people in the United States was brought to America from France early in the 19th century. In 1815 a group of men in Hartford, Connecticut became interested in the establishment of a school for deaf children but lacked information on the proper means of educating the deaf. One of these gentlemen, Dr. Mason Cogswell, was particularly interested since his own daughter Alice was deaf and had been taught on an experimental basis by a young minister, Dr. Thomas Hopkins Gallaudet.

As a result, Dr. Gallaudet was sent abroad to investigate methods then being used in England. His efforts there met with failure until he was introduced to the Abbe Sicard in London who invited him to cross the Channel and visit his school in Paris which had been founded in 1755 by the Abbe de l'Eppe. The Abbe, who is said to have been the inventor of the sign language, eventually published a volume describing both his sign system and his method of educating the deaf.

After Dr. Gallaudet had spent several months studying educational methods as well as signs, he was ready to return to America. Accompanying him was a young deaf instructor from the French school, Laurent Clerc, who had proved most helpful and who agreed to assist in the new American school. In America the French sign language was enlarged and modified, eventually becoming the basis of the American language of signs which today is considered one of the most refined and complete sign systems in the world.

The first permanent school for the deaf was established in Hartford, Connecticut in 1817. It was many years later, after Thomas Hop-

kins Gallaudet had seen the establishment of a number of schools for the deaf across the United States, that he also envisioned the establishment of a college. This dream was passed on to his son, Edward Miner Gallaudet, who was responsible for establishing Gallaudet College, the world's first and only college for deaf students located in Washington, D.C. The charter for the college was signed in 1864 by President Abraham Lincoln.

Fingerspelling, the use of hand positions to represent the letters of the alphabet, is much older than the language of signs. The positions of the fingers of the hand do, to some extent, resemble the printed letters of the alphabet. Illustrations of the manual alphabet have been found to exist early in the Christian era. Latin Bibles of the 10th century show drawings of such hand positions and it is known that persons who lived in enforced silence, such as monks of the Middle Ages, used fingerspelling as a means of communication. Most of the European countries use a single-handed alphabet while England's alphabet requires the use of two hands. Today each country that has a manual alphabet uses its own version, which is therefore understood only by users of that particular system.

The question is often asked whether the sign language is universal. Although signs are used in many countries, each has developed its own system which has been standardized to some extent within that country. In recent years, an international sign language has been developed that crosses national barriers and permits communication between deaf persons of many countries. It is useful for international events such as conferences and Olympic Games for the Deaf. It is a known fact that persons who understand the language of signs find they can communicate with deaf persons across language barriers more easily than is possible with hearing people using spoken languages.

In educational circles the language of signs is gaining respectability and a number of colleges and universities are now accepting proficiency in signs in fulfillment of the doctoral requirement for proficiency in a foreign language. Among the colleges that have accepted sign language in place of another language are New York University, American University, and the University of Minnesota.

The sign language is looked upon by some as a new art form and is used in performances by the National Theater of the Deaf, a professional drama group, as a means of presenting deaf people and their language to a hearing world. Also being introduced is signed interpretation of music, a beautiful and expressive means of portraying the feeling, emotion, and rhythm of songs. Both deaf and hearing people are enjoying new experiences through communicating in the language of signs, making it possible for them to live together with true understanding and mutual enrichment.

Terminology

Adventitiously Deaf—Those who are born with normal hearing but in whom the sense of hearing becomes nonfunctional later through illness or accident.

Audiogram—A graph on which hearing test results are recorded.

Congenitally Deaf—Those who are born deaf.

Deaf—Those in whom the sense of hearing is nonfunctional for the ordinary purposes of life.

Expressive Skill—The ability to express oneself in the language of signs and fingerspelling.

Fingerspelling (also called **The Rochester Method**)—Use of the manual alphabet to form words or sentences.

Hard-of-hearing—Those in whom the sense of hearing, although defective, is functional with or without a hearing aid.

Interpreting—A signed and fingerspelled presentation of another person's spoken communication.

Lipreading, Speechreading—The ability to understand the oral language or speech of a person through observation of his lip movement and facial expression.

Manual Alphabet—The 26 different single-hand positions representing the 26 letters of the alphabet.

Manual Communication—Communication by use of signs and fingerspelling.

Oralism, Oral Training—A method of training or educating a deaf person through speech and speechreading without employing the language of signs or fingerspelling.

Post-lingual Deaf—Those who become deaf after language is acquired.

Prelingual Deaf—Those who become deaf before language skills are acquired.

Receptive Skill—The ability to understand what is expressed in both fingerspelling and in the language of signs.

Reverse Interpreting—An oral presentation of another person's signed and fingerspelled communication.

Sign Language—A language that uses manual symbols to represent ideas and concepts. The term is usually used to describe the language used by deaf people in which both manual signs and fingerspelling are employed.

Simultaneous Communication—The use of manual communication simultaneously with oral communication.

Simultaneous Method—A method of training or educating deaf persons through the simultaneous use of manual and oral communication.

Total Communication—A philosophy of educating the deaf child which advocates the use of any and all means of communication to provide unlimited opportunity to develop language competence. Included are the following: speech, amplification (hearing aids), speechreading, gesturing, signs, fingerspelling, pantomime, reading, writing, pictures, and any other possible means of conveying ideas, language, and vocabulary.

The Art of Signing

You, the new learner, are embarking on a journey into a community that enjoys communication. You have decided that signs are important and should be learned. Your enthusiasm is high and your first course in signs will give you the skills with which to begin conversing with deaf people.

As is true with any language, the more one speaks with a native user of the language, the more fluent one becomes. If you will associate with adult deaf people, carry on conversations, attend their social and athletic events, you will find your communication skills improving rapidly within a short time. However, one should usually count on a period of 1 or 2 years before attaining an adequate level of competency. To become a proficient interpreter for the deaf, an additional learning period of 1 or 2 years is required.

Variations in Signs

The signs described in this manual are a compilation of those most commonly used among the American deaf people. For the most part, these signs are the ones used and understood in all parts of the country. However, as is true with the spoken language, regional differences do exist and it is not difficult to adjust to them.

There is also a variation in the way different people make the same sign. The sign "see" for instance, is taught as proceeding from the eyes. However, some signers have a habit of making this sign at the side of the face or even letting the fingertips touch the right cheek. Such variations are quite normal and should be expected. It may be difficult for the beginning sign-language student to adjust to seeing signs made somewhat differently from the way he was taught in the classroom but it is important to be flexible about this and to be patient in the process.

Combining Signs, Speech, and Fingerspelling

As you sign and fingerspell, it is important to develop the skill of speaking and signing at the same time (called the simultaneous method of communication). This is not a simple matter, particularly for those who have a habit of speaking rapidly and who would therefore have difficulty in maintaining a smooth flow of language while attempting to combine the two modes of communication. The sign should begin at the same time the word is spoken. This is true also of fingerspelling but this is, of course, more difficult. (Further explanation of combining speech with fingerspelling is covered in the section on fingerspelling.) Interpreters do not vocalize while signing but do form words on the lips.

The concept of speaking or of forming words on the lips is emphasized to a much greater extent today than it was in the early days of sign language when speech was not as much a part of the deaf child's training. Since deaf children are taught speech and lipreading (also called speechreading) very early, it is important for all signers either to vocalize or to use the lips at all times. Signers are cautioned, however, not to engage in exaggerated mouthing of words. Only the normal amount of lip movement is necessary. Those whose lip movements are difficult to read should attempt to develop the necessary clarity if they intend to work with deaf people in any extensive capacity.

Initializing Signs

There is a growing trend to initialize signs, that is, to begin the sign with the first letter of the desired word. This makes it possible for the signer to be specific in portraying the exact word instead of making a sign that represents a concept and could therefore be used for any one of three or four words.

An example is the basic sign for "group" which can be initialized to form the following words: family, organization, class, department, society, association, group, workshop, team. The basic concept remains while the letter of the alphabet used to begin the sign distinguishes each one to give the exact word. Initializing is helpful and acceptable if it is not overdone. In other words, an initial should not be added if the sign already has a specific meaning. The sign for "happen," for instance, is always read as such and does not require the initial "h" to clarify it.

Plurals and Tenses

When signing with adult deaf persons no special word endings are needed to show the plural form since context usually provides this information. Sometimes a sign is repeated several times to represent the plural form. Tense is usually obvious from context but past tense can be shown by adding the sign "finished" or "past."

Grammatical Forms

No difference is shown for the different grammatical forms of the same word and usually the noun, adjective, and adverb will be signed exactly alike. As an example, "love," "loving," and "lovingly" are all signed in the same way but lip movement and context give clues as to the intended form. Traditionally, a sign for the suffix "er" has been added to denote a person (law—lawyer; sing—singer). Also in common use is the signed suffix "er" or "est" forming the comparative (warm—warmer—warmest). Some current sign systems advocate the use of additional markers or fingerspelled endings to facilitate learning in educational settings. These are described in chapter 2.

Possessives

Possessives are indicated by adding an "s" to the end of the fingerspelled or signed word and twisting the wrist so that the fingers and thumb are facing up, still in the "s" position.

Facial Expression and Body Language

Facial expression and body language are equally as important as the hand positions, if not more so. It is necessary that all of these be coordinated to properly convey the intended meaning. Signs showing emotions such as happiness or sadness should show the appropriate expression on the face. When the sign "tired" is made, the whole body indicates a sag, while the sign for "strong" calls for a show of strength by throwing the body back and the chest forward.

Head movement and facial expression can completely change the meaning of a sign. For instance, when the sign for "like" is accompanied by a pleasant expression it is clearly indicative of enjoyment, while exactly the same sign accompanied by a negative shaking of the head will portray dislike. Deaf persons do not focus so much on reading each other's hands as they do on reading the face and the overall body language.

Speed, Motion, and Force of Signs

A sign can be made slowly or with speed, it can be static or have motion, it can be made gently or with force. All of these elements are an important part of portraying the full meaning of your message. You may "love" a person by gently crossing your hands over your chest or you may indicate a stronger feeling by clasping the hands more tightly to the chest and even adding a rocking motion. The sign for "beautiful" takes on different shades of meaning when facial expression, size, strength, and feeling are added in varying degrees. The spoken equivalent of the word will then be one of the following: lovely, pretty, attractive, beautiful, or gorgeous.

Speed of the sign also influences meaning. For example, the sign "hurry" is moved more rapidly when one is saying, "Hurry, we're leaving now," than when saying, "Don't hurry, we have plenty of time." When the sign for "growing up" is made (raising the down-turned palm) a difference is shown in using the phrase in the following statements: "My boy is beginning to grow up now," and, "It seems as if my son grew up overnight!" In the latter, the sign is made with a faster and higher upward movement. The sign for "require" becomes "demand" when made more forcibly. The more forceful the sign and the stronger the facial expression, the stronger the feeling in either the positive or negative direction.

Signers are cautioned not to use excessive

9

motion but to limit the movement to that which is necessary to make the sign clear, unless some type of emphasis is intended. Unusually large, flowing motion may be desired for a particular type of oratory, but crisp, precise signs are desirable for ordinary conversation and speeches.

Signs follow each other in a natural sort of progression and a pause is made at the end of a thought. The pause is equivalent to the drop in voice that usually comes at the end of a sentence.

Direction of the Sign

Direction is an integral part of the language of signs. The same sign made in different directions can give opposite meanings. "Give," for instance, can be moved away from you to indicate you are giving to someone else, but moved toward you to show someone is giving to you. The sign "there" simply points in the intended direction. The points of the compass (north, south, east, and west) are signed by moving the initial letter in the appropriate direction.

Spatial Relationships and Background

The position of the hand when signing and fingerspelling is usually in front of the chest in a comfortable location. The clothing becomes the backdrop against which signs are read and it is therefore desirable when signing for a considerable length of time to wear a solid color that is in contrast to the skin color of the hands. The eyes of the reader tire quickly and signers should be considerate of their audience in this respect. In this category are interpreters, teachers, and speakers who must be read by deaf people for long periods of time. A good solid contrasting color of clothing as well as a background that is free of design will help alleviate eye strain on the part of the reader.

The size of your signs will be determined by the number of people for whom you are signing and the distance to be covered. Signs should be increased in size according to the increase in the number of persons reading signs and the distance to be covered. On a one-to-one basis, or for very small groups, signs do not extend much beyond the body area. The larger the group and the greater the distance to be covered, the less fingerspelling is advisable since there is no way to enlarge the fingerspelled configuration. Although the human voice can be amplified electronically, signs can only be amplified by increasing their size. As signs increase in size, they are also paced somewhat less rapidly in order to facilitate understanding.

Left-handed or Right-handed Signing

Signs are pictured in this manual for the right-handed individual but should be made in reverse by those who are left-handed. For those who say they could sign either way, it will be important to make a decision during the first lesson. It is suggested that such persons try some fingerspelling and signs first with one hand and then with the other, then decide which is most comfortable and proceed with the dominant hand. It is not a good practice to make some signs with one hand and some with the other unless this is done as a means of showing a spatial relationship or for other special emphasis.

Understanding Signs

It is common for new signers to have difficulty understanding other persons signing to them. This is true with spoken languages as well. You may have learned French and felt you spoke it very well only to find you were not able to understand a word the Frenchman said to you when you arrived in Paris. To understand native users of any language requires exposure over a period of time. Do not be discouraged by this problem if you encounter it. It requires skill as well as a keen mind and a quick eye. Magicians say, "The hand is quicker than the eye," and this often seems to be the case when hands and fingers are moving very rapidly.

Deaf people will be patient with you when you do not understand them but you will have to be patient with yourself as well. Association with users of sign language is the best way to improve your receptive skill. When available, films and videotapes of signers are also helpful in improving your understanding of this language.

Importance of Signing

Deaf people recognize the importance of signing since it is their means of daily communication within the family and with the deaf community. It has been called "the mother tongue" of deaf people and is as valuable for social interaction as is speaking to the hearing person. Even deaf children are able to express their wants by means of simple signs long before they are able to speak.

Hearing children of deaf parents have been known to communicate their wants to parents by means of a few simple signs before the age of 1, which is earlier than they are normally able to express their needs by means of speech. Early use of signs will stimulate the mind and lessen the frustration that so often accompanies deafness with its communication barrier.

The usefulness of sign language extends beyond the realm of the deaf, for it has been found useful by people with speech loss due to accidents or neurological problems, by laryngectomees, and even by divers for underwater communication. In fact, the full extent of its usefulness has yet to be explored.

The Language Pattern of Signs

The signs contained in this manual may be used in either the grammatical word order of the English language or in ASL (American Sign Language, also called AMESLAN), which has its own grammatical system and other distinguishing features. A brief explanation follows:

Signing in English Grammatical Word Order

In this system, signs are simply added to words as they are spoken in the English grammatical order. Within this system are two subsystems: First is that used by those deaf adults who follow the grammatical order of the English language but who do not sign articles or infinitives and who use shortcuts, using one sign to represent several words. Also included is some ASL (described in this section). It is important to recognize that there is a great deal of language variation within this subsystem based on background experiences, deafness in family members, education, age, region of the country, and other factors.

The second subsystem is the method being promoted by some educators, formalizing signs into a system that parallels the English language exactly through the use of markers (prefixes, suffixes, plural endings, tenses, and various word-form changes). Also included are signs to designate articles and infinitives. This use of English along with signs, markers, and fingerspelling is generally supported for classroom use in order to give students an exact representation of the English language.

This manual contains a section showing the markers that have been used traditionally by the deaf and another section showing the newer markers which are not generally needed or used by adults. Deaf adults have not, as a rule, felt it necessary to include the newer markers as a part of their every-day language even when using some form of manual English. Some of the terms used to describe the use of signs along with formal English are the following: manual English, straight English, signed English, and signing exact English.

Signing in the American Sign Language Pattern (ASL or AMESLAN)

Linguists are studying the pattern used by deaf persons when they communicate in ASL. Studies are showing that this is indeed a unique and recognizable language that has its own grammatical pattern. A brief description of some of the characteristics of ASL follows:

1) ASL condenses wherever possible and often makes use of facial expression and body language rather than words to convey nuances.
2) ASL omits articles (a, an, the).
3) ASL often uses just one sign plus body and facial expression for a complete statement. Example: In reply to a question, an affirmative answer is often given by signing the word *finish*. This one sign, plus the intensity and expression with which it is made can mean any one of the following: "I've already done that." "Yes, I did." "Sure, I did that." "Of course I have!" "It's completed." "That's enough!"
4) ASL uses one sign concept to cover several English words. Example: Although the phrase "after a while" contains three words, it is made with one sign representing the concept "later." The sign for "past" can also mean "in the past," "once upon a time," or "a long time ago," depending on how large the sign is made.
5) ASL shows tense by context or by adding such signs as: past, finished, later, not yet, and after a while.
6) ASL presents short sentences in various word orders, any of which are acceptable.

11

The sentence: "I ate at noon," could be signed in any of the following ways: "finish eat noon," "noon finish eat," or "eat finish noon."

7) Long sentences seem to follow the time sequence in which the events occurred. While in English we would say: "I didn't get to work until noon yesterday because I had an accident," ASL users would say: "Yesterday happened me accident; work arrive noon."

8) ASL uses little fingerspelling.

The above are not meant to be hard-and-fast rules but are presented to give the new signer some insight into the ASL language pattern. Attempts are being made to formally describe ASL, and although it is being taught in some sign courses, the best way to become proficient in this method of communication is to socialize with deaf people who enjoy communicating in this language form which is truly their own. It should be pointed out that Ameslan is used by deaf persons with high verbal skills as well as by those with minimal language competency.

Combination of English and ASL

A combination of English and Ameslan is often seen. As a rule this takes place when English word order is being used and ASL phrases are thrown in for convenience.

Communicating Effectively

One of the important skills to be developed by the signer is that of communicating with each deaf person on an appropriate educational and cultural level in either the English or the ASL pattern. To determine the language level and language pattern used by a deaf person, it is necessary to carry on a conversation and watch for the amount of fingerspelling as well as the word order and the vocabulary level being used. Observe indications of understanding such as nods at appropriate places, a negative shaking of the head, a questioning look, or a slight frown. Check on yourself when you feel you are not being understood and, if necessary, start all over again, changing your pattern somewhat.

It will be observed that the more education a deaf person has had, the more he tends to fingerspell to convey the exact word he has in mind. Do not be embarrassed by having to repeat or by not being understood. Haven't you been misunderstood by your hearing friends and haven't they asked you to repeat at times also?

It is important to be aware of the fact that the deaf person's lack of competency in English usage is not a measure of his intelligence. English is a second language to those who lost their hearing before language was acquired (prelingual deafness) and it must therefore be learned artificially. Speech also is learned artificially, particularly by those deaf persons whose hearing loss is so severe that they do not benefit by the use of amplification. Good speech or the lack of it is also no measure of intelligence.

Deafness by its nature imposes an extremely severe educational handicap. Language is usually acquired by hearing and when this sense is impaired, language is learned through observing, by reading speech on the lips, by reading, and through intensive classroom work. The outcome is a wide difference in language facility among deaf people. In fact, some deaf persons are mistakenly thought of as mentally retarded when they are judged by their written work. The age at which deafness occurs is the factor that most greatly influences speech and language development.

Fingerspelling

Fingerspelling is an important part of the communication system of deaf persons. It is simply the American alphabet written in the air instead of on paper. There are 26 hand positions, some of which are exact representations of the printed block letter.

Fingerspelling is used in combination with the language of signs for proper nouns, names and addresses, and for words that have no sign. Its importance cannot be overrated and it is therefore essential for the beginner to concentrate on developing both expressive and receptive skills in order to become proficient.

Alexander Graham Bell, who appeared before a Royal Commission in 1888 to give evidence on teaching the deaf, commented: "For we want that method, whatever it is, that will give us the readiest and quickest means of bringing English words to the eyes of the deaf, and I know of no more expeditious means than a manual alphabet."

Hand Position

The palm of the hand should face the audience at a slight angle with the arm being held in a comfortable natural position. Since it is important to see lip movement, the hand should not be held in a position that will block the view of the mouth. Neither should the hand be held so far from the mouth that the lips cannot be read simultaneously with the fingerspelling.

Flow and Rhythm

Each letter should be made clearly, distinctly, and crisply with a slight pause between words. This pause is shown by holding the last letter of a word for a moment before beginning the first letter of the next word. The hands do not drop between words. If there is movement while fingerspelling, it should be a gradual move to the right but there is no need to bounce letters or to push letters forward in an attempt to be clear.

Some letters and combinations of letters are more easily made than others and there is often a tendency to spell these more rapidly than the more difficult ones but this is not advisable. It is not necessary to be concerned with speed since this is a natural by-product of practice. However, it is important to establish and maintain rhythm in fingerspelling since this aids readability.

Vocalization

The words you fingerspell should be spoken simultaneously but individual letters should not be vocalized. One- and two-syllable words present no problem but longer words are a challenge. It is possible to develop skill in simultaneous fingerspelled communication by practicing in syllabic units. (Interpreters use silent lip formation since vocalization would interfere with the speaker's presentation.)

Double Letters

When double letters are formed the hand is opened slightly before repeating the second letter of the series. Letters such as "c" and "l" are already open and are simply moved from left to right (or to the left if you are left-handed) with a very slight bounce. In other words, the repeated letter is not merely moved over to the right, since a clear separation is needed to indicate that the letter is being made twice. The movement for the letter "z" is simply repeated. Try the following words using the principles outlined above:

Aaron	soccer	beet	apple	rolling
cool	sunny	offer	hurry	letter
better	chubby	haggle	swimming	dazzle
summer	massive	padded	spelling	fizz

Capitalized Abbreviations

To distinguish a word from an abbreviation, it is necessary to circle the individual letters very slightly when they represent names of places, organizations, etc. Try a few: U.S.A.; N.A.D. (National Association of the Deaf); R.I.D. (Registry of Interpreters for the Deaf).

Reading Fingerspelling

Fingerspelling should be read in the same way you read the words on this page, in units instead of letter by letter. As you read fingerspelling, first short words and then longer ones, do not allow your partner in conversation to slow down when you do not understand, because this will tend to get you into the habit of reading letters instead of syllables or words. If you do not understand the word being spelled, ask the person with whom you are practicing to repeat at the same rate, even if a great deal of repetition is required. This forces you to read in word units and will increase your comprehension more rapidly.

Practice Hints

It is suggested that you begin fingerspelling two- and three-letter words, gradually increasing the length of words, breaking them down into syllables, until a smooth flow is attained. Speech or lip movement should always accompany fingerspelling and signs as you practice.

It would be well to find a partner with whom to fingerspell but if this is not possible try looking into a mirror. You will then see yourself as others do, you will become aware of word-unit formations, and you will also be surprised at the errors that will be clearly visible and that can be corrected before bad habits are formed.

The following are examples of one- and two-syllable words that will be helpful in developing your skill:

an	bat	ban	bane	date	dated
at	cat	can	cane	fate	hated
it	fat	Dan	dane	gate	fated
he	hat	fan	lane	hate	mated
of	mat	man	mane	late	rated
so	pat	pan	pane	mate	
as	rat	ran	wane	pate	
be	sat	tan		rate	
up	vat	van			

bet	bid	old	older	ham	cot
get	did	bold	bolder	jam	dot
jet	hid	cold	colder	Pam	got
met	lid	fold	folder	ram	hot
net	rid	gold	holder	Sam	jot
pet		hold	solder	tam	lot
set		mold			not
wet		sold			rot
		told			

For additional word lists and practice material see the bibliography for a reference to Guillory's manual, *Expressive and Receptive Fingerspelling for Hearing Adults.*

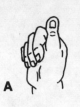 A

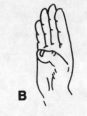 B

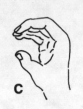 C

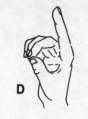 D

 E

 F

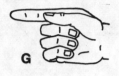 G

 H

 I

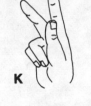 J

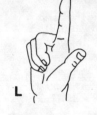 K

 L

 M

 N

 O

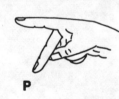 P

 Q

 R

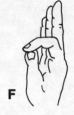 S

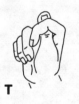 T

 U

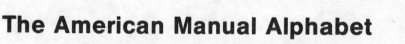 V

 W

X

Y

Z

The American Manual Alphabet

Drawings show a side view. In actual practice the letters should face the persons with whom you are communicating.

1
Family Relationships

MALE

Grasp the imaginary brim of a hat with four fingers and thumb.
Origin: Tipping the hat.
Usage: the first *male* in the family.
Note: Although this is primarily a basic sign intended as a prefix, it is often used alone to indicate any male.

FEMALE

Move the inside of the thumb of the right "A" down along the right cheek toward the chin.
Origin: Represents the old-fashioned bonnet string.
Usage: male and *female* applicants.
Note: Although this is primarily a basic sign intended as a prefix, it is often used alone to indicate any female.

MAN

Sign "MALE"; then bring the flat hand, palm down, away from the head at the level of the hat.
Origin: Indicating the height of the male.
Usage: *man* of the house.
Note: The sign listed for "gentleman" is often used instead.

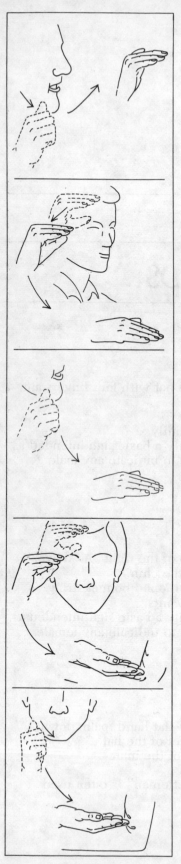

WOMAN

Sign "FEMALE"; then bring the flat hand, palm down, away from the face at the level of the cheek.
Origin: Indicating the height of the woman.
Usage: a young *woman*.
Note: The sign listed for "lady" is often used instead.

BOY

Sign "MALE"; then bring the right open hand down to about waist level, palm down.
Origin: A male of small stature.
Usage: an active *boy*.
Note: The hand would be brought considerably lower for a 3-year-old child than for a 12-year-old.

GIRL

Sign "FEMALE"; then bring the right open hand down to about waist level, palm down.
Origin: A female of small stature.
Usage: a pretty *girl*.
Note: See note under "boy."

SON

Sign "MALE"; then place right hand (palm up) in the crook of the left arm.
Origin: A male baby.
Usage: our only *son*.

DAUGHTER

Sign "FEMALE"; then place the right hand (palm up) in the crook of the left arm.
Origin: A female baby.
Usage: my successful *daughter*.

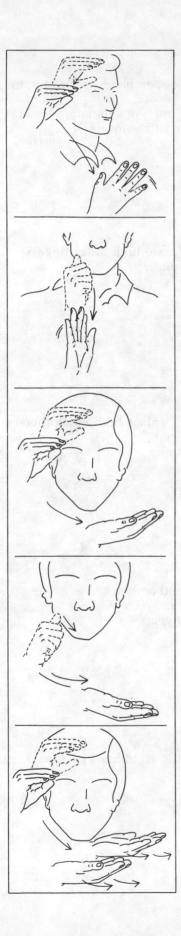

GENTLEMAN

Sign "MALE"; then make the sign for "FINE" (tip of "FIVE" hand at the chest).
Origin: A man with a ruffle is a gentleman.
Usage: a real *gentleman*.
Note: This sign is also used for "man."

LADY

Sign "FEMALE"; then make the sign for "FINE" (tip of the "FIVE" hand at the chest).
Origin: A lady with a ruffle.
Usage: *Ladies* and gentlemen.
Note: This sign is also used for "woman."

FATHER

Sign "MALE"; then open the right hand and move it toward the left, palm up. (Note: A small child makes this sign by placing the tip of the index finger on his forehead; the next step is placing the thumb of the "FIVE" hand on the forehead.)
Origin: Man holding a baby. (Originally made with two hands.)
Usage: *Father's* Day.

MOTHER

Sign "FEMALE"; then open the right hand and move it toward the left, palm up. (Note: A small child makes this sign by placing the tip of the index finger on his chin; the next step is placing the thumb of the "FIVE" hand on the chin.)
Origin: Woman holding a baby. (Originally made with two hands.)
Usage: a new *mother*.

GRANDFATHER

Sign "MALE"; then swing open hands, palms up, to the left twice just below chin level.
Origin: Same as for "father" but one generation back.
Usage: old *grandfather* clock.

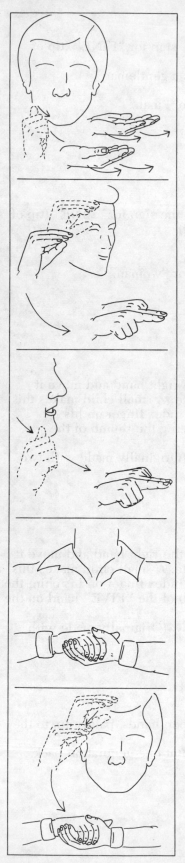

GRANDMOTHER

Sign "MOTHER"; then swing open hands, palms up, to the left twice just below chin level.
Origin: Same as for "mother" but one generation back.
Usage: *Grandmother* was babysitting for us.

BROTHER

Sign "MALE" and "SAME" (place both index fingers side by side, pointing to the front).
Origin: Male in the same family.
Usage: older *brother*.

SISTER

Sign "FEMALE" and "SAME" (place both index fingers side by side, pointing to the front).
Origin: Female in the same family.
Usage: youngest *sister*.

MARRY

Clasp the hands, with right hand on top.
Origin: Clasping the hands in marriage.
Usage: happily *married* for 10 years.

HUSBAND

Sign "MALE"; then clasp hands, right hand on top.
Origin: Male who is married.
Usage: a good *husband*.

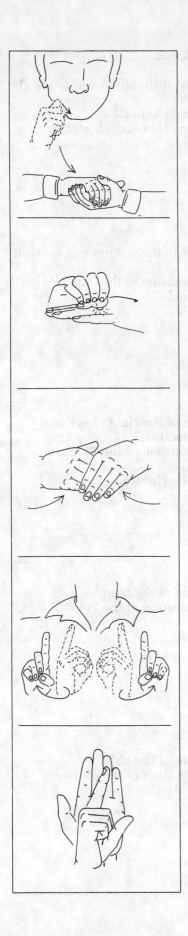

WIFE

Sign "FEMALE"; then clasp hands as in "MARRIAGE."
Origin: A female who is married.
Usage: my *wife's* parents.

ENGAGEMENT (To be married)

Place the right "E" on the fourth finger of the left hand.
Origin: The engagement ring is placed on the finger.
Usage: Beth is *engaged* to Don.

WEDDING

With palms facing the body and fingers pointing forward,
bring the right hand into the left between the thumb and
index finger; left hand grasps right.
Origin: Hands placed together in the wedding ceremony.
Usage: Eddie and Barbara had a beautiful *wedding*.

DIVORCE

Place the "D" hands before you, palms slightly inward,
and give them a quick twist outward and away from each
other ending with palm side out.
Origin: Initial hands moved away from each other
indicating a separation.
Usage: The *divorce* rate is high in America.

IN-LAW

Place the right "L" against the palm of the left hand.
Origin: This is the sign for "law" representing that which
is in the book.
Usage: Rosemary is my sister-*in-law*.

STEPMOTHER, STEPFATHER, etc.

Place the "L" before you, twist it slightly inward; add the sign for "mother," "father," etc.
Origin: Second mother or second father.
Usage: an understanding *stepmother* and *stepfather*.

UNCLE

Place the right "U" at the side of the temple and move it downward in a wavy motion.
Origin: An initial sign at the location of the "male" sign.
Usage: The kids like *Uncle* Hank.

AUNT

Place the right "A" at the side of the right cheek and move it downward in a wavy motion.
Origin: An initial sign at the location of the "female" sign.
Usage: *Aunt* Ruth is good to the children.

NEPHEW

Shake the letter "N" at the side of the temple.
Origin: An initial sign at the location of the "male" sign.
Usage: six *nephews*.

NIECE

Shake the letter "N" at the side of the chin.
Origin: An initial sign at the location of the "female" sign.
Usage: three *nieces*.

COUSIN

Shake the letter "C" at the side of the cheek.
Origin: An initial sign made between the locations of the "male" and the "female" signs.
Usage: eight *cousins*.

FAMILY

Place the "F" hands in front of you, palms facing forward; draw hands apart and away from you; turn until the little fingers touch.
Origin: An inital sign for a group.
Usage: Your *family* tree can be traced.

BABY, INFANT, CHILD

Place the right hand in the crook of the left arm and the left upturned hand under the right arm; then rock.
Origin: Rocking the baby.
Usage: *baby* girl.
mother and *infant*.
a month-old *child*.

CHILD, CHILDREN

Pat the head of an imaginary child. For the plural, repeat the motion several times.
Usage: an only *child*.
nine *children* in the family.

KID (informal)

Extend the little finger and index finger (other fingers and thumb closed); place the hand, palm-side down, just above the upper lip and wiggle the hand slightly.
Origin: Wiping the nose, as children often do.
Usage: "I started as an average *kid*, I finished as a thinkin' man" (Rudyard Kipling).

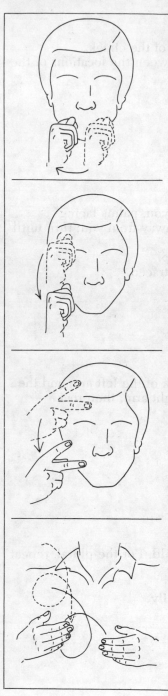

TWINS

Place the right "T" on the left side of the chin, then on the right.
Usage: pretty *twin* girls named Janna and Jenny.

ADULTS

Place the "A" at the side of the forehead, then at the side of the chin.
Origin: An initial sign at the location of the "male" and "female" signs.
Usage: The *adults* sat around talking.

PARENTS

Place the middle fingertip of the "P" hand at the side of the forehead, then on the side of the chin.
Origin: An initial sign at the location of the "mother" and "father" signs.
Usage: We all belong to a *parents'* organization.

GENERATION, DESCENDANTS, ANCESTORS, POSTERITY

Both open hands, palms facing back, come down from the right shoulder in a rolling motion. (Can be done in reverse also.)
Origin: The sign for "born" is repeated several times as it moves from past to present (or from present to past).
Usage: the next *generation; ancestors* from Ireland; many *descendants;* leave it for *posterity.*

2

Pronouns, Question Words, & Endings

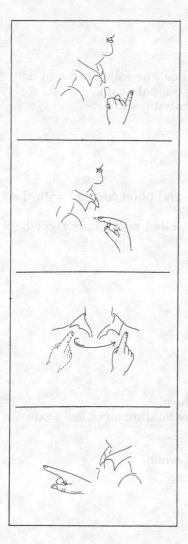

I

The "I" hand is placed at the chest.
Origin: Using the initial letter while indicating self.
Usage: *I* will go with you.

ME

Point the right index finger at yourself.
Origin: Indicating self.
Usage: Speak to *me*.
Note: This sign is also used for the personal pronoun "I."

WE, US

Place the index finger at the right shoulder and circle it forward and around until it touches the left shoulder. The initial "W" or "U" is used by some.
Origin: Pointing to self, then to others and back to self.
Usage: *we*, the people.
　　　　Come and help *us*.

YOU

Point the index finger out. For the plural, point the index finger out and move from left to right.
Origin: Natural sign.
Usage: *You* have one vote.
　　　　All of *you* are improving.

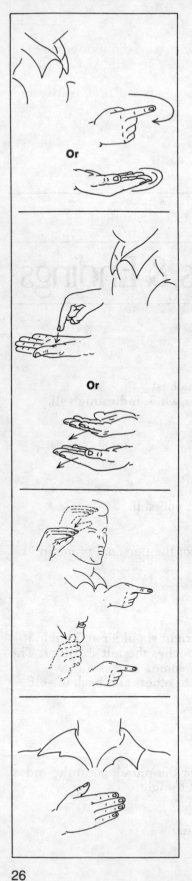

THEY, THEM, THOSE, THESE

Point the index finger toward the object and move it toward the right. Or, direct the upturned hand forward and right.
Origin: Indicating the object.
Usage: *they* agree.
      hear *them* sing.
      those chairs.
      these papers.

THIS

1) Place the tip of the right index finger into the left open palm.
Origin: Pointing to a specific object.
Usage: *This* is my book.

2) When indicating time and area, the following sign is used: Drop the hands before you, palms up.
Usage: Give us *this* day our daily bread.
      This farm is for sale.

HE, HIM, SHE, HER

Sign "MALE" or "FEMALE" and point forward with the index finger.
Note: These words are often spelled rather than signed.
Usage: *He* is young.
      Give the letter to *him*.
      She sings well.
      We offered *her* a job.

MY, MINE

Place the open palm on the chest.
Origin: Showing possession by holding an object against the chest.
Usage: This is *my* country.
      These children are all *mine*.

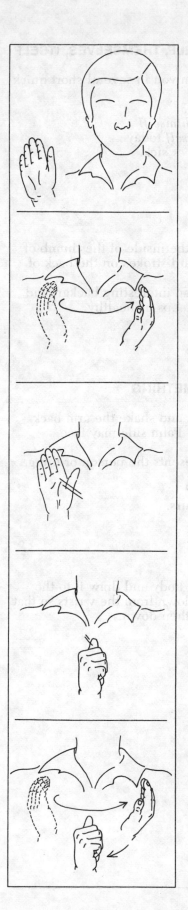

HIS, HER, THEIR

Face the palm out, directing it toward the individuals. (Sometimes the sign for "MALE" or "FEMALE" precedes the sign for clarity.)
Origin: The open palm, indicating possession, is directed toward the person.
Usage: *his* choice.
       her dog.
       their home.

OUR

Place the right hand, slightly cupped, at the right shoulder with thumb side against the body, circling around until the little-finger side touches the left shoulder.
Origin: Open palm indicating the possessive, as concerning self and others.
Usage: We are thankful for *our* freedom.

YOUR

Face the palm out, directing it forward.
Origin: The open palm indicating the possessive is directed toward the person to whom you are speaking.
Usage: *Your* idea is good. (For the plural form, move the palm forward and then toward the right.)

SELF, MYSELF

Strike the "A" hand, palm side facing left, against the chest several times.
Usage: We all need more *self*-control.
       I hurt *myself* yesterday.

OURSELVES

Sign "OUR" and "SELF."
Usage: seeing *ourselves* as others see us.

YOURSELF, HIMSELF, HERSELF, THEMSELVES, ITSELF

Direct the "A" hand away from you in several short quick movements.
Usage: You drew that *yourself?*
He painted the house *himself!*
She does not seem *herself* today.
They worried *themselves* sick.
The vase fell by *itself.*

EACH, EVERY

Hold up the left "A" and use the inside of the thumb of the right "A" to make downward strokes on the back of the left thumb.
Usage: *Each* person here has an interesting background.
Exercising *every* day keeps us healthy.

SOMEONE, SOMEBODY, SOMETHING

Hold up the right index finger and shake the arm back and forth slightly, left to right. Palm side may face forward or self.
Origin: The index finger represents the person or thing.
Usage: *Someone* is coming.
Is *somebody* laughing?
I hear *something* upstairs.

ANY

Place the "A" hand before the body and draw it to the right while moving it up and down from the wrists so that the thumb points first up and then down.
Usage: *Any* child knows that.

ANYONE, ANYBODY

Sign "ANY" and "ONE."
Usage: *Anyone* may come.
Anybody home?

ANYTHING

Sign "ANY" and "THING" (drop the slightly curved open right hand before you, palm facing up; move it to the right and drop it again).
Usage: *Anything* can happen here.

EVERYBODY, EVERYONE

Sign "EACH" and "ONE."
Usage: *Everybody* is welcome.
  The invitation is for *everyone*.

OTHER, ANOTHER

Move the "A" hand slightly up and to the right turning the thumb up and over toward the right.
Origin: The thumb is pointing in the direction of another person.
Usage: *Other* nurses helped us.
  They came from *another* hospital.

EACH OTHER, ONE ANOTHER, ASSOCIATE, SOCIALIZE, FELLOWSHIP

Circle the right "A" which is pointing down in a counterclockwise motion around the thumb of the left "A" which is pointing up.
Usage: they like *each other*; have concern for *one another*; *associate* with good people; *socializing* at a party; *fellowship* with my friends.

THAT

Place the right "Y" on the left palm.
Usage: Who is *that* girl? *That's* right! It costs *that* much?
Note: As a conjunctive, "that" should not be signed as in the sentence, "I know *that* you are right." In such cases either omit the word or spell it.

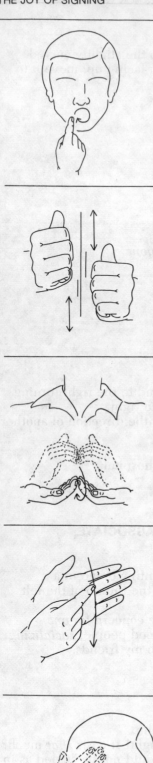

WHO

Describe a circle around the pursed lips toward the left with the index finger.
Origin: The index shows the lip movement.
Usage: *Who* is coming for dinner tonight?

WHICH, WHETHER

Place both "A" hands before you with palms facing each other and raise and lower them alternately.
Origin: Is it this hand or that one?
Usage: *Which* is your coat?
I can't decide *whether* to work or play.

HOW

Place the curved hands back to back with fingers pointing down; turn hands in this position until fingers point up.
Usage: *How* is your family?

WHAT

Draw the tip of the right index downward across the left open palm.
Usage: *What* kind of work do you do?

WHY

Touch the fingertips to the forehead and draw them away, forming a "Y" (palm facing self).
Usage: *Why* can't you travel around the world with me?

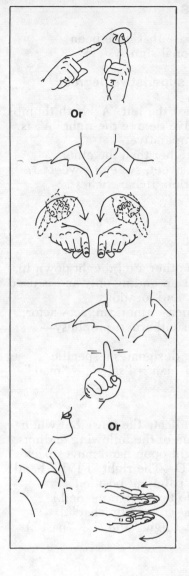

WHEN

Left index is held up facing you; right index faces out and describes a circle in front of the left index and comes to rest on the tip of the left index.

Or,
Point the index fingers forward with palms up; bring them to the center, ending with index fingers side by side (palms down). This sign is similar to "happen" and is usually used to ask when something happened.

Usage: *When* shall we meet?

WHERE

Hold up the right index finger and shake the hand back and forth quickly from left to right.
Usage: *Where* are you going?

Or,
Both open hands, palms up, are circled outwardly (right hand clockwise and left hand counterclockwise).

Usage: Dr. Roberts visited the place *where* he was born.

WHATEVER, WHOEVER, etc.

Make the sign for the desired pronoun and add "ANY." Sometimes the question word (what, who, etc.) is used alone without the ending. Another alternative is to use the sign for "no matter."
Usage: Do *whatever* you can to help.
　　　　Whoever is interested may go.
　　　　Come *whenever* you can.

ARTICLES

A, AN, THE—As a rule, articles are omitted in the language of signs as used by deaf adults. However, in manual English systems, they are included for educational purposes. In these cases, they are made as follows: A—Move the right "A" slightly to the right; AN—fingerspell; THE—Turn the "T" from a palm-left to a palm-forward position.

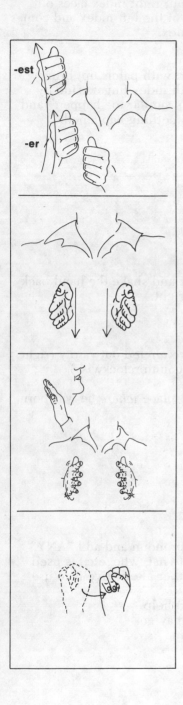

COMMONLY USED ENDINGS

The following endings are those that have been commonly used in the traditional sign system.

-ER, -EST (Comparative and superlative degree)

Raise the right "A" up and past the left "A," both thumbs pointing up. For the superlative degree the right "A" is raised higher than for the comparative.
Origin: One is shown to be higher than the other.
Usage: long, long*er*, long*est;* sweet, sweet*er*, sweet*est;* large, larg*er*, larg*est;* rich, rich*er*, rich*est.*

"PERSON" ENDING

Both open hands facing each other are brought down in front of the body. This sign is an ending only and is used following verbs, occupations, and locations.
Usage: teach—teacher; America—American; act—actor; law—lawyer; south—southerner; prophesy—prophet.
Note: When the word ending designates a specific person, use that sign, as: salesman = "sales" + "man."

PAST TENSE

Ordinarily the context will indicate the tense but when past tense must be shown, one of the following endings may be used: PAST—The right open hand moves back over the shoulder. FINISHED—The right "FIVE" hand is turned from a palm-in to a palm-out position.
Usage: Yesterday I drove. (No tense sign needed.)
I *went* to town. (Sign "go" + "finished".)
I *studied* that subject. (Sign "study" + "past".)

'S or S' (Possessives)

Twist the right "S" inward. This ending may be used both after signs and after fingerspelled words.
Usage: president's men; Sandy's children; women's club; brother's house; Mike's pipe; people's choice.

PLURALS

The most common way of indicating the plural form is to repeat the sign several times. Often the context will show that a word is plural and no change or addition is needed.
Usage: three mice = "THREE" + "MOUSE"
churches on every corner (repeat the sign for "church" several times, i.e., strike the "C" on the wrist several times).

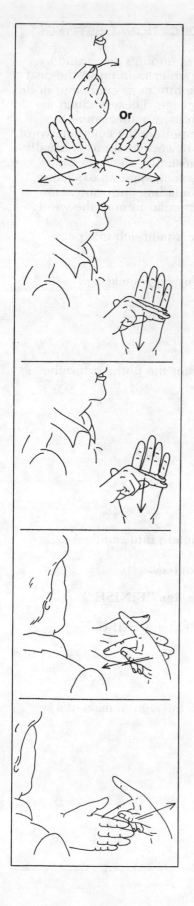

NEGATIVE PREFIXES—UN, IM, IN, DIS, IL

Use the formal sign for "NOT" preceding the intended word.
Usage: *im*polite—not polite; *in*capable—not capable; *im*possible—not possible; *dis*interested—not interested; *un*important—not important; *il*legal—not legal.

The following endings have become common in recent years and are now used to some extent by deaf adults:

-MENT

Place the side of the right "M" against the left palm (which has fingertips pointing up); move the "M" downward.
Usage: develop*ment* of the system.

-NESS

Place the side of the right "N" against the left palm (which has fingertips pointing up); move the "N" downward.
Usage: Deaf*ness* is increasing.

PRE-

Place the back of the right "P" against the left palm and move the "P" away from the palm toward self.
Origin: Based on the sign for "before."
Usage: Renee's deafness is *pre*lingual.
The meeting was *pre*arranged.

POST-

Place the palm side of the right "P" against the back of the left hand and move the "P" away from the hand.
Origin: Based on the sign for "after."
Usage: The patient needs *post*-operative care.

WORD ENDINGS USED IN EDUCATIONAL SETTINGS

Following are some of the word endings advocated by educators for classroom use in order to improve the deaf child's vocabulary and to make him more proficient in the correct use of the English language. These endings are not ordinarily used by deaf adults. An alternative to adding word endings is fingerspelling the complete word. Among deaf adults, a word in its various forms is usually represented by one sign. For instance, the same sign denotes any of these words: expect, expects, expecting, expectant, expectation. Speechreading and context are called upon to identify the particular form of the word.

ING—Move the right "I" from a palm-left to a palm-forward position.

Usage: think(*ing*); walk(*ing*); lov(*ing*); seek(*ing*.)

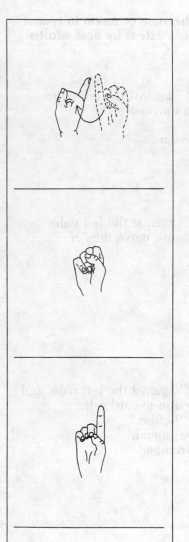

S (Plural)—Add an "S" for either the plural or for the third person singular.

Usage: chair(*s*); walk(*s*).

D (Past)—Add a "D" to the sign to indicate the past.

Usage: help(*ed*); excit(*ed*); learn(*ed*).

For the irregular form add the sign "FINISH."

Usage: taught—sign "TEACHER + FINISH."

N (Participle)—Add an "N" to the sign to make it a participle.

Usage: spok(*en*); brok(*en*).

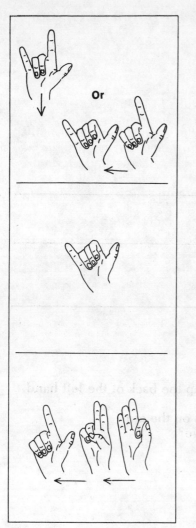

LY (Adverbs)—Form a combination of "L" and "Y" (thumb, index, and little finger up) and move the hand downward. Or, fingerspell "LY".

Usage: nice*(ly)*; slow*(ly)*.

Y (Adjectives)—Add a "Y" to the sign to make it an adjective.

Usage: sleep*(y)*; rain*(y)*.

-FUL—fingerspell at the end of the sign.

Usage: use *(ful)*; meaning *(ful)*.
Note: Some prefer to make the sign for "full."

3

Time

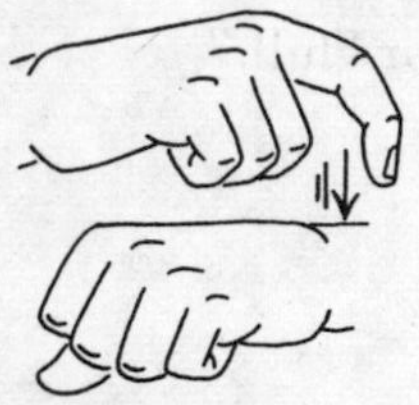

TIME

Crook the index finger and tap the back of the left hand several times.
Origin: Pointing to the watch on the arm.
Usage: What *time* do you have?

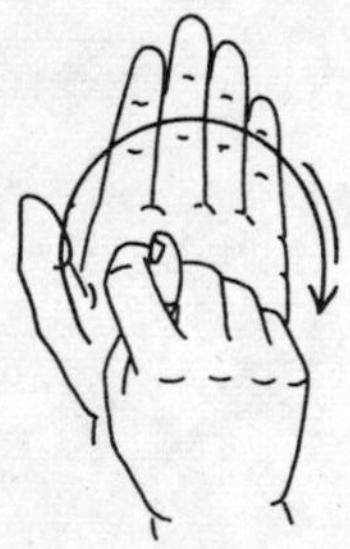

TIME

Make a clockwise circle with the right "T" in the left palm. This sign is used in the abstract sense.
Origin: Indicating the movement of the clock.
Usage: in medieval *times*.

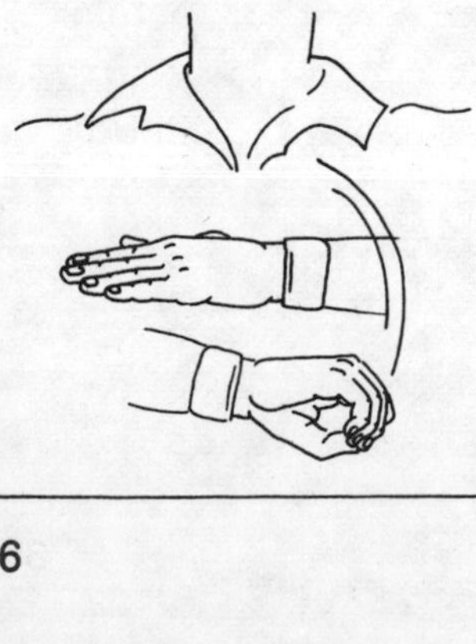

SUNRISE, SUNSET

The left arm is held in front of the body pointing right with the palm down. The right "O" starts below and moves upward (or downward) behind the left forearm.
Origin: The sun appearing or disappearing beyond the horizon.
Usage: *Sunrise* will be at five.
a golden *sunset*.

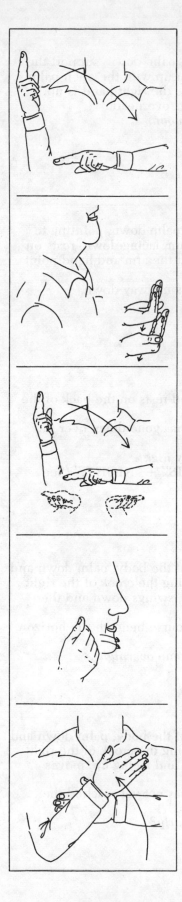

DAY

The right arm, with index finger pointing out, palm up, is moved in a short arc from right to left (or from left to right) while the left index touches the inside of the right elbow. ALL DAY is signed with a complete arc.
Origin: Indicates the course of the sun.
Usage: a long, hard *day;* the first *day* of the week.

NOW, CURRENTLY

Place both bent hands before you at waist level, palms up. Drop the hands slightly.
Origin: Indicates time that is immediately before you.
Usage: *Now* is the time to act.
　　　　currently performing at the Kennedy Center.

TODAY

Sign "THIS" and "DAY." (The order may be reversed.)
Usage: What are you doing *today?*

DAILY, EVERY DAY

Place the side of the "A" hand on the cheek and rub it toward the chin several times.
Origin: Indicating several tomorrows.
Usage: *daily* bread.
　　　　drive to work *every day.*

MORNING

The fingertips of the left hand are placed in the crook of the right arm; the right arm moves upward (palm up).
Origin: Shows the sun coming up.
Usage: See you in the *morning.*

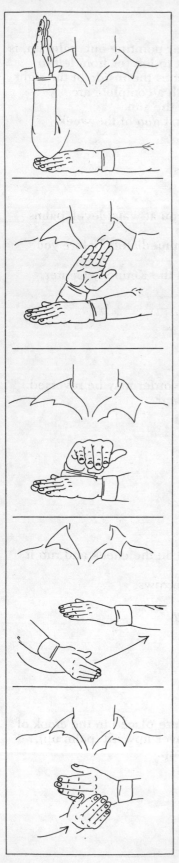

NOON

The fingertips of the left hand, palm down, support the right arm which is held straight up with the open palm facing left. (Or, sign "12" while the right hand is up.)
Origin: Indicates that the sun is overhead.
Usage: The luncheon starts at *noon*.

AFTERNOON

The left arm is in front of you, palm down, pointing to the right. The right forearm, palm facing down, rests on the back of the left hand so that the arm and hand point slightly upward.
Origin: Indicates that the sun is halfway down.
Usage: this *afternoon* at four.

NIGHT

The wrist of the right bent hand rests on the back of the left open hand.
Origin: Indicates that the sun has gone down over the horizon.
Usage: went to a meeting every *night*.
TONIGHT—Sign "THIS" + "NIGHT." (See "today.")

ALL NIGHT, OVERNIGHT

The left hand is held in front of the body, palm down and pointing right, fingertips touching the crook of the right arm. The right arm, palm open, swings down and then toward the left.
Origin: The sun moves in its course beneath the horizon.
Usage: slept well *all night*.
stayed at my friend's home *overnight*.

EARLY (in the morning)

The left hand is held in front of the body, palm down and pointing right, fingertips touching the crook of the right arm. The right arm, palm open and facing up, moves upward slightly.
Origin: The sun in its course has not yet reached the horizon.
Usage: Do you like to get up *early?*

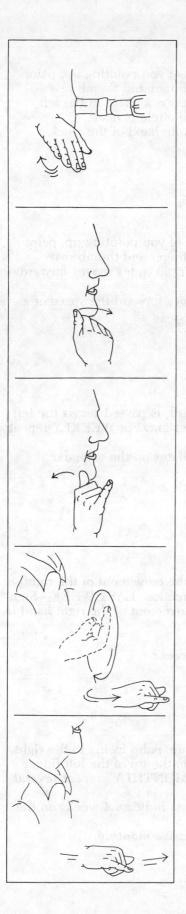

LATE, NOT YET

Place the right hand near the hip with fingers pointing down and palm facing back. Hand is moved back and forth several times.
Origin: You are behind those who have already arrived.
Usage: always *late; not yet* here.

TOMORROW

Touch right side of the chin with thumb of "A" and direct it slightly up and forward in a semicircle.
Origin: Indicates the time that is before you.
Usage: "One today is worth two *tomorrows* "(Benjamin Franklin).

YESTERDAY

Touch right side of the chin with thumb of the "Y" hand and describe a semicircle up and back toward the ear. (This sign can be made with the "A" hand.)
Origin: Initial sign moved back to represent time behind you.
Usage: *yesterday* is gone.

FOREVER, EVERLASTING, ETERNAL

Sign "ALWAYS" (a circle in front of you) and "STILL" (as described below).
Usage: now and *forever; everlasting* peace; *eternal* hope.

STILL, YET

Move the right "Y" hand forward, palm facing down. This sign is used only in a continuing sense.
Usage: that word is *still* used.
      The book is read *even yet*.
      He is experienced, *yet* slow.
Note: When the words *not yet* are used, sign "LATE."

HOUR

The left hand is held in front of you pointing up, palm facing right. The right index finger and thumb rest against the left hand and describe a circle in the left palm, twisting the wrist as the circle is made.
Origin: Representing the minute hand of the clock.
Usage: 3 *hours* ago.

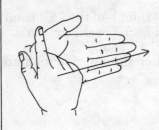

MINUTE, SECOND

The left hand is held in front of you pointing up, palm facing right. The right index finger and thumb rest against the left hand and the right index moves forward slightly.
Origin: The minute hand moves forward the space of a minute.
Usage: 15 *minutes* late.
Wait a *second*.

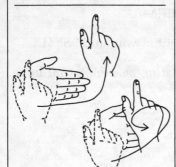

WEEK

Right index hand, palm forward, is passed across the left palm which is pointing to the right. For WEEKLY repeat several times.
Origin: Indicates one row of dates on the calendar.
Usage: 52 *weeks* in a year.
weekly meetings.

NEXT WEEK, LAST WEEK

Sign "WEEK" and continue the movement of the right hand in an up-left-forward direction. LAST WEEK—Sign "WEEK" and continue the movement of the right hand in an up-and-back direction.
Usage: See you *next week*.
What happened *last week?*

MONTH, MONTHLY

The left index finger is held up, palm facing to the right. The right index is moved from the tip of the left finger down to the last joint. (For "MONTHLY" repeat several times.)
Origin: The tip and three joints indicate 4 weeks on the calendar.
Usage: twice a *month;* bills arrive *monthly*.

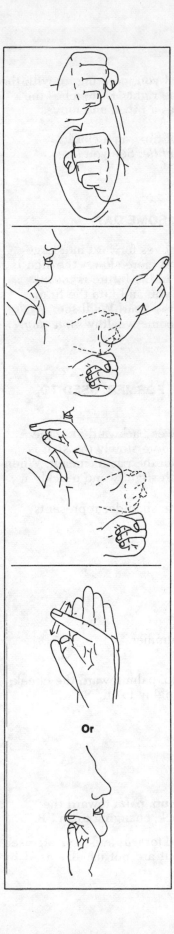

YEAR

With palms facing in, the right "S" revolves forward and around the left "S" coming to a halt resting on the left "S."
Origin: The earth revolving around the sun.
Usage: during a school *year*.

NEXT YEAR, LAST YEAR

NEXT YEAR—Place the right fist on the thumb side of the left fist; then move the right hand up and forward into a "ONE" position.

LAST YEAR—Place the right fist on top of the left fist; then move the "ONE" hand back.
Note: These signs can be made in such a fashion with any number, usually up to five.
Usage: a new job *next year*.
a vacation in Hawaii *last year*.
met her *3 years ago*.
See you at the convention *in 2 years*.

ANNUAL—Sign "NEXT YEAR" several times.
Usage: our *annual* business meeting.

RECENTLY, A LITTLE WHILE AGO, JUST, LATELY

The left hand is held in front of you, pointing up with palm facing right. Place the little finger side of the right "ONE" hand against the left palm and move the right index up and down.
Origin: Backwards on the clock.

Or, place the right curved "ONE" hand at the right cheek, palm facing back, and move it back and forth slightly.
Origin: Time that is behind you.
Usage: Something happened to me *recently*.
Paul ate *a little while ago*.
Peggy *just* arrived.
not feeling well *lately*.

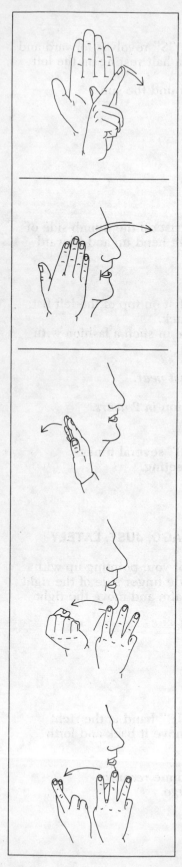

AFTER A WHILE, LATER

The left hand is held in front of you, pointing up with the palm facing right. The tip of the right "L" touches the center of the left palm, acting as a pivot, and moves forward.
Origin: Indicates the passing of time on a clock.
Usage: I'll come back *after a while*. See you *later*.

FUTURE, BY AND BY, LATER, SOME DAY

Raised arm, palm facing left, moves forward in a large semicircle. Note: The larger and more slowly the sign is made, the greater the distance in the future is meant.
Origin: Indicating time before you and into the future.
Usage: a good *future; later* in the year; We'll see progress *by and by*. become wealthy *some day*.

PAST, AGO, LAST, PREVIOUS, FORMER, USED TO, WAS, WERE

The open hand facing back moves backward over the right shoulder. The larger and more slowly the sign is made, the greater the distance in the past is meant. When the sign is moved back and forth slightly and quickly it means "recently" or "lately."
Origin: Movement back over the shoulder represents time behind you.
Usage: *past* president.
long time *ago*.
last month.
previous occupation.
former home.
He *used to* drive.
Laura *was* here in May.
We *were* traveling all summer.

WAS—The right "W" is held up, palm toward the cheek; then the hand moves back, changing to an "S."

WERE—The right "W" is held up, palm toward the cheek; then the hand moves back, changing to an "R."

Note: The initial signs described for *was* and *were* are used in some educational settings but are not usually used by deaf adults.

WILL

Raised right arm with open palm toward cheek, moves forward. (This sign is used only as a verb.)
Origin: Moving ahead toward the future.
Usage: I *will* succeed.

WOULD

Place the right "W" near the side of the face, palm toward cheek; move the hand forward into a "D" position.
Origin: The sign for "will" becomes "would" when initials are used.
Usage: *Would* you flirt?

IS, AM, ARE, BE

Place the tip of the index finger at the mouth; move it forward, still upright.
Origin: This sign represents the verb "to be" and indicates that breath is still there.
Note: The initial signs described for *is, am, are, be, would, were,* and *was* are used to show clear distinctions between the words but are not usually used by deaf adults.
Usage: This *is* the way.
Yes I *am* angry.
We *are* improving every day.
How wonderful *to be* at home again.
She *was* in Mexico for a month.
We *were* in St. Petersburg for a week.

AGAIN, REPEAT, OFTEN

The right curved hand faces up, then turns and moves to the left so that the fingertips touch the left palm which is pointing forward with the palm facing right. OFTEN— Repeat the sign for "AGAIN" several times.
Usage: Say that *again*.
repeat please.
I'd like to see Kathy more *often*.

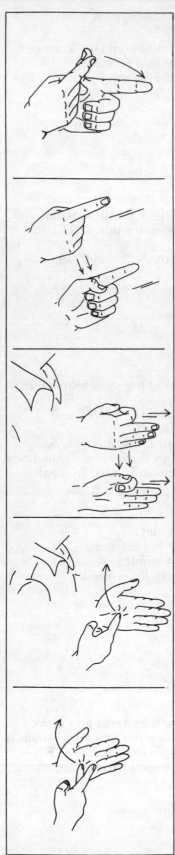

THEN

Place the left "L" in front of you with the thumb pointing up; then using the right index touch first the left thumb, then the left index finger.
Origin: First the thumb, then the next finger.
Usage: *then* we left town.

REGULAR

Place the little-finger edge of the right "G" hand on the index-finger edge of the left "G"; move both hands forward and strike together again.
Usage: went to the doctor *regularly*.

FAITHFULLY

Place the little-finger edge of the right "F" on the index-finger edge of the left "F"; move both hands forward and strike them together again.
Origin: The sign for "regular" made with an "F."
Usage: Lowell attends church *faithfully*.

ONCE

Tip of the right index touches the center of the left palm and comes toward the body and up in a quick circular movement.
Usage: It only happened *once*.

TWICE

Touch the left palm with the middle finger of the right "TWO" hand and bring it toward you and up.
Usage: Take the pills *twice* a day.

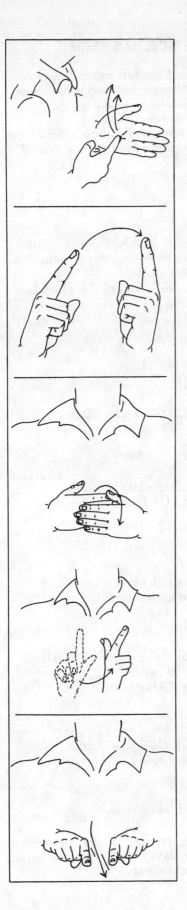

SOMETIMES, OCCASIONALLY, ONCE IN A WHILE

The sign for "ONCE" is repeated several times.
Usage: *Sometimes* we go swimming in the ocean.
The girls go biking *occasionally*.
We jog *once in a while* but not regularly.

UNTIL

Direct the right index finger in a forward arc and touch the left index which is pointing up.
Usage: It was hard to wait *until* summer for our vacation.

NEXT

The left open hand faces the body; the right open hand is placed between the left hand and the body and then passes over the left.
Origin: Over and on the other side of the object.
Usage: the *next* train.

When "next" is used to indicate that it is someone's turn, the following sign is usually used: Place the "L" before you, palm out; make a quick turn to a palm-in position. Point the sign toward the person whose turn it is.
Usage: *your turn*.

DURING, WHILE

Both index fingers, palms down and pointing forward, separated slightly, are pushed slightly down and then forward.
Origin: Hands moving forward show time moving on.
Usage: *during* the war; *while* we worked.

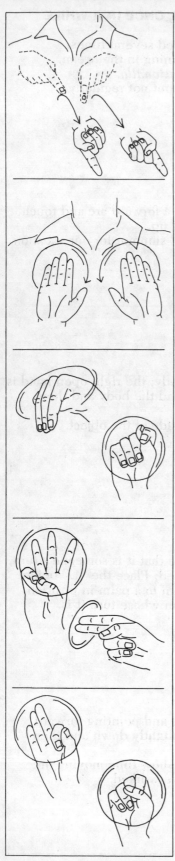

SINCE, ALL ALONG, EVER SINCE, HAS BEEN

Right index finger at right shoulder, left index finger in front of it; both index fingers are circled under-back-up-forward ending with both index fingers facing up.
Origin: From the past to the present.
Usage: *since* Wednesday; *ever since* childhood; deaf *from* birth; doing it *all along;* How long *has it been?*

SUNDAY

Both hands are held in front of the body, fingers pointing up and palms out. Both hands are moved in opposite circular motions.
Origin: Represents the large open doors of the church.
Usage: a quiet *Sunday* afternoon.

MONDAY

The right "M" describes a small clockwise circle.
Usage: blue *Monday.*

TUESDAY

The right "T" describes a small clockwise circle.
Usage: The program is planned for *Tuesday.*

WEDNESDAY

The right "W" describes a small clockwise circle.
Usage: a *Wednesday* afternoon appointment.

THURSDAY

Form a "T" and an "H" and describe small clockwise circles. (Often made with the "H" only.)
Usage: You can ride with me on *Thursday.*

FRIDAY

The right "F" describes a small clockwise circle.
Usage: left for the weekend on *Friday.*

SATURDAY

The right "S" describes a small clockwise circle.
Usage: a busy *Saturday.*

Note: When referring to a regular day of the week such as "every Monday," "on Thursdays," etc., form the initial letter and draw the hand straight down.

4
Mental Action

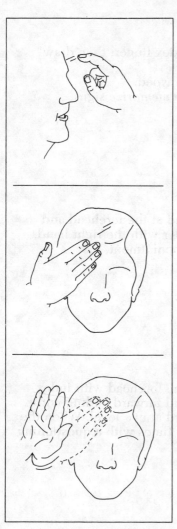

MIND, MENTAL, BRAIN

Tap the forehead with the curved index finger.
Origin: Indicating the location of the mind.
Usage: Good *mental* health is important.
What's on your *mind?*
The *brain* is very complex.

KNOW, KNOWLEDGE

Pat the forehead.
Origin: A natural sign indicating knowledge.
Usage: *Know* thyself!
A little *knowledge* can be dangerous.

DON'T KNOW, DIDN'T KNOW

Sign "KNOW" and then turn the palm out away from the head.
Origin: "KNOW" + "NOT."
Usage: We really *don't know* everything.
He *didn't know* the answer.

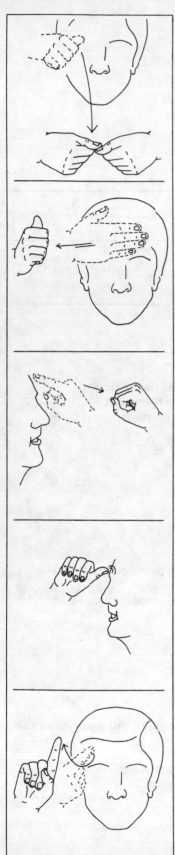

REMEMBER

Place the thumbnail of the right "A" on the forehead and then on the thumbnail of the left "A." (Originally the first part of the sign was "KNOWLEDGE" but later became the "A.")
Origin: Knowledge that stays.
Usage: *Remembering* names is not easy.

FORGET

Wipe across the forehead with the open hand, ending in the "A" position.
Origin: Knowledge that has been wiped off the mind.
Usage: Don't *forget* to call me next week.
　　　Forgetfulness is a sign of age.

MEMORIZE

Touch the forehead with the index finger; then draw away into an "S."
Origin: The thought is firmly grasped.
Usage: Association helps you to *memorize* signs.

REMIND

Place the thumb of the "A" hand at the forehead and twist it. Or, tap the right shoulder with the right hand.
Usage: *Remind* me about the appointment.

FOR

Point toward the right side of the forehead with index finger; then circle downward and forward ending with the index finger pointing forward at eye level. When the sign is repeated quickly several times with a questioning look, it means, "What for?"
Usage: I have a gift *for* you!

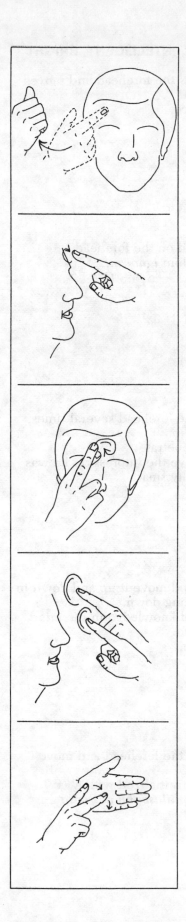

BECAUSE

Touch the forehead with the index finger; then draw it slightly up and to the right forming an "A." (This sign is sometimes begun with the open hand.) Note: When the words *for* and *since* are used to mean *because,* the sign for "BECAUSE" should be used as in the examples below.
Usage: *because* of her illness; *since* we did not know; can't go *for* it is raining.

THINK, THOUGHTS, MEDITATE, CONSIDER

The index finger faces the forehead and describes a small circle. Two hands are sometimes used to show deep thought.
Origin: Something is going around in the mind.
Usage: *think* deeply; *meditate* often; kind *thoughts*; *consider* the problem.

REASON

The "R" hand revolves in front of the forehead.
Origin: Making the "THINK" sign with an "R."
Usage: My *reason* for coming here is obvious.

WONDER, CONCERN

Point one or both index fingers toward the forehead and revolve them slowly as in "THINK." The face should show a concerned expression. (The right "W" is sometimes used.)
Origin: Slow and deliberate thinking.
Usage: Do you sometimes *wonder* about the future?
I have a deep *concern.*

MEAN, INTEND, PURPOSE

The fingertips of the right "V" are placed against the left open hand, the "V" facing out; the "V" is turned and again placed into the palm, the "V" facing in.
Usage: What do you *mean?*
My nurse had good *intentions.*
What's the *purpose* behind all this activity?

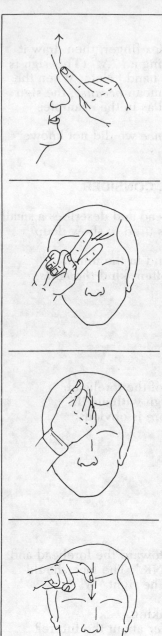

CLEVER, BRILLIANT, SMART, INTELLIGENT, BRIGHT

Index or middle finger touches the forehead and moves upward with a shaking motion.
Origin: The mind has brilliance.
Usage: *clever* idea.
    brilliant scientist.
    smart child.
    intelligent speaker.
    bright girl.

IGNORANT

Place the back of the "V" hand on the forehead.
Usage: Lack of schooling left him *ignorant*.

STUPID

Strike the "A" hand against the forehead several times, palm facing in.
Origin: Thick skull, hard to penetrate.
Usage: For some reason he gave the impression he was *stupid*, but he was really smart.

WISE

Crook the right index finger and move it up and down in front of the forehead, palm facing down.
Origin: Indicating the depth of knowledge in the mind.
Usage: a *wise* counselor helped.
    the *wisdom* of Solomon.

PHILOSOPHY

Place the right "P" in front of the forehead and move it up and down.
Origin: The sign for "wise" is initialized with a "P."
Usage: Have you studied the *philosophy* of Plato?

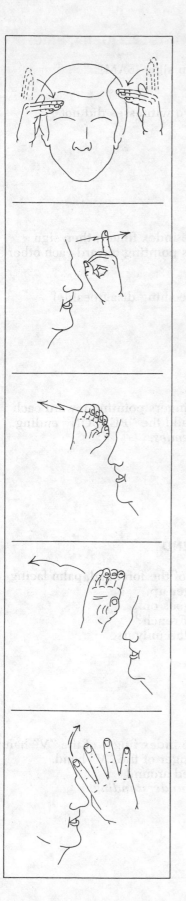

HOPE, EXPECT

Touch the forehead with the index finger; then raise the open palms so they face each other, the right hand near the right forehead and the left hand at the left. Both hands bend to a right angle and unbend simultaneously.
Origin: Thinking and beckoning for something to come.
Usage: *hope* for the best; *expect* changes.

IDEA

Touch the forehead with the tip of the "I," palm facing in; move it forward, palm still facing in.
Origin: A little thought comes forward.
Usage: Explain your *idea*.

OPINION

Place the "O" in front of the forehead; move it forward.
Origin: The sign for "idea" is made with an "O."
Usage: Your *opinion* is valuable.

CONCEPT

Place the "C" in front of the forehead; move it forward.
Origin: The sign for "idea" is made with a "C."
Usage: the *concept* of equality.

INVENT, DEVISE, MAKE UP, CREATE

The "FOUR" hand, index finger touching the center of the forehead, pushes upward the full length of the forefinger.
Origin: A thought coming out of the mind.
Usage: Bell *invented* the telephone.
     The child *made up* that story.
     We *devised* a new method.
     We saw the artist's latest *creation*.
Note: This sign is not used for the creation of the heavens and the earth.

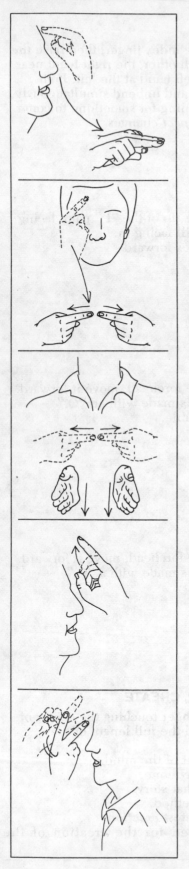

AGREE, CORRESPOND

Touch the forehead and then sign "SAME."
Origin: Thinking the same.
Usage: I *agree* with you.
The stories of the two witnesses did not *correspond*.

DISAGREE

Touch the forehead with the index finger; then sign "OPPOSITE" (index fingers pointing toward each other pulled apart).
Origin: Thinking opposite.
Usage: *Disagree* without becoming disagreeable!

ENEMY, FOE

Sign "OPPOSITE" (index fingers pointing toward each other are pulled apart) and add the "PERSON" ending.
Usage: He's made many *enemies*.
Friend or *foe?*

UNDERSTAND, COMPREHEND

Place the "S" hand in front of the forehead, palm facing self, and snap the index finger up.
Origin: Suddenly the light goes on.
Usage: Do you *understand* French?
I can't *comprehend* the universe.

MISUNDERSTAND

Touch the forehead with the index finger of the "V" hand and then with the middle finger of the "V" hand.
Origin: The thought is turned around.
Usage: I'm sorry for the *misunderstanding*.

PROBLEM

Place the knuckles of the bent "U" hands together and twist them back and forth from the wrist.
Usage: a personal *problem*.

WORRY, TROUBLE, CARE, ANXIOUS

Right open hand, palm facing left, passes in front of the face and down toward the left shoulder. Same motion is made alternately with the left hand several times.
Origin: Everything is coming at you.
Usage: *Worry* can cause illness.
What's the *trouble?*
Few people are free from *care*.
When Joel didn't come home Roz became *anxious*.

BURDEN, BEAR, FAULT, OBLIGATED, RESPONSIBILITY

Place both hands on the right shoulder. "Responsibility" is often signed using the "R" hands in this position.
Origin: Carrying a load on the shoulder.
Usage: a heavy *burden*; difficult to *bear*; that was my own *fault*; an *obligation* to my family; she felt *responsible*.

PRESSURE

Hold up the left index finger, palm side to the right; place the palm of the right open hand against the left index and push forward.
Origin: Bringing pressure to bear on someone.
Usage: Students put *pressure* on their principal.

CONFLICT, CROSS-PURPOSES

Hold the left index in front of you; move the right index across it.
Origin: Instead of the index fingers being together as in "agree" they cross to show conflict.
Usage: *conflicting* opinions.
our ideas *clashed*.
We were at *cross-purposes*.

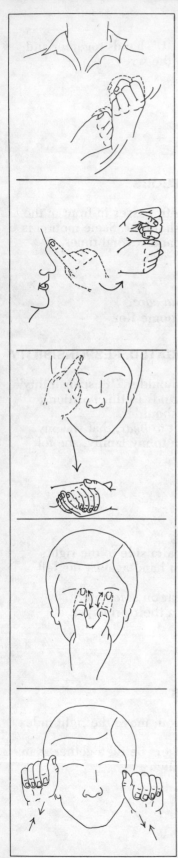

TRUST, CONFIDENCE

Bring both hands slightly to the left closing them to "S" positions, the right one slightly below the left.
Origin: Holding on to something.
Usage: Jamie *trusts* his parents.
Have *confidence* in yourself.

FAITH

Touch the forehead with the index finger; raise both hands slightly to the left closing them into "S" positions with the left "S" above the right.
Origin: Grasping the thought.
Usage: very strong *faith*.

BELIEVE

Touch the forehead with the index finger and clasp the hands.
Origin: Holding onto the thought.
Usage: I *believe* you're telling the truth.

DON'T BELIEVE, SKEPTICAL

Place the bent "V" in front of the eyes, palm in; crook and uncrook the "V" several times.
Usage: I *don't believe* that tale.
I'm *skeptical!*

DOUBT

Place the "A" hands in front of the face, palms facing forward, and move them up and down alternately. (Note: The above sign for "don't believe" is also used for "doubt.")
Origin: The up-and-down movement suggests uncertainty.
Usage: I have some *doubts* about that.

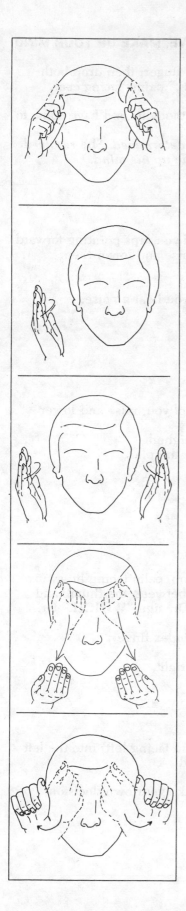

SURPRISE, ASTONISHED

Snap both index fingers up from under the thumbs (other fingers closed) at the sides of the eyes.
Origin: Eyes opened wide in surprise.
Usage: *surprise* party.
astonishing news.

SEEM, APPEAR, LOOK, APPARENTLY

Place the right curved hand, pointing up, at the side of the head and give it a quick turn so that the palm faces you. ("Look" may be signed by tracing a circle around the face.)
Origin: Suddenly the palm appears.
Usage: room *seems* warm; he *appears* confused; weather *looks* good; *Apparently* we took the wrong road.

COMPARE

Make the sign for "APPEAR" with both hands and look at the palms as if comparing them.
Origin: Comparing the palms.
Usage: We *compared* our handwriting.

OBEY

Both "A" hands, with palms facing the body, are dropped from eye level, opening into bent positions, facing up.
Origin: Hands coming down in obedience.
Usage: Why not *obey* the law?
My dog is *obedient*.

DISOBEY

Both "A" hands are in front of the face at eye level and then make a quick turn outward so that they face forward. (Sometimes made with only one hand.)
Origin: Hands refusing to come down in obedience.
Usage: Several soldiers *disobeyed* the order.

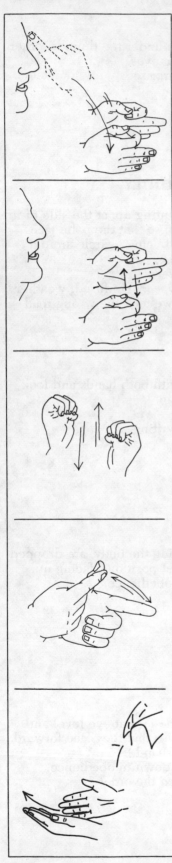

DECIDE, DETERMINE, RESOLVE, MAKE UP YOUR MIND

Touch the forehead with index finger; then drop both hands in front of you into an "F," palms facing each other.
Origin: You have weighed the thoughts and have come to a decision.
Usage: The jury *decided*. I am *determined*. She *resolved* to do better. Julian *made up his mind*.

IF

Place the "F" hands in front of you, tips pointing forward and palms facing each other; raise and lower them alternately in short motions.
Origin: The thought is weighed.
Usage: Don't be frightened *if* you hear a noise.

EVALUATE

Place both "E" hands in front of you; raise and lower them alternately.
Origin: Something is being weighed.
Usage: An expert will *evaluate* the plan.

OR, EITHER

Place the left "L" in front of you, palm facing in; swing the right index back and forth between the thumb and index fingers of the left hand. Or, sign "WHICH." Or, fingerspell.
Origin: Is it the thumb or the index finger?
Usage: one *or* the other.
either book will be all right.

ALL RIGHT, RIGHT

Place the right open hand (palm facing left) into the left open hand and move it forward.
Usage: That's *all right*.
You have a *right* to make your own decision.

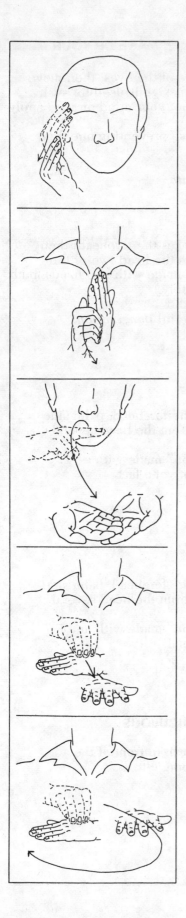

EXPERIENCE

Place the tips of the open "AND" hand at the right temple (at approximately eye level) and close to an "AND" position as you draw the hand slightly down and away from the head.
Origin: The hair at the temples is turning white (a person with experience is an older person).
Usage: Many years of *experience* made him an expert.

EXPERT, SKILLFUL, PROFICIENT, COMPETENT

Grasp the lower edge of the left open hand with the right fingertips, which are closed against the palm, and pull away.
Usage: *expert* typist.
       skilled mechanic.
       proficient signer.
       competent physician.

PROVE, PROOF, EVIDENCE

Touch the mouth with the index finger; then place the back of the right open hand in the left palm.
Origin: Place it where one can see it.
Usage: *Prove* your point!
       The judge wants *proof*.
       Here's the *evidence*.

ADVISE, ADVICE, COUNSEL, AFFECT

Place the tips of the right "AND" hand on the back of the left open hand (palms down) and open the right as it is moved forward.
Usage: Wise men accept *advice*. You cannot *advise* a fool. Lawyers give *counsel*. Your mood *affects* me. We found a good marriage *counselor*. (Add "PERSON" ending.)

INFLUENCE

Place the fingertips of the right "AND" hand on the back of the left open hand (as in "ADVISE"); then circle left-forward-right.
Usage: Don't underestimate the power of *influence*.

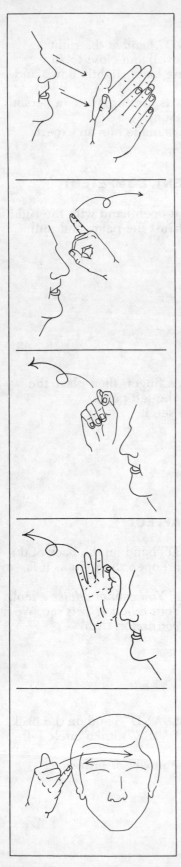

ATTENTION, CONCENTRATE

Place open hands at either side of the eyes; then move both hands forward. (Note: This sign is used for such phrases as: "pay attention," "put your mind on it," "apply yourself.")
Origin: Like blinders on a horse preventing one from looking to the right or the left.
Usage: Please *pay attention*.
      I'm trying to *concentrate*.

IMAGINATION

Place the "I" hand so that it faces the forehead; then circle it upward and away from the head two or three times. (This sign is frequently made with two hands, both hands making the sign alternately.)
Origin: Thoughts floating around.
Usage: Children have a wonderful *imagination*.

THEORY

Place the "T" hand in front of the forehead, palm side left; circle it upward and away from the head several times.
Origin: The sign for "imagination" made with a "T."
Usage: It's only a *theory* and not yet a fact.

FICTION, FANTASY

Place the "F" hand in front of the forehead, palm side left; circle it upward and away from the head several times.
Origin: The sign for "imagination" made with an "F."
Usage: Good *fiction* is educational.

FOOLISH, SILLY, ABSURD, RIDICULOUS

Shake the "Y" hand back and forth in front of the forehead several times, palm facing left.
Usage: *foolish* error.
      silly girls.
      absurd belief.
      ridiculous action.

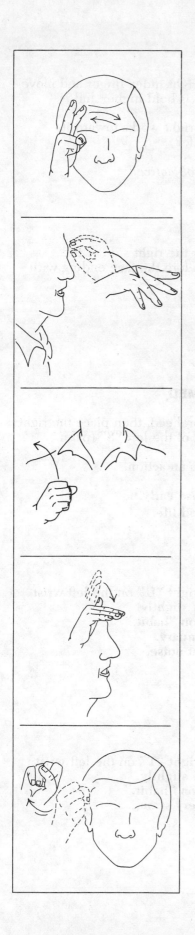

CARELESS

Pass the "V" hand back and forth in front of the forehead, palm facing to the left.
Usage: The fire started because of *careless* smoking.

DON'T CARE

Place the tips of the right "AND" hand on the forehead and open it as you turn it and throw it forward. Informally this sign is sometimes made from the nose with either the index finger or the tips of the "AND" hand.
Usage: I *don't care,* I'm going anyway.

REFUSE, WON'T

Hold up the right "S" hand, palm facing left, and draw it back forcefully toward the right shoulder. At the same time, the head turns slightly to the left.
Usage: He *refused* to cooperate. I *won't!*

STUBBORN, OBSTINATE

Place the thumb of the right open hand against the side of the head, palm facing forward, and bend the hand forward.
Origin: Like a mule.
Usage: That's a *stubborn* animal.
  He was *obstinate* and refused to listen.

REBEL, STRIKE

Hold up the right "S" and give it an outward twist.
Origin: Represents the head turning suddenly away.
Usage: *rebel* against authority.
  workers went on *strike.*

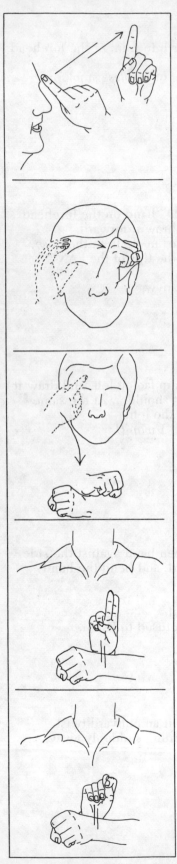

GOAL, AIM, OBJECTIVE

Touch the forehead with the right index finger and move it toward the left index which is held higher and is pointing up.
Origin: Left hand is the goal, right works toward it.
Usage: What is your *goal* in life?
Aim for perfection.
Can you explain your *objective?*

GUESS

Place the right "C" hand near the right side of the forehead and pass the hand before the face ending with the "S" position.
Origin: Catch it in the air.
Usage: *Guess* what happened.

HABIT, CUSTOM, ACCUSTOMED

Place the right index at the forehead, then place the right "A" (palm down) on the wrist of the left "S" (palm leftward); push downward.
Origin: Your mind is bound to an action.
Usage: a reading *habit*.
It was his *custom* to rise early.
Accustomed to the good life.

USUALLY, USED TO

Place the inside wrist of the right "U" on the left wrist (left hand closed); push down slightly.
Origin: An initial sign based on "habit."
Usage: It *usually* snows in January.
I'm not *used to* all that noise.

TRADITION

Place the inside wrist of the right "T" on the left wrist (left hand closed); push down slightly.
Origin: An initial sign based on "habit."
Usage: Some *traditions* are very strong.

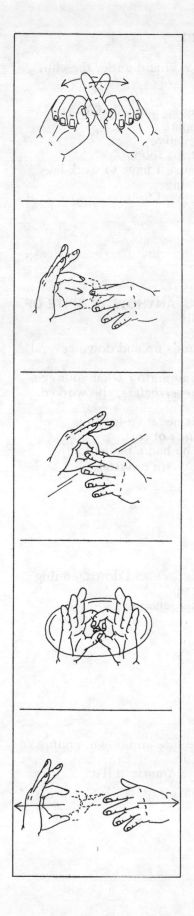

BUT

Cross the index fingers, palms facing out, and draw them apart.
Origin: Based on the sign for "different." The word *but* suggests a difference.
Usage: The car is old *but* looks new.
    We don't have money; *however*, we will borrow. (Sign "BUT.")

JOIN, UNITE, OF

Hook the right index and thumb into the left index and thumb (other three fingers separated). "Of" is usually spelled.
Origin: Showing a connection.
Usage: Mr. Morgan *joined* the organization.
    He *united* with the church.
    Would you like to become a member *of* our club?

CONNECTION, COMBINE, BELONG TO, RELATIONSHIP, ASSOCIATION

Sign "JOIN" and move the hands in this position away from yourself and back several times.
Usage: I don't see any *connection*. We *combined* our efforts. She *belongs to* a health club. We have a good *relationship*. We *associate* daffodils with spring.

COOPERATION, UNITED

Sign "JOIN" and move the hands in this position right-forward-left in a circular motion.
Usage: We all *cooperated* in the project.
    We *united* as a group.

DISCONNECT, RELEASE, LET GO

The hands in the "JOIN" position are disconnected.
Origin: Releasing your connection.
Usage: Our phone was *disconnected* yesterday.
    I'm glad to be *released* from the obligation.
    He refused to *let go* of his responsibilities.

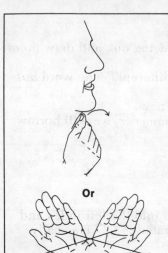

NOT, DON'T, DOESN'T, DIDN'T

Place the thumb of the right "A" hand under the chin and direct it forward.

Or, more formally: Cross the open hands before you, palms down, and draw them apart.
Origin: Natural sign for the negative.
Usage: I'm *not* planning any trips soon.
    Don't wait for me because I have to work late.
    Bill *doesn't* smoke any more.
    He *didn't* think it was good for him.

NO MATTER, NEVERTHELESS, ANYHOW, IN SPITE OF, REGARDLESS, EVEN THOUGH

Brush the tips of both open hands up and down several times, palms facing up.
Usage: Everyone is welcome, *no matter* what your age.
    She had a headache; *nevertheless,* she worked.
    I'm going *anyhow.*
    He came *in spite of* his negative feelings.
    I'll buy the TV *regardless* of cost.
    He came *even though* he had a bad cold.
    Any color is alright; it *doesn't matter.*

HONOR

Bring the "H" hand toward the face and down, ending with the "H" fingers pointing up.
Usage: He brought *honor* to his school.

RESPECT

Bring the "R" hand toward the face and down, ending with the "R" fingers pointing up.
Usage: We show *respect* for the American flag.

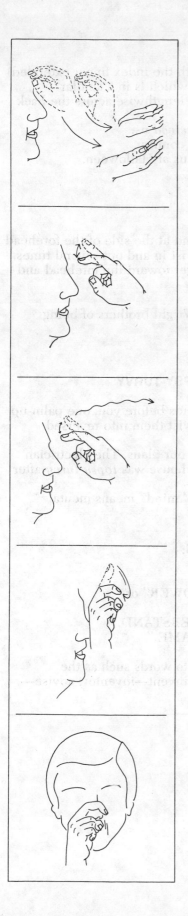

INFORM, INFORMATION, NEWS, NOTIFY

Place the "AND" hands at the forehead; move them
down and away from you, ending with open palms up.
Origin: Knowledge is passed on to others.
Usage: Be sure to *inform* your lawyer.
      The *information* came through the newspaper.
      Did you receive any *news*?
      We *notified* all members.

SUSPECT, SUSPICION, SUSPICIOUS

Crook and uncrook the index finger in front of the
forehead several times (palm facing self).
Origin: Question in the mind.
Usage: The police *suspected* the man.
      My *suspicions* were true.
      His actions made me *suspicious*.

DREAM

Touch the forehead with the index finger and draw it
away, crooking and uncrooking the finger several times,
palm facing you.
Origin: The mind going off into fantasies.
Usage: *Dreams* sometimes come true.

PUZZLED

Draw the back of the index finger toward the forehead
and crook it.
Origin: A question in the mind.
Usage: That *puzzles* me!

FOOL

Place the crooked right index against the nose and move
the head down slightly as if the finger is pulling the head
down.
Usage: Don't try to *fool* me.

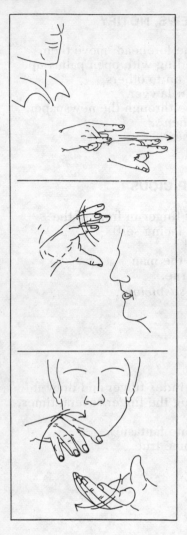

DECEIVE, BETRAY, TRICK

Place the right "Y" hand (with the index finger extended) on the back of the left hand, which is in a similar position, and slide it forward lengthwise across the back of the left.
Usage: I suspect that she *deceived* us.
The spy *betrayed* his country.
The children *tricked* us at Halloween.

CRAZY

Place the curved "FIVE" hand at the side of the forehead and give the hand a quick twist in and out several times. Or, point the right index finger toward the forehead and circle several times.
Origin: Brains are twisted.
Usage: People accused the Wright brothers of being *crazy*.

FOULED UP, BUNGLED, TOPSY-TURVY

Place the curved "FIVE" hands before you, one palm-up and the other palm-down. Twist them into reversed positions.
Usage: That really *fouled up* our plans. The electrician *bungled* the job. The house was *topsy-turvy* after the children left.
Note: This sign preceded by "mind" means mental confusion.

MISCELLANEOUS NOTES:

a strong *will*—"MIND."
will-power—"MIND" + "POWER" or "DETERMINATION."
realize—"KNOW" or "UNDERSTAND."
resemble—"APPEAR" + "SAME."

Add the "PERSON" ending to words such as the following: dream—dreamer; invent—inventor; advise—adviser.

5

Emotion and Feeling

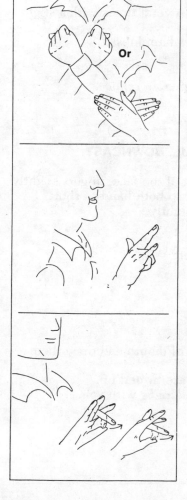

LOVE

The "S" hands are crossed at the wrist and pressed to the heart. (Or use the open hands.)
Origin: Pressing to one's heart.
Usage: my first *love*.

I LOVE YOU

Form a combination of "I," "L," and "Y" (thumb, index, and little finger extended) and direct the palm forward.
Usage: The hand is directed toward the intended
persons.

HATE, DETEST, DESPISE

Snap the middle fingers of both hands as the hands are pushed away from you.
Origin: Pushing away.
Usage: *hate* to clean house.
He *detests* arrogance.
Honest people *despise* lying.

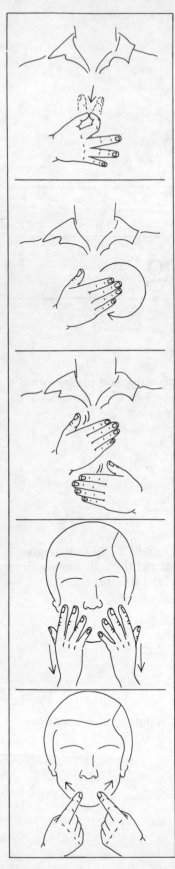

LIKE

Place the thumb and forefinger against the chest (other fingers separated) and draw them away from the body, closing the two fingers. Or, use the sign for "please" described below.
Origin: The heart is drawn toward an object.
Usage: Who *likes* ice cream?

PLEASE, PLEASURE, ENJOY, LIKE

Rub the chest with the open hand in a circular motion.
Origin: Rubbing the heart to indicate pleasure.
Usage: *Please* come for a visit.
It's a *pleasure* to see you.
They *enjoyed* their swim.
I *like* spaghetti very much.

HAPPY, GLAD, REJOICE, JOY

The open hands pat the chest several times with a slight upward motion.
Origin: Patting the chest shows happiness.
Usage: feel *happy*.
glad to hear the news.
The good news made people *rejoice*.
full of *joy*.

SAD, DEJECTED, SORROWFUL, DOWNCAST

Hold both open hands in front of the face, fingers slightly apart and pointing up; then drop both hands a short distance and bend the head slightly.
Origin: Long-faced and gloomy.
Usage: a *sad* face.
dejected because he left.
a *sorrowful* event.
She looked *downcast*.

LAUGH

Place index fingers at corners of mouth and draw them upward several times.
Origin: Corners of the mouth are turned up.
Usage: "*Laugh* and the world *laughs* with you...."

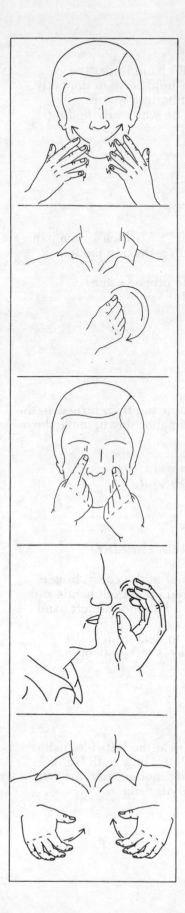

SMILE, CHEERFUL, PLEASANT, FRIENDLY

Place the "FIVE" hands near the sides of the mouth, wiggle the fingers as the hands are moved outward and upward toward the ear.
Origin: Smiling from ear to ear.
Usage: a beautiful *smile*.
       cheerful bus driver.
       pleasant people.
       friendly teacher.

SORRY, REGRET, APOLOGIZE

Rub the "A" hand in a circular motion over the heart.
Origin: Indicating pressure on the heart.
Usage: I'm *sorry*.
       I *regret* my words.
       Did you *apologize?*

CRY, WEEP, TEARS

Draw the index fingers down the cheeks from the eyes several times.
Origin: Tears coursing down the cheeks.
Usage: Please don't *cry!*
       Beth *wept* for joy.
       no more *tears*.

CROSS, GROUCHY

The curved hand with fingers slightly separated, is bent and unbent several times in front of the face, palm in.
Origin: The face is twisted.
Usage: The teacher was *cross*.
       grouchy every morning.

ANGER, WRATH

Place the curved "FIVE" hands against the waist and draw up against the sides of the body.
Origin: Tearing the clothes in anger.
Usage: He spoke in *anger*.
       The preacher talked about the *wrath* of God.

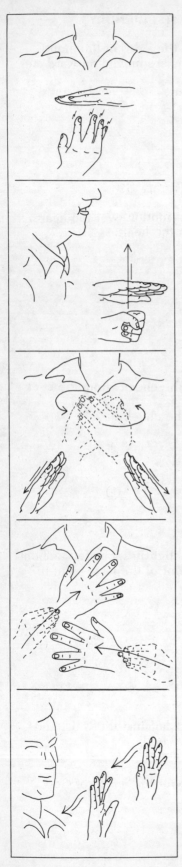

BOILING, BURNING (in anger)

Wiggle the curved right "FIVE" hand under the downturned left palm which is held close to the body.
Origin: Simulates the action of boiling water.
Usage: I watched his face and he was really *boiling.*

BLOWUP, BLOWING ONE'S TOP

Place the right palm on the left "S" (which is in a palm-left position); lift the palm off in a shaking motion.
Origin: The lid blew off.
Usage: We had a *blowup* in the office yesterday.
     The boss *blew his top!*

PEACE

Right palm is placed on left palm and then turned so the left palm is on top; both hands palms down, move down and toward the sides.
Origin: A handshake of peace.
Usage: People want *peace,* not war.
     The forest looked so *peaceful.*

AFRAID, SCARED, FRIGHTENED, TERRIFY

Hold both "AND" hands in front of the chest, fingers pointing toward each other; then open both hands and move the right hand toward the left and the left hand toward the right, palms facing self.
Usage: *afraid* to swim; *scared* to death; the noise *frightened* us; earthquakes *terrify* people.

FEAR, DREAD

Both "FIVE" hands are held up at the left side, palms facing out, right hand behind left. Draw both hands toward self with a slight shaking motion from the wrist.
Origin: Hands held up to ward off danger.
Usage: My cat *dreads* water.
     Do you *fear* snakes?

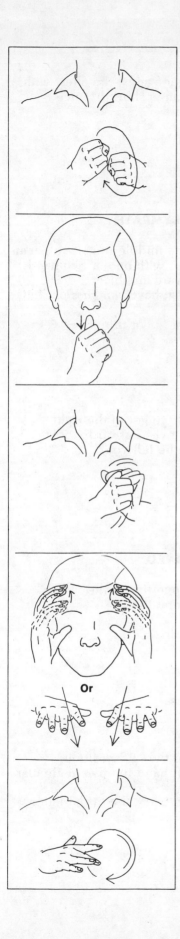

SUFFERING, AGONY

The right "S" revolves forward and around the left "S," both palms facing self. The sign is made with feeling.
Origin: Inner turmoil.
Usage: His *suffering* was almost more than he could bear.
The patient seemed to be in great *agony*.

PATIENT, ENDURE, BEAR, SUFFER

Place the thumbnail of the right "A" against the lips and draw downward.
Origin: Closing the mouth and suffering in silence.
Usage: Mothers need *patience*.
can't *endure* any more.
How can you *bear* the noise?
suffered with a toothache.
Can you *put up with* those neighbors?
I can't *stand* it.

GRIEF, CRUSHED

Place the "A" hands together, palm to palm, and twist them near the heart.
Origin: The heart is crushed.
Usage: My heart was *grieved*.
He was *crushed* when he heard the sad news.

SHOCKED, DUMBFOUNDED

Place the "C" hands at the sides of the eyes; open the "C's" to become larger.
Origin: The eyes open wide suddenly.
Or, both open "FIVE" hands, palms facing down, are pushed slightly forward while the body suddenly straightens.
Origin: The body stiffens.
Usage: His language *shocked* his mother.
The announcement *shocked* everyone.
I was *dumbfounded*.

APPRECIATE

With the right hand in a "FIVE" position, use the middle finger to draw a circle over the heart (left-down-right-up).
Origin: Touching the heart to show appreciation.
Usage: We *appreciate* your assistance.

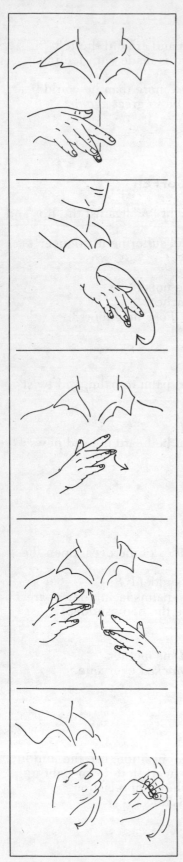

FEEL, SENSATION

Place the tip of the middle finger against the chest with other fingers extended; draw it up a short distance.
Origin: The finger feels the heart.
Usage: What do you *feel*?
That's an odd *sensation*.

MERCY, PITY, COMPASSION, SYMPATHY

Sign "FEEL" and, still using the middle finger, stroke an imaginary person in front of you (with one or two hands).
Origin: Feeling is extended toward an object.
Usage: show *mercy*; *pity* the dog; have *compassion*; letter of *sympathy*.
Note: Use also for "poor you" or "poor thing."

FEEL HURT

Touch the heart with the middle finger of the right "FIVE"; give the hand a quick twist outward.
Usage: Did you *feel hurt* when he left you?

EXCITED, THRILLED, STIMULATED

Alternately brush the middle fingertips of the "FIVE" hands upward on the chest several times.
Origin: The feelings are stirred.
Usage: very *excited* about the trip.
thrilled with the award.
Work *stimulates* him.

EMOTION

The sign for "FEEL" is used in the "E" position, alternating the right and the left hand in upward circular motions.
Origin: Feelings from the heart, using the initial letter.
Usage: Ann has strong *emotions*.

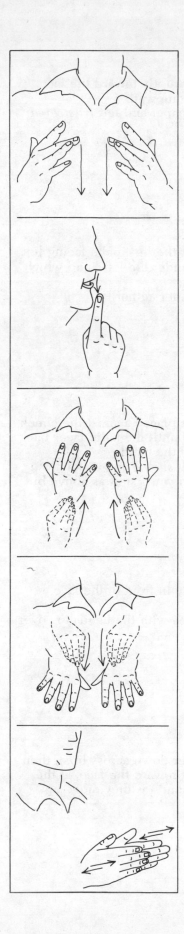

DISCOURAGED, DISAPPOINTED

Both middle fingers move down the chest side by side.
Origin: Feelings sink.
Usage: felt lonely and *discouraged*.
The loser was *disappointed*.

LONELY, LONESOME

Draw the index finger down across the lips, palm facing left.
Origin: Silent and alone.
Usage: *lonely* and without a friend.
lonesome and alone in the city.

INSPIRED

Place the closed "AND" hands against the front of the body at the waist (pointing upward, palm side in); move both hands up, gradually opening to a "FIVE" position at the chest.
Origin: Life and feelings rise to the surface.
Usage: Music can *inspire!*

DEPRESSED

Place the closed "AND" hands on the chest (pointing downward with palm side toward chest); move both hands down, opening to a "FIVE" position.
Origin: Inner feelings move down and inward.
Usage: Losing a job can be very *depressing*.

ENTHUSIASTIC, EAGER, ZEALOUS, INDUSTRIOUS, ANXIOUS

Flat hands, palm to palm, are rubbed together.
Origin: A natural motion indicating enthusiasm.
Usage: full of *enthusiasm*.
always *eager* to please.
Show *zeal* for your program.
working *industriously*.
anxious to learn new signs.

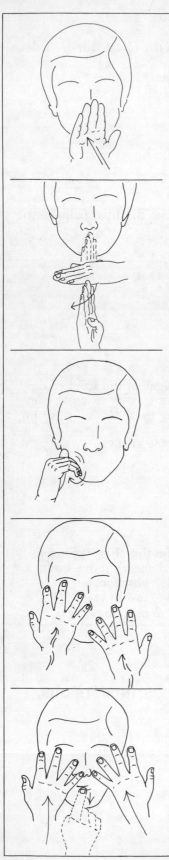

FRUSTRATED

The back of the hand moves abruptly toward the face.
Origin: Coming up against a stone wall.
Usage: He couldn't finish the paper and felt *frustrated*.

HUMBLE, MEEK

The right "B" is placed against the lips, palm facing left, and is then passed down and under the left hand which is open with palm facing down.
Origin: One is willing to be under authority.
Usage: a *humble* log cabin.
      meek, not boastful.

ASHAMED, SHAME

The back of the curved hand is placed against the cheek, palm down, and is then turned until the palm faces back.
Origin: Hiding the face behind the hand.
Usage: *ashamed* of himself; felt *shame* and anger.
Note: When saying, "Shame on you," start as above but continue away from your face.

EMBARRASS, BASHFUL, SHY

Hands move upward alternately in front of the face (palms in).
Origin: Wanting to hide the face with the hands to cover confusion.
Usage: easily *embarrassed*.
      young and *bashful*.
      shy, not bold.

BLUSH

Sign "RED" (brush index finger down across lips); then place the "AND" hands, palms toward the face, at the sides of the cheeks and open hands as they move up.
Origin: Face becoming red.
Usage: Darlene *blushes* easily.

FLIRT

Place the thumbs of the "FIVE" hands together, palms facing down in front of the face (or just below it); wiggle the fingers.
Origin: The fluttering eyelashes.
Usage: He *flirted* and she blushed.

KISS

Place the fingertips at the mouth and then on the cheek.
Origin: A kiss on the mouth and cheek.
Usage: He *kissed* her goodbye.

HEART

Trace a heart on the chest with index fingers. (The middle fingers may be used instead.)
Origin: Natural sign.
Usage: from the bottom of my *heart*.

VALENTINE

Use the "V" hands to trace a heart on the chest.
Origin: Initializing the "heart" sign.
Usage: Trixie received a pretty *valentine*.

KIND, GRACIOUS

The open hand is placed on the body over the heart and is then moved up-out-in-up around the left open hand which faces the body pointing to the right.
Origin: As if winding a bandage around the arm.
Usage: a *kind* father.
     a *gracious* lady.

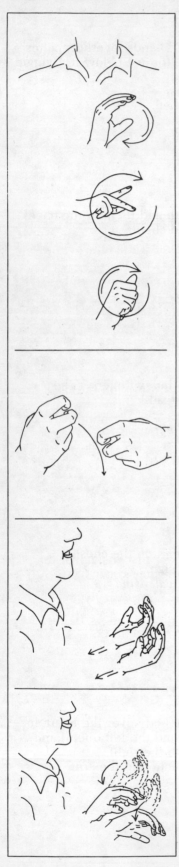

CHARACTER

Describe a circle over the heart with the right "C" hand, palm facing left.
Origin: The initial letter over the heart.
Usage: a man of good and strong *character*.

PERSONALITY

Describe a circle over the heart with the right "P" hand.
Usage: a pleasant *personality*.

ATTITUDE

Describe a circle over the heart with the right "A."
Usage: an *attitude* toward women.

MEANNESS

The knuckles of the bent right middle and index fingers strike the knuckles of the left bent middle and index fingers in a sharp downward stroke (palms facing self).
Origin: A quick striking motion.
Usage: *mean* little boys.

WANT, DESIRE

Place both curved "FIVE" hands in front of you, palms up, and draw them toward you several times.
Origin: Drawing an object toward oneself.
Usage: *want* a new car.
       desire your advice.

DON'T WANT

Place both curved "FIVE" hands in front of you, palms up; turn them over quickly to a palms-away position.
Origin: Wants are turned down.
Usage: I *don't want* to leave.
       Tom *doesn't want* to work.

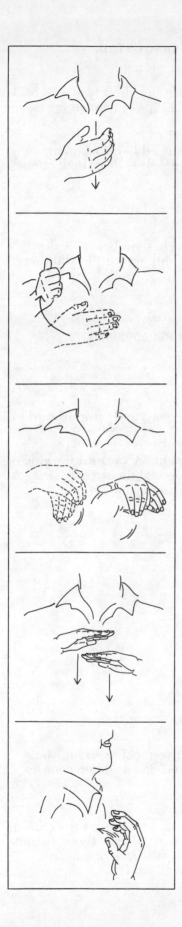

WISH

Place the "C" hand just below the throat, palm facing in, and draw it down.
Origin: This is the sign for "hunger."
Usage: I *wish* I could travel around the world.

RATHER, PREFER

Place the open hand on the chest; move the hand away toward the right and up into an "A" position. (An alternate sign for "prefer" is to touch the chin with the middle finger.)
Origin: A combination of the signs for "like" and "better."
Usage: I'd *rather* fly than drive.
　　　　prefer dark meat (use the alternate sign).

COMFORTABLE, COMFORT

Using curved hands, stroke forward first on the back of the left and then on the back of the right hand.
Origin: Stroking the hands as if warming them.
Usage: *comfortable* in front of the fireplace.
　　　　needing *comfort* at this time.

SATISFY, CONTENT, RELIEVED

Both open hands, palms down, are placed against the chest, right above the left, and pushed down.
Origin: Inner feelings are quieted.
Usage: *Satisfy* your desire.
　　　　content with your decision.
　　　　heard the news and felt *relieved*.

COMPLAIN, OBJECT, PROTEST, GRIEVANCE, GRIPE

The curved "FIVE" hand is placed against the chest in a quick movement.
Usage: *complained* about the service in the restaurant.
　　　　I *object* to that.
　　　　a written *protest*.
　　　　Discuss your *grievance*.
　　　　always *griping*.

DISCONTENT, DISSATISFIED, DISGUSTED, AGGRAVATED

The curved "FIVE" hand against the chest is moved back and forth slightly while the fingertips remain on the chest.
Origin: Inner feelings are stirred.
Usage: Her facial expression showed her *discontent*.
constant *dissatisfaction;* feeling *disgusted;* often *aggravated.*

PRIDE, PROUD, ARROGANT

Place the "A" hand against the chest and move it slowly upward. For "arrogant" tilt the chin upward in addition to using the "A" hand.
Origin: Inner feelings rise.
Usage: *proud* parents;
pride in your success.
arrogance makes a person unpopular.

BOAST, BRAG

Place the "A" hand against the chest and push upward in several short, quick movements.
Origin: Self pushed forward.
Or, place the thumbtip of the right "A" against the side of the body just above the waist several times.
Usage: *boasting* about your accomplishments.
Bragging again?

VAIN, VANITY

Place the "V" hands in front of you, palms facing you, and move the "V" fingers up and down simultaneously.
Origin: All eyes looking at me.
Usage: beautiful but *vain.*
Vanity tends to alienate.
Note: This sign is not used in the sense of fruitless effort, futility, or uselessness, as: he tried *in vain.* Use substitute words such as: without success, failed, or of no use.

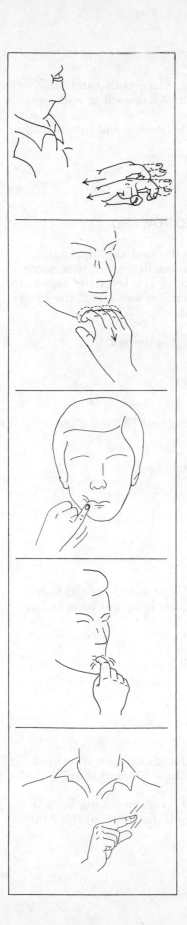

SELFISH

Point the "V" hands forward (palms down) and draw
them back towards you, crooking the fingers.
Origin: Drawing everything toward oneself.
Usage: He acted *selfish* and refused to share.

STINGY, MISERLY

Use the right hand in a clawed position and scrape
downward on the chin.
Usage: He was careful with his money, not *stingy*.
Mr. Scrooge, a *miserly* old man.

JEALOUS

Place the "J" finger in the corner of the mouth and twist
it.
Origin: The corner of the mouth is turned down.
Usage: Timmy is *jealous* of his new baby brother.
Note: This sign may be interchanged with the following
one.

ENVY

Bite the end of the index finger.
Origin: Biting the finger in envy.
Usage: His skill made me *envious*.
Note: This sign and the one above may be interchanged.

CONSCIENCE, GUILTY

Place the side of the right "G" against the heart and
strike several times.
Origin: Indicates the beating of the heart, feeling guilty.
Usage: His *conscience* is bothering him.
Do you feel *guilty* about doing that?

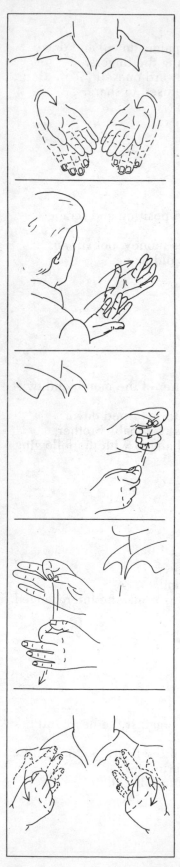

CONFESS, ADMIT

With fingertips pointing down, place both hands against the body, draw them up and forward, ending with open hands facing up.
Origin: That which is within is brought out into the open.
Usage: an honest *confession*.
  I *admit* my ignorance.

TEND, TENDENCY, INCLINED TOWARD

Hands open, middle fingers extended slightly, palms facing up; right middle finger touches heart, then moves upward and away from the body. The left hand moves in exactly the same way, but is farther away from the body.
Origin: Feelings are extended.
Usage: *tend* to gain weight.
  inclined toward outdoor activities.

REVENGE

Strike the fingertips of the modified "A" together several times (palms facing in).
Origin: Picking at each other.
Usage: I will *get even* (take revenge).

UNFAIR

The fingertips of the right "F" (palm facing left) move downward in a quick motion, touching and passing the left "F" (palm right).
Origin: As if striking something.
Usage: That's *not fair!*
  a grievance about *unfair* treatment.

COURAGEOUS, BRAVE

Place the tips of the "FIVE" hands high on the chest near the shoulders and bring them forward into "S" positions.
Usage: He had the *courage* to stand up for his beliefs.
  The land of the free, and the home of the *brave*.

6
People, Occupations, and Money

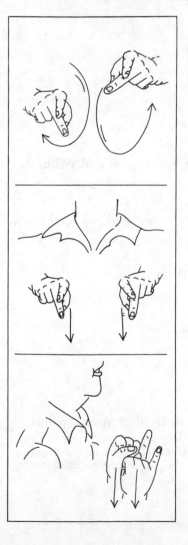

PEOPLE

Using both "P" hands, circle them alternately toward the center.
Usage: The U.S. government is responsible to the American *people*.

PERSON, PERSONAL

With both hands in the "P" position bring the hands down in front of the body, a short distance apart.
Usage: a fine *person;* her *personal* business.

INDIVIDUAL

Both "I" hands facing each other are brought down in front of the body, a short distance apart. For the plural, repeat, moving the sign slightly to the right. (Some prefer to use the open hand, palms pointing forward.)
Usage: We worked as *individuals,* each one responsible for part of the project.

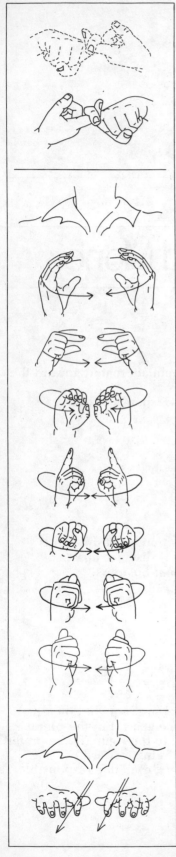

FRIEND

Hook the right index over the left which is palm-up and repeat in reverse.
Origin: Representing a close-knit association.
Usage: my best *friend*.

GROUP, CLASS, COMMUNITY, ORGANIZATION, DEPARTMENT, SOCIETY, TEAM

Place the "C" hands in front of you; draw them apart to the sides and around to the front until the little fingers touch.
Note: Use of the "C" hands encompasses any group. Distinctions may be made by initializing as follows:

C—CLASS, COMMUNITY
Usage: a *class* in school; a *community* of nuns.

G—GROUP
Usage: a *group* of doctors.

O—ORGANIZATION
Usage: a women's *organization*.

D—DEPARTMENT
Usage: *Department* of Health, Education, and Welfare.

S—SOCIETY
Usage: the Ladies' Aid *Society;* interested in *social* work.

T—TEAM
Usage: We're proud of our college *team*.

A—ASSOCIATION
Usage: a scientific *association*.

AUDIENCE

Place the curved "FIVE" hands in front of you, palms down, and move them forward.
Origin: Rows of people in front of you.
Usage: We were surprised to see such a large *audience*.

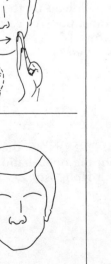

CHARACTER

Place the right "C" against the left palm and move it forward in a complete circle. ROLE—Use the right "R" as above.
Usage: a *character* in the play; What is your *role?*

NEIGHBOR

Sign "NEAR" (the back of the right bent hand approaches the inside of the left bent hand, both palms facing the body); add the "PERSON" ending.
Origin: A person who lives nearby.
Usage: a good *neighbor.*

SWEETHEART

Place both "A" hands together, palms facing the body; bend and unbend the thumbs.
Origin: Two people nodding to each other.
Usage: *sweethearts* since childhood.

BACHELOR

Place the right "B" first at the right side of the chin, then at the left.
Usage: a popular *bachelor.*

SCOUTS

Place the index tip of the right "U" at the forehead (palm forward).
Origin: The scout salute.
Usage: the Boy *Scouts* of America.

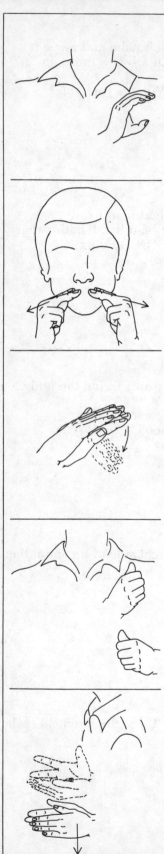

POLICE, COP

Place the right "C" at the left shoulder, palm facing left.
Origin: The policeman's badge worn on his uniform.
Usage: The *police* protected us. Call the *cops!*

THIEF, ROBBER

Use both "N" hands and stroke across the upper lip to the sides.
Origin: Indicating the mask worn over the lower part of the face.
Usage: The *thief* stole a bicycle.

HYPOCRITE, IMPOSTOR

Place the right open hand on the back of the left open hand; bend both hands together.
Usage: They felt he was a *hypocrite*.
His actions showed him to be an *imposter*.

SOLDIER, ARMY

Place the right "A" against the left shoulder, palm facing body, and the left "A" on the left side of the waist. (The sign for "ARMY" should be followed by the "group" sign made with a "C" representing a body of soldiers.)
Origin: Soldier presenting arms.
Usage: tomb of the unknown *soldier*.
a large *army*.

SAILOR

Sign "SHIP" and add the "PERSON" ending. Or, show the bell-bottom trousers with the open hands.
Usage: Our *sailors* arrived in Hong Kong.

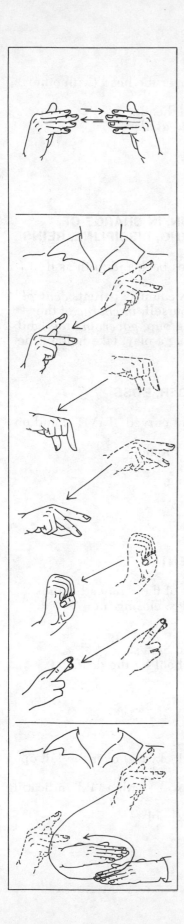

WAR, BATTLE

Place the bent "FOUR" hands in front of the body, fingertips pointing toward each other, palms down; move the hands first to the right, then to the left in front of you.
Origin: The armies forcing each other back, first one and then the other.
Usage: marching to *war*. The *battle* is over.

KING

Place the right "K" against the left shoulder, then against the right waist.
Origin: The initial letter combined with the stole worn by royalty.
Usage: the *king* of England.

QUEEN

Sign as in "KING" using a "Q."
Usage: *Queen* for a day.

PRINCE, PRINCESS

Sign as in "KING" using a "P."
Usage: the student *prince*.
Note: For *princess*, precede this sign with "GIRL."

EMPEROR

Sign as in "KING" using an "E."
Usage: the *emperor* of Japan.

ROYAL

Sign as in "KING" using an "R."
Usage: the *royal* throne.

KINGDOM

Sign "KING" and then make a counterclockwise circle with the right open hand over the left open hand, both palms down.
Origin: A combination of the sign for "KING" and "OVER" showing his authority over the land.
Usage: ruler of a great *kingdom*.

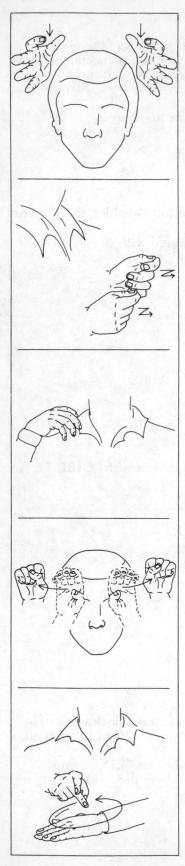

CROWN, DIADEM

Bring both "C" hands down over the head (with other fingers extended).
Origin: Placing a crown on the head.
Usage: a golden *crown*; a royal *diadem*.

REIGN, RULE, CONTROL, RUN, IN CHARGE OF, MANAGE, GOVERN, DIRECTING, DISCIPLINE, REINS

Move both modified "A" hands back and forth as if holding reins.
Usage: a king *reigns*; *rules* his country; parents *control* children; *discipline* yourself; *in charge* of the building; *managing* a group; *governing* the land; *run* a meeting; *directing* a play; take hold of the *reins*.

CAPTAIN, CHAIRMAN, OFFICER, BOSS

Place the fingertips of the right curved "FIVE" hand on the right shoulder.
Origin: Authority rests on the shoulder.
Usage: a *captain* in the army.
      chairman of the meeting.
      a naval *officer*.
      my new *boss*.

PRESIDENT, SUPERINTENDENT

Place both "C" hands in front of the forehead, palms forward; draw them to the sides, closing into "S" positions.
Origin: Horns of authority.
Usage: *president* of the United States.
      superintendent of a school for the deaf.

PRINCIPAL

Circle the right "P" (counterclockwise) over the left open hand which is palm-down.
Origin: Making the sign for "over" with a "P," indicating the principal is over others.
Usage: *principal* of the high school.

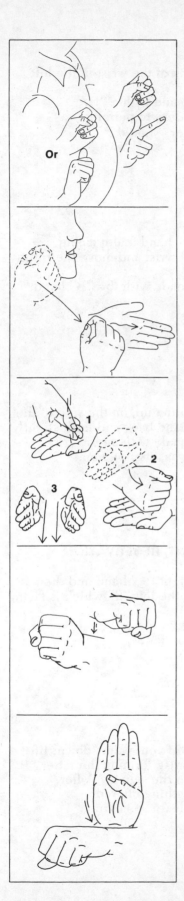

ASSISTANT

Place the thumb tip of the right "L" against the left fist. (Sometimes made with the right "A.")
Usage: Mr. Martin is *assistant* to the president.

SECRETARY

Take an imaginary pencil from the ear, write into the left hand and make the "PERSON" ending.
Origin: A person who takes notes.
Usage: Teri is my good *secretary*.

TREASURER

Sign "MONEY" and "COLLECTION"; add the "PERSON" ending.
Origin: A person who collects money.
Usage: *treasurer* of the organization.

WORK

The right "S" facing down is struck several times on the wrist of the left "S."
Origin: Activity of the hands.
Usage: "All *work* and no play makes Jack a dull boy." (Ben Franklin).

BUSINESS

Place the right "B" hand, pointing up, at the left wrist and strike several times.
Origin: The sign for "work," made with a "B."
Usage: We set up our *business* last year.

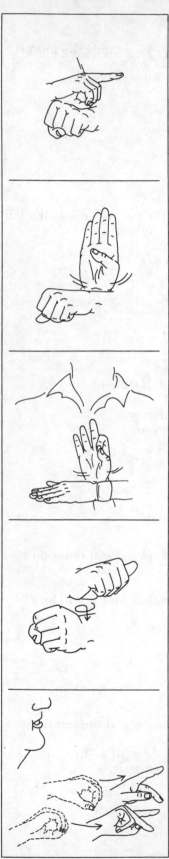

DUTY

Place the right "D" on the back of the wrist of the left closed hand.
Origin: The sign for "work," made with a "D."
Usage: Every one of us had a *duty* to perform.
Note: This sign is often used for "should."

BUSY

Place the wrist of the right "B" hand (palm facing forward) on the side of the left wrist and move the right hand back and forth slightly.
Origin: The sign for "work," made with the "B" hand.
Usage: We all lead a *busy* life.

FUNCTION

Place the right "F" hand, pointing up, on the side of the left wrist and move the right hand back and forth slightly.
Origin: The sign for "work," made with an "F."
Usage: Every part of the body has its *function*.

ENGAGEMENT, APPOINTMENT, RESERVATION

Make a small circle with the right "A" hand and then place the wrist on the wrist of the left "S" which is facing right.
Origin: Indicating one is bound.
Usage: a dinner *engagement* tonight.
   a 4 o'clock *appointment*.
   a plane *reservation*.

OPPORTUNITY

Place both "O" hands in front of you, palms down; lift both hands slightly from the wrist, forming the letter "P." Or, raise both open hands as in the sign for "offer."
Origin: An opportunity is something offered.
Usage: a good *opportunity* to learn something.

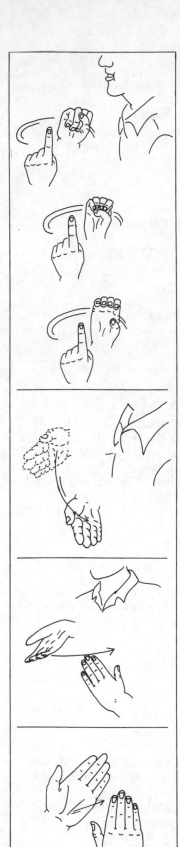

SITUATION

Hold up the left index finger; circle it with the right "S" from left to right.
Origin: Being in the middle of something.
Usage: finding yourself in a difficult *situation*.

ENVIRONMENT

Sign as above, using the "E" hand.
Usage: living in a good *environment*.

CIRCUMSTANCE

Sign as above, using the "C" hand.
Usage: I would like to explain the *circumstances* of the case.

HIRE

Bring the right open hand toward the body, palm facing up.
Usage: *Hire* the handicapped.

FIRED

Hold up the left open hand, fingertips up and palm in; pass the upturned right hand toward you across the top of the fingertips, toward the left.
Origin: As if the head were cut off.
Usage: The boss had reasons for *firing* the men.

DISMISSED, LAID OFF

Move the tips of the right fingers across the lower edge of the left hand in a quick motion.
Origin: Wiped off.
Usage: Class is *dismissed*.
       laid off for a month.

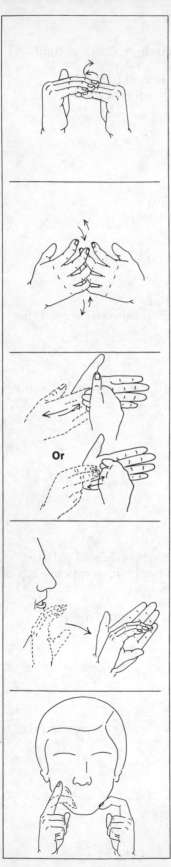

BUILD

Place the palm of one hand on the back of the other; alternate hands and repeat several times.
Origin: Placing one brick upon another.
Usage: This house is *built* well.

MACHINE, FACTORY, MOTOR, ENGINE

Lock the fingers of the curved "FIVE" hands, palms facing you, and shake them up and down.
Origin: Gears in motion.
Usage: a large new *machine*; a *factory* worker.
a powerful *motor*; an old *engine*.

PAINT

Using the fingertips of the right open hand as a brush, draw them back and forth across the left palm. Or, use two fingers if indicating painting with a smaller brush.
Origin: The actual motion of painting.
Usage: He *painted* the house white. The nurse *painted* Mercurochrome on the cut.

PICTURE, PHOTOGRAPH

Place the right "C" at the side of the face, palm facing forward; then place the "C," with palm still facing forward, against the left open palm.
Origin: The face is put on a card.
Usage: I never saw that *picture* before.
I thought it was a good *photograph*.

CAMERA, TAKE A PICTURE

Make a "C" with each hand, using only the thumb and index fingers, palms facing each other; move the right index up and down.
Origin: Holding a small camera and taking a picture.
Usage: Where's your *camera*?
Will you *take a picture* for me?

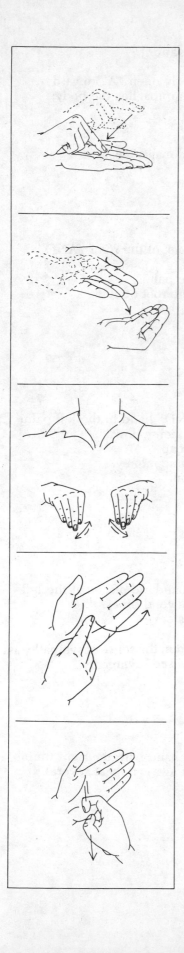

PRINT, NEWSPAPER

The right "G," palm down, picks the imaginary type and places it in the left palm.
Origin: Natural motion of old-style typesetting.
Usage: The book was *printed* in 1977.
　　　　Did you read the morning *paper?*

BUY, SHOPPING, PURCHASE

Place the back of the "AND" hand into the left palm and lift it out to the right, still in the "AND" position. (For "SHOPPING" repeat the sign several times.)
Origin: Putting out money.
Usage: Money cannot *buy* everything.
　　　　We were out *shopping* all afternoon.
　　　　Russia *purchased* wheat from the U.S.A.

SELL, STORE, SALE

Both "AND" hands, pointing down, are held in front of you, moving back and forth from the wrist.
Origin: Holding up an item for sale.
Usage: We *sold* the house.
　　　　our best *sales*man (add the "man" sign).
　　　　The grocery *store* is near our home.
　　　　Some women like garage *sales*.

PAY

Place the tip of the right index finger in the left palm and move the index finger out to the right.
Origin: Pointing to the money which is paid out.
Usage: Buy now, *pay* later.
　　　　high monthly *payments*.

COST, PRICE, CHARGE, FINE, TAX

Place the left palm in front of you, facing right; strike the right crooked index finger against the left palm and down, palm facing you.
Origin: Indicating that a part of the money is taken.
Usage: the high *cost* of living.
　　　　price of meat.
　　　　Painters *charge* by the hour.
　　　　paid a $10 fine.
　　　　Sales *tax* is 4%.

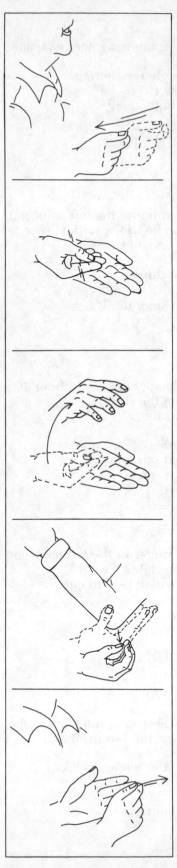

SUBSCRIBE, DRAW (Compensation)

Draw the right, modified, slightly open "A" toward yourself, closing the "A" as it approaches the body; repeat several times.
Origin: Pulling it in.
Usage: He *draws* social security.
We *subscribe* to several magazines.

MONEY, FUNDS

Strike the left palm with the back of the right "AND" hand several times.
Origin: Counting coins into the palm.
Usage: The love of *money* is the root of evil.
Our *funds* are low.

RICH, WEALTHY

Place the back of the right "AND" hand in the left palm and then lift it out, right palm facing down.
Origin: Showing money in a heap.
Usage: A *rich* uncle left her some money.
We are a *wealthy* nation.

POOR

The open fingers of the right hand are placed at the left elbow and pulled downward several times.
Origin: Indicating the ragged sleeve.
Usage: a *poor* family.
Note: This sign is not to be used in the sense of sympathy as in "poor Suzie." For this usage see "sympathy."

DOLLARS

Grasp the tips of the left open hand with the right thumb and four fingers; pull the right away. Repeat several times.
Origin: Counting out the bills.
Usage: 100 *dollars*.

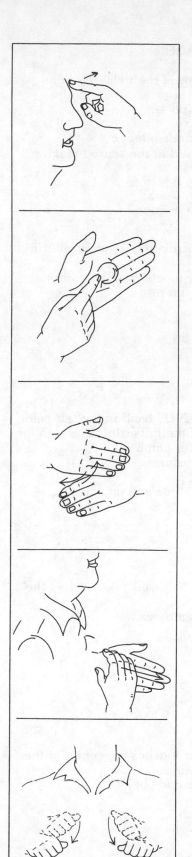

CENTS (Used with a number)

Touch the forehead and follow by making the desired number.
Usage: Do you have a *nickel* or a *dime?* (Nickel—
      "CENT" + "FIVE"; Dime—"CENT" + "TEN.")

COINS

Draw a small circle in the left palm with the right index.
Origin: Tracing the shape of the coin in the hand.
Usage: a *coin* collector.

CHANGE (Money)

Place the little-finger edge of the right open hand on the index edge of the left open hand and move the right slightly from side to side.
Origin: As if dividing it up.
Usage: Do you have *change* for a dollar?

CHECK

Place the tips of the right "C" against the left open palm and draw the right hand toward the tip of the left hand.
Origin: Indicating the size and shape of the check.
Usage: If I pay by *check* I have a good record.

DEPOSIT

Place the "A" hands in front of you and then move them away from each other to the sides as the wrists turn slightly.
Usage: You will have to leave a *deposit* of $25.

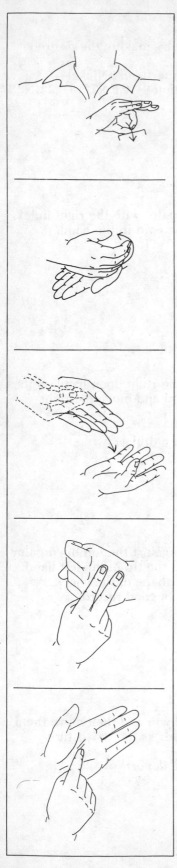

PROFIT, BENEFIT, ADVANTAGE

Place the thumb and index tips of the right "P" in an imaginary breast pocket.
Origin: Placing money in the pocket.
Usage: Make a *profit*.
It's to your *benefit* (or *advantage*).
Note: This sign is not to be used in the sense of taking advantage.

EARN

Draw the right curved hand across the left palm starting at the fingertips.
Origin: As if gathering money together in the palm.
Usage: Your money can *earn* interest.

SPEND, WASTE

Place the back of the right "AND" hand in the left palm and open it as you slide it off the fingertips. The sign for "WASTE" is made with greater emphasis.
Origin: Money slides off the palm.
Usage: Don't *spend* it all!
That's a *waste* of both time and money.

SAVE (As saving money)

Place the inside of the right "V" against the back of the left wrist.
Usage: "A penny *saved* is a penny earned" (Ben Franklin).

OWE, DEBT, DUE

The tip of the right index finger touches the center of the left palm several times.
Origin: Pointing to where the money belongs.
Usage: I *owe* you $5.
Our national *debt* is high.
Payment is *due* next week.

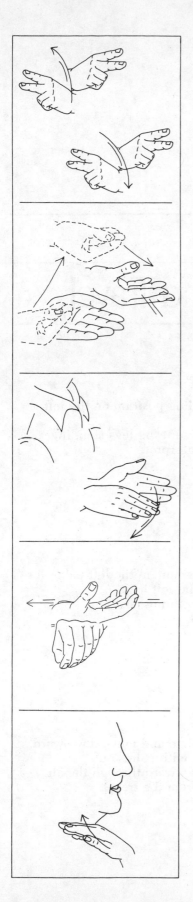

BORROW, LEND

Make the sign for "KEEP" (the right "V" on top of the left "V" crossing at the wrist); draw it either toward or away from the body as the case may be.

Usage: People *borrow* money to buy cars (toward body).
Banks will *lend* you money (away from body).
I made application for a *loan* (toward body).

EXPENSIVE

Place the back of the right "AND" hand into the left palm; lift the right hand out and draw it away, opening it somewhat and then giving it a slight quick twist to the right.

Usage: very *expensive* clothes.

CHEAP

Place the index-finger side of the right open palm against the left palm and brush downward.

Usage: I think my shoes look *cheap*.
That store has *cheap* clothes.

BEG

Place the back of the right curved "FIVE" hand on the back of the left hand; draw it back several times.

Origin: Hand extended in a begging position.

Usage: *beg* for help.

BROKE

Strike the little-finger side of the downturned hand against the right side of the neck.

Usage: I spent all my money and now I'm *broke!*

7
Physical Movement and Travel

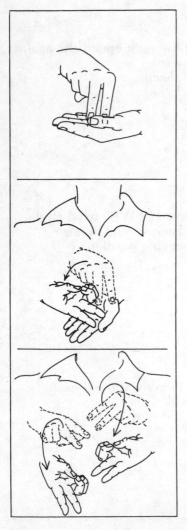

STAND

Place the right "V" in a standing position on the left palm.
Origin: The two fingers represent the legs standing.
Usage: Melba will *stand* to interpret.

FALL

Place the "V" in a standing position on the left palm; let the "V" fall, palm down, into the left hand.
Origin: From a standing to a reclining position.
Usage: Don't run, you may *fall*.

FALLING

Both hands in "V" positions rotate and move downward, palms out, then in, and ending with palms out.
Origin: An object tumbling downward through the air.
Usage: The leaves are *falling* from the trees.

SLIDE

Sign "STAND" and slide the "V" forward on the left palm.
Origin: Moving from a standing position to a slide.
Usage: It's icy, you may *slide* (or *slip*).

LIE, RECLINE

Place the back of the right "V" hand in the left palm.
Origin: Fingers represent a reclining position.
Usage: *lie* on the grass; *reclining* on the couch.

GET UP, ARISE

The right "V" with fingers pointing up and facing you is raised and then placed in a standing position on the left palm.
Origin: Rising to a standing position.
Usage: It's time to *get up*.
　　　　They all *arose* and sang.

DANCE

Place the right "V" in a standing position on the left palm and swing the "V" back and forth.
Origin: The motion of the body in dancing.
Usage: Barbara was known for her graceful *dancing*.

JUMP

Place the right "V" in a standing position on the left palm; lift the "V," bending the knuckles, and return to a standing position.
Origin: Bending the knees in jumping.
Usage: Children *jump* and play.

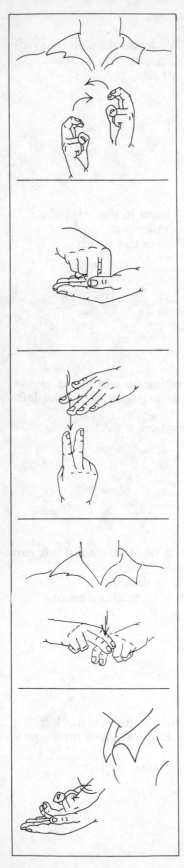

CLIMB

Place the curved "V" hands before you facing each other; move them upward alternately in stages. (To climb a rope form "S" positions, hand over hand, as in actual climbing.)
Usage: Mountain *climbing* can be dangerous.
He *climbed up the rope* to the window.

KNEEL

Bend the knuckles of the right "V" and place in the left palm.
Origin: Fingers are in the kneeling position.
Usage: The visitor *knelt* before the queen of England.

DROWN

Place the right "V" (palm toward you) between the index and middle fingers of the left open hand, which is facing down, and slide it down with a slightly wavy motion.
Origin: Left hand represents the water level and right hand is sinking.
Usage: No one knew the cause of her *drowning*.

SIT, CHAIR

The right curved index and middle fingers are placed crosswise on the left curved index and middle fingers, both palms facing down.
Origin: Fingers represent the seated person and the chair.
Usage: I *sat down* for a few minutes.
We will need about 50 *chairs* for the meeting.

RESTLESS

The back of the curved "V" is placed in the left palm and is twisted from side to side slightly, with a motion from the wrist.
Origin: As if squirming in a seat or lying restlessly in bed.
Usage: feeling *restless* while waiting.
feel *restless* and can't sleep.
I *tossed and turned* all night.

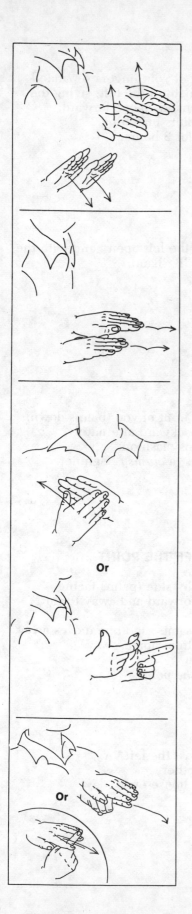

RISE, BE SEATED

Both open hands move up with palms up, or move down with palms down.
Origin: The natural motion of asking people to rise or to be seated.
Usage: Will the audience please *rise*.
　　　　Everyone *be seated* please.

WALK

Open hands, palms down, are moved in a forward-downward motion alternately.
Origin: Representing feet walking.
Usage: Brisk *walking* is good exercise.

RUN

The right open palm, facing up, brushes outward to the right from under the left open palm.

Or, hook the index of the right "L" under the thumb of the left "L" and move hands forward in a quick motion.
Usage: Daily *running* helps keep you well.

ESCAPE, RUN AWAY

Place the right index under the left open hand which is facing down, and move it forward and out toward the right.

Or, place the right index pointing up between the index and middle fingers of the left open hand (palm down); move the right index away in a quick motion.
Usage: *escaped* during the night.
　　　　often *ran away* from home.

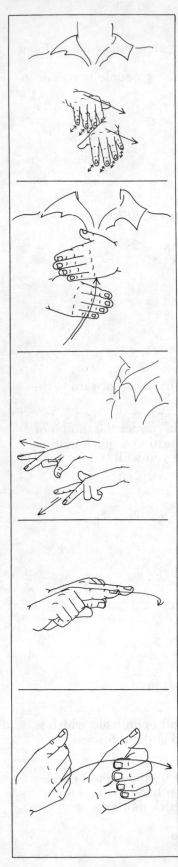

MARCH

Place both bent hands in front of you, fingers separated and palms facing down, right behind the left; swing the fingers back and forth as both hands move forward.
Origin: Indicating rows of soldiers marching.
Usage: The soldiers *marched* for 3 hours.

KICK

Strike the little-finger edge of the left open hand with the index-finger edge of the right "B" hand.
Origin: The motion of kicking.
Usage: *kicked* by a horse.

AWKWARD, CLUMSY

Place the "THREE" hands in front of you (palms down) and move them forward and backward alternately.
Origin: As if walking in a clumsy fashion.
Usage: feel *awkward* on skates; a *clumsy* beginner.

STRAY, DEVIATE, DIVERT, OFF THE POINT

Place both index fingers side by side (palms facing down); move the right index forward and away toward the right.
Origin: Fingers begin as for "same" and one moves away.
Usage: Our cat *strayed away* from home.
　　　　deviated from the truth.
　　　　Our discussion is *off the point*.
　　　　cars were *diverted*.

PASS

Move the right "A" forward past the left "A."
Origin: One hand passes the other.
Usage: Many people *pass* our house every day.
　　　　A new law was *passed*.

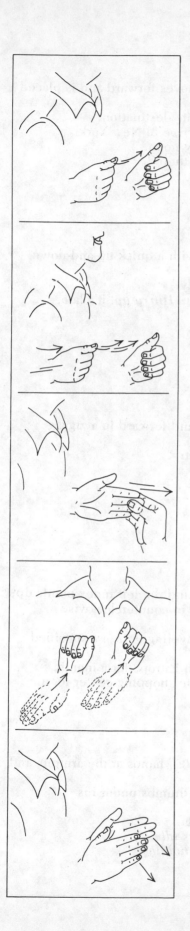

FOLLOW, FOLLOWER, DISCIPLE

Place the right "A" behind the left "A" and move them both forward. (Add the "PERSON" ending for the noun.)
Origin: One hand follows the other.
Usage: *follow* the leader.
Some people are *followers*.
12 *disciples*.

CHASE

Sign "FOLLOW" more vigorously.
Origin: One hand following the other rapidly.
Usage: Police *chased* the thief and caught him.

LEAD, GUIDE

Grasp the tip of the left open hand with the right fingertips and thumb and pull forward.
Origin: Right hand leading the left.
Usage: *lead* the horse to water; our Indian *guide*.

DEPART, LEAVE, WITHDRAW

Place the open hands in front of you toward the right, palms down, with fingertips pointing forward; draw the hands back and up into "A" positions.
Origin: Hands moving away as if one is withdrawing.
Usage: The train *departs* at 10:30.
What time are you *leaving?*
She *withdrew* from the room.

LEAVE, NEGLECT, ABANDON

Place open hands in front of you, palm facing palm, tips to the right; give them a downward twist from the wrist.
Origin: Downward movement suggests leaving something.
Usage: *Leave* your books here.
Don't *neglect* your practice.
We didn't need our coats so we *left* them in the car.
The parents *abandoned* their children.

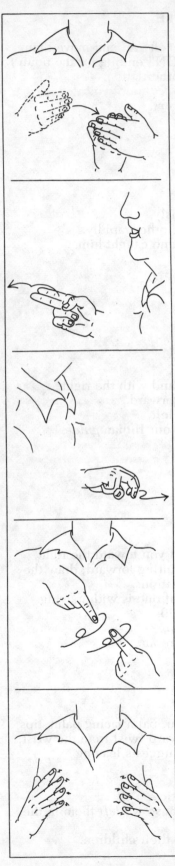

ARRIVE, REACH, GET TO

The right slightly bent hand moves forward and is placed in the left open palm.
Origin: The hand "arrives" at its destination.
Usage: When will the plane *arrive* in New York?
We *reached* Chicago by noon.
What time did you *get* there?

HURRY

Move the right "H" forward with a quick up-and-down movement.
Origin: Moving forward rapidly.
Usage: *Hurry,* it looks like rain. *Hurry up,* it's late.

TRAVEL, TRIP, JOURNEY

Move the right curved "V" hand forward in a zigzag movement, palm facing down.
Usage: *travel* to another country.
trip to northern Italy.
a long *journey.*

TRAVEL AROUND

The right index points down and the left index points up; they circle around each other in counterclockwise movements.
Note: This sign represents traveling *within* a specified area rather than *to* an area.
Usage: We *traveled around* in Europe for a month.
We *went around* in the shopping center for a while.

VACATION, IDLE, HOLIDAY

Place the thumbs of the "FIVE" hands at the armpits and wiggle the four fingers.
Origin: A man standing with thumbs under his suspenders.
Usage: a *vacation* in Bermuda.
never working, always *idle.*
July 4th is a national *holiday.*

VISIT

The "V" hands, pointing up and facing you, are rotated up-out-down-in-around each other.
Origin: Represents people in circulation.
Usage: Why not *visit* the Smithsonian Institute?

SUITCASE

Using an "S" hand, lift an imaginary suitcase by the handle.
Usage: Linda took two red *suitcases* on her trip.

AUTOMOBILE, CAR, DRIVE

Place the "S" hands in front of you, palms facing each other, and move them up and down alternately as if driving a car.
Note: When indicating that one is driving to a destination, the "S" hands are moved forward.
Usage: a beautiful, new *car*; *drove* around sightseeing;
He *drove* right to the hospital (second description above).

RIDE

Place the right curved "V" in the slightly opened left "O," and move them forward.
Origin: Placing yourself in the vehicle.
Usage: May I *ride* with you?

GET IN, GET OUT

Place the bent "V" in the left "O" or remove the right "V," as the case may be.
Usage: Hurry and *get in*, we have to leave.
Two people *got out of* the car.
I *stepped out of* my role.
I *removed myself from* the situation.

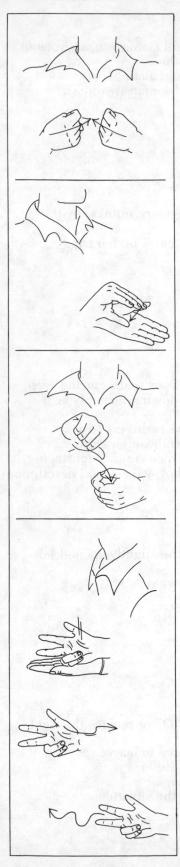

COLLISION, ACCIDENT

Bring the knuckles of the "S" hands forcibly together (palm side toward the body).
Origin: Two vehicles colliding.
Usage: Two large ships *collided*. We saw a bad *accident* on the highway.

FLAT TIRE

Place the thumb of the open "AND" hand on the left palm and bring the right to a closed "AND" position.
Origin: Showing the tire deflating.
Usage: arrived late because of a *flat tire*.

GASOLINE

Move the thumb of the right "A" into the left "O."
Origin: Pouring gas into the tank.
Usage: will need *gas* soon.

PARKING

Place the right "THREE" hand on the left open palm, all fingertips pointing forward.
Origin: The right hand is the car and the left represents the street.
Usage: We drove and drove but couldn't find a place to *park*. The signs said, "No *Parking*."

Note: The "THREE" hand is used to represent the actual car movement as pictured: 1) backing into a parking space, 2) moving in and out of traffic.

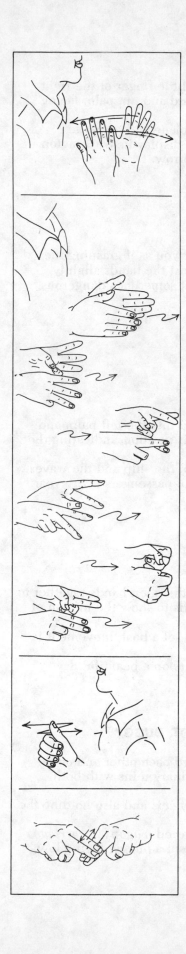

TRAFFIC

The open "FIVE" hands, facing each other pointing up, move slightly back and forth alternately.
Origin: Indicating the flow of traffic in two directions.
Usage: *Traffic* is heavy on Friday afternoons.

WAY, ROAD, PATH, STREET, HIGHWAY

Place both open hands in front of you, fngers pointing forward and palms facing each other; move both hands forward with a slight zigzag motion.
Origin: Showing the pathway.
Usage: the *way* to Los Angeles.
　　　The *road* is very narrow.
　　　a *path* through the woods.
　　　a busy *street*.
　　　a new, improved *highway*.
Note: Initials are sometimes used in educational settings, such as:
W—way

R—road

P—path

S—street

H—highway

BACK AND FORTH

Move the "A" hand forward and backward several times.
Usage: *back and forth* to work every day.
　　　She was impatient and walked *back and forth* constantly.

TRAIN, RAILROAD

Rub the right "H" back and forth on the back of the left "H," both palms down.
Origin: Movement on the tracks.
Usage: The *train* arrives in Philadelphia at 5 p.m.
　　　Railroad travel can be very comfortable.

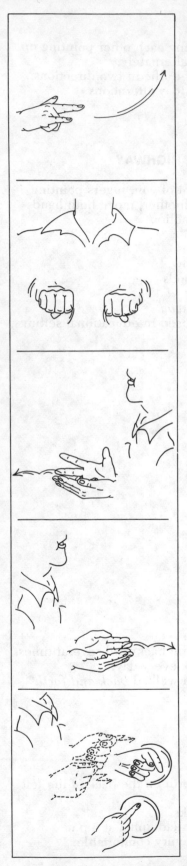

AIRPLANE, FLY

Extend the thumb, index, and little finger of the right hand and move the hand forward and up, palm facing down.
Origin: Showing wings of the plane and take-off.
Usage: The first *airplane* is on display in Washington. We *fly* to London tomorrow.

MOTORCYCLE

Place the "S" hands in front of you as if grasping the handlebars of a motorcycle; twist the hands slightly.
Usage: *Motorcycles* are fun but sometimes dangerous.

SHIP

Place the right "THREE" hand into the left palm and move the hands together in this position, indicating the motion of the waves.
Origin: Represents the masts of the ship and the waves.
Usage: *Ships* carry thousands of passengers every year.

BOAT

Place the little-finger edge of the open hands together to form a boat and move the hands to show the motion of waves.
Origin: Hands are in the shape of a boat; movement is natural.
Usage: People enjoy their *boats* on a beautiful day.

WAGON, CARRIAGE, CHARIOT, BUGGY

Point both index fingers toward each other and circle them forward; then hold imaginary reins with both modified "A" hands.
Origin: Indicating the large wheels and also holding the reins of the horse.
Usage: People traveled in covered *wagons*. a *carriage* and four horses; a ride in a *buggy*; Swing low, sweet *chariot*.

8

Opposites

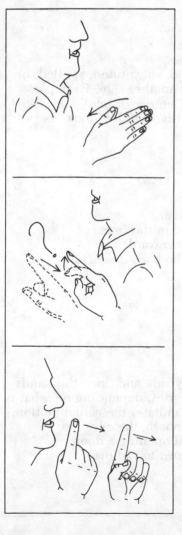

ASK, REQUEST

Place the open hands palm to palm and draw them toward the body.
Origin: Hands held as in prayer.
Usage: *Ask* for help. What is your *request*?

QUESTION

Draw a question mark in the air with the index finger; draw it back and direct it forward as if placing the dot below the question mark.
Usage: That *question* is hard to answer.

ANSWER, REPLY, RESPOND

Place the tip of the right index, palm facing left, at the lips; place the left index, pointing up, in front of it; move both hands out ending with the index fingers pointing forward. ("Reply" and "Response" are often made with "R's.")
Usage: *answer* my letter; a quick *reply*; an intelligent *response*.

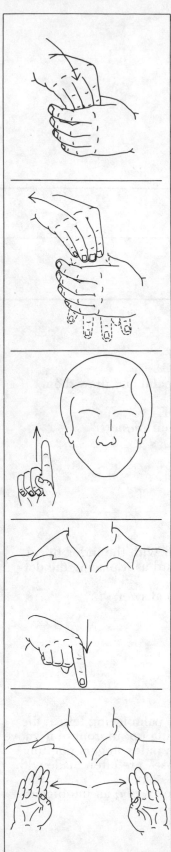

IN

Place the closed fingertips of the right hand into the left "C" hand.
Origin: Placing something in the left hand.
Usage: You live *in* America.

OUT

The right open "AND" hand, facing the body and pointing down, becomes a closed "AND" as it is drawn up through the left "C" which then becomes an "O."
Origin: Moving out of the left hand.
Usage: Republicans are *out*, Democrats are in.

UP

Point up with the index finger.
Usage: The cat is *up* in the tree.
Note: This sign is often omitted, substituted, spelled, or included within the context of another sign. Examples: stand *up* (omit); sun *up* (sign "sunrise"); time's *up* (sign "time" and "finish"); look *up* (the sign for "look" is directed upward).

DOWN

Point down with the index finger.
Origin: A natural gesture, used in the sense of descending, going down or downward.
Usage: *down* in the valley; Who lives *downstairs?*

OPEN

Place both open hands side by side and draw the hands apart. The sign for "OPEN" varies, depending on what is being opened. Often the sign imitates the actual motion, as in opening a window, the mouth, the eyes, etc.
Origin: Hands move apart as if opening a door.
Usage: The White House is *open* to visitors.

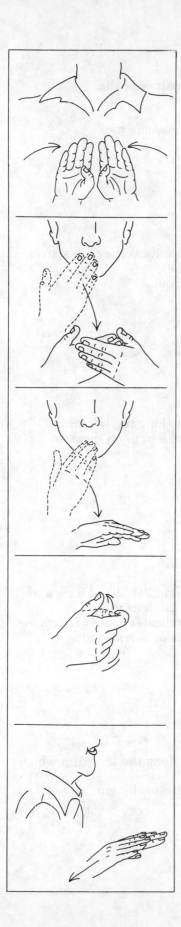

CLOSE, SHUT

Draw both open hands toward each other until the index fingers touch. The sign for "CLOSE" or "SHUT" varies depending on what is being closed.
Origin: Hands come together as if a door is closing.
Usage: I'm cold, please *close the door.*

GOOD, WELL

Touch the lips with the fingers of the right hand and then move the right hand forward placing it palm up in the palm of the left hand.
Origin: It has been tasted and smelled and offered as acceptable.
Usage: *good* food; doing *well* at work.

BAD

Touch the lips with the fingers of the right hand and then turn the palm down.
Origin: It has been tasted and smelled and turned down.
Usage: That tastes *bad.*

FAST, QUICK, RAPID, IMMEDIATELY, SUDDENLY, RIGHT AWAY

The right thumb is snapped out of the curved index finger as if shooting a marble. May be made with both hands.
Origin: As fast as shooting a marble.
Usage: *fast* train; *quick* thinking; *rapid* growth; needs help *immediately;* storm came *suddenly;* the children obeyed *right away.*

SLOW

Stroke down the back of the left hand slowly with the right hand.
Origin: The hand is moving slowly.
Usage: a *slow* learner.
Slow down, I can't understand your fingerspelling.

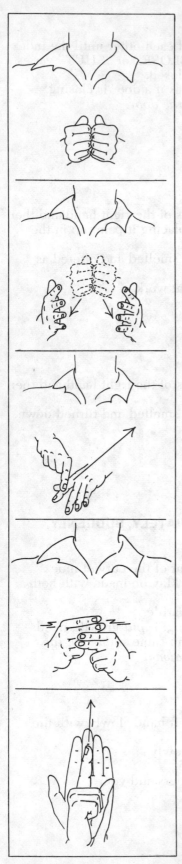

WITH, ACCOMPANY

Place the "A" hands together, palm to palm.
Origin: One hand with the other.
Usage: Come *with* your friend.
I'm afraid, will you *accompany* me?

WITHOUT

Sign "WITH"; then open the hands as they are separated.
Origin: Hands no longer together.
Usage: He acted *without* a reason.

LONG

Draw the right index finger up along the left arm.
Origin: The finger is measuring length on the arm.
Usage: a *long* time.

SHORT (in length), SOON, BRIEF

Rub the middle finger of the right "H" hand back and forth along the index finger of the left "H."
Origin: The short movement indicates a short length.
Usage: a *short* story; coming *soon*; a *brief* visit.

TALL

Pass the right index finger up along the left palm which is pointing upward.
Origin: Upward movement indicates height.
Usage: a *tall* man.

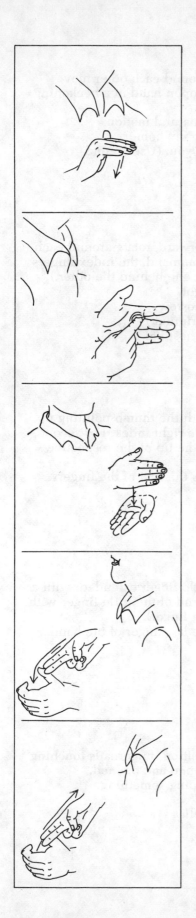

SHORT (in height), LITTLE, SMALL

Hold the right open hand in front of you, palm facing down; lower it slightly.
Origin: The lowered hand indicates short stature.
Usage: a *short* man; a *little* girl; a *small* boy.

START, BEGIN, COMMENCE

The tip of the right index makes a half-turn between the index and middle fingers of the left open hand.
Origin: Indicating a screw or a key being turned.
Usage: *Start* the car.
　　　Begin a new job.
　　　will *commence* at 2 o'clock.

STOP, CEASE

Little-finger side of the right open hand is brought down sharply to a position across the left open palm.
Origin: The right hand is placed emphatically on the left to form a barrier.
Usage: All the noise *stopped*.
　　　His breathing *ceased*.
　　　The men *quit* working at 3 o'clock.

PARTICIPATE, JOIN

Place the right "U" into the left "C."
Origin: Placing yourself in a situation.
Usage: Would you like to *participate?*
　　　Come on, *join in!*

QUIT, RESIGN

Place the right "U" into the left "C" and then pull it out again in a quick motion.
Origin: Taking yourself out of a situation.
Usage: I *quit!*
　　　The president *resigned*.

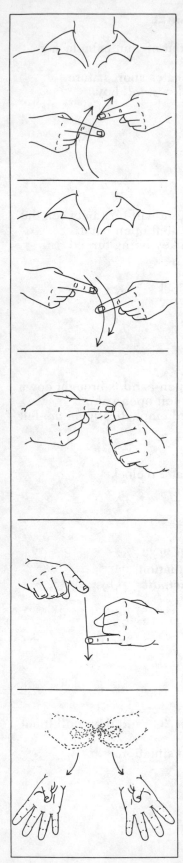

COME

Index fingers rotating once around each other move toward the body. Or, use the open hand in a beckoning motion.
Origin: Using the hands in a natural motion.
Usage: When can you *come* to my home?
   Come, I'm waiting for you. (Use second description.)

GO, GOING, WENT

Index fingers as they move forward, rotate around each other once. (When giving a command, the index fingers are swung down and forward, one behind the other.)
Usage: I *go* to work every night.
   She's *going* home tomorrow.
   Go! (Use second description.)
   Dr. Allen *went* to the hospital.

FIRST

Hold up the left "A" hand with the thumb pointing up and strike it with the tip of the right index. For second, third, fourth, and fifth, touch the tip of the respective fingers.
Origin: The thumb represents the first of the fingers.
Usage: in the *first* place.

LAST, FINAL, END

Hold the left "S" with the little finger extended; with a downward motion strike the end of the little finger with the right index finger (or little finger).
Origin: The little finger is the last finger of the hand.
Usage: *last* day of the week.
   the *end* of the world.
   the *final* decision.

LOSE, LOST

Both hands in the "AND" position, fingernails touching and palms facing up, are dropped and opened.
Origin: The open hands dropping something.
Usage: *lost* your car keys.
   always *lose* my umbrellas.

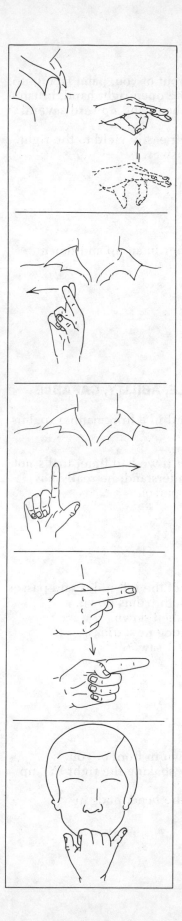

FIND, DISCOVER

Place the open hand in front of you, palm down; draw the thumb and forefinger together and lift up as if picking up something.
Origin: The natural motion of picking up something.
Usage: can't *find* the check; *found* time for his family; *discovered* a bird's nest.

RIGHT

Direct the "R" hand toward the right.
Origin: Showing a rightward direction.
Usage: sit on the *right*.

LEFT

Direct the "L" hand toward the left.
Origin: Showing a leftward direction.
Usage: *left* at the next corner.

RIGHT, CORRECT, PROPER, APPROPRIATE

The little-finger edge of the right "G" hand is placed on the index of the left "G" hand so that both index fingers point forward, one above the other. For "PROPER" and "APPROPRIATE" make the sign twice.
Usage: that's *right*; *correct* answer; *proper* clothing; *appropriate* behavior.

WRONG, MISTAKE, ERROR

The "Y" hand touches the chin, palm facing in.
Usage: the *wrong* way.
made a *mistake*.
my *error*.

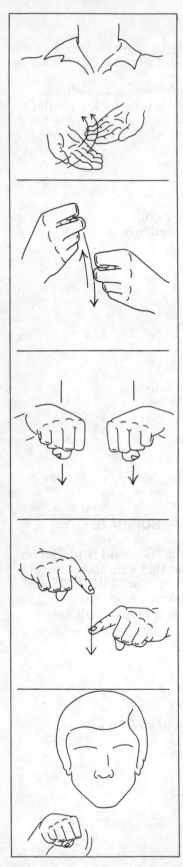

EASY, SIMPLE

Place the curved left hand in front of you, palm facing up. Using the little-finger side of the open right hand, brush under the fingertips of the left hand and upward several times.
Origin: The fingertips of the left easily yield to the right.
Usage: *easy* lesson; a *simple* answer.

DIFFICULT

Both bent "V's" strike each other in an up and down movement.
Usage: a *difficult* exam.

CAN, COULD, POSSIBLE, ABLE, ABILITY, CAPABLE

Move both "S" hands downward in a firm manner (palms down).
Origin: The fist indicates power.
Usage: *can* sign well; we *could* if we had time; that's not *possible*; not *able* to understand; he really has *ability*; a very *capable* person.

CAN'T, COULDN'T

The right index strikes the tip of the left index and passes it in a downward movement, both palms down.
Origin: The finger can't be pushed down.
Usage: You *can't* teach an old dog new tricks.
  I *couldn't* believe what I saw.

YES

Shake the right "S" up and down in front of you. Agreement is also indicated by shaking the right "Y" up and down.
Origin: The fist, representing the head, nods in agreement.
Usage: *Yes*, I will go.

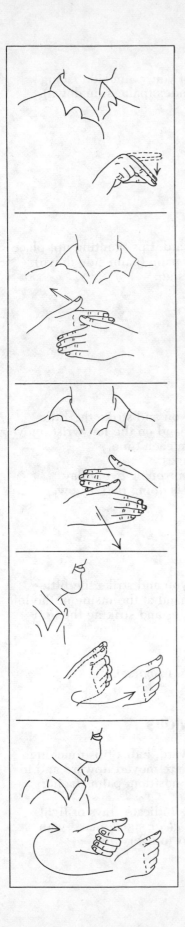

NO

Make an abbreviated "N" and "O" by bringing the index, middle finger, and thumb together in one motion.
Usage: *No,* I won't.

BEFORE

Open hands are facing you and the right is drawn away from the left toward the right shoulder.
Origin: Back over the shoulder always indicates the past.
Usage: the day *before* yesterday; come *ahead* of time. Buy your ticket *in advance.*

AFTER

Place the left open hand in front of you, palm facing you and fingers pointing right; place the right palm against the back of the left hand and then move the right forward, away from the left.
Origin: Indicates forward movement from a fixed location.
Usage: Come *after* 7 o'clock.

AHEAD

Place the "A" hands close together facing each other and move the right "A" in front of the left "A."
Origin: One in front of the other.
Usage: *ahead* of me in line.

BEHIND

Place the "A" hands close together facing each other and move the right "A" behind the left "A." To indicate that one is behind in accomplishment, place the right "A" behing the left "A" and draw the right back some distance.
Usage: hiding *behind* the door.
I was *behind* in my studies. (Use second description above.)

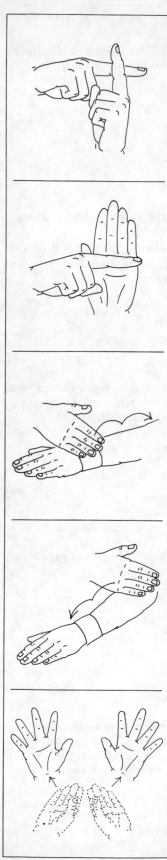

POSITIVE

Place the left index in front of you, palm side facing right; cross it with the right index (palm side down).
Origin: Natural sign.
Usage: Think *positively.*

NEGATIVE

Face the left open palm outward, tips pointing up; place the right index across the left palm (palm side down).
Origin: Indicating the minus sign.
Usage: a *negative* attitude.

IMPROVE

Place the left arm in front of you and strike the little-finger side of the right open hand on the left wrist; move it up in stages striking the arm each time.
Origin: Moving upward in stages.
Usage: Your interpreting is *improving* every day.
   She was very sick but is *doing better* now.

WORSEN, DETERIORATE

Place the left arm in front of you and strike the little-finger side of the right open hand at the inside of the left elbow, moving it down in stages and striking the arm each time.
Origin: Going downhill.
Usage: His health *deteriorated.*
   The patient's condition is *worsening.*

LIGHT, BRIGHT, CLEAR, OBVIOUS

Both "AND" hands point forward, index tips touching; open the fingers as the hands are moved upward and to the sides ending in a "FIVE" position, palms facing forward.
Origin: Opening of the fingers indicates rays of light.
Usage: no *light;* a *bright* day; *clear* signs; make your
   meaning *clear; obvious* to everyone.

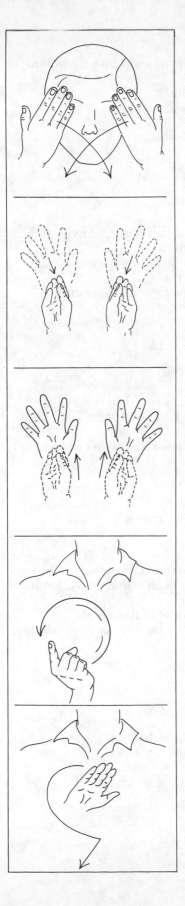

DARK, DIM

The open hands, palms facing you and pointing up, are crossed in front of the face.
Origin: Indicates darkness when eyes are covered.
Usage: a very *dark* night.
      The room was *dim.*

LIGHTS OUT, TURN OFF THE LIGHT

The open "AND" hands are brought down to the closed "AND" positions.
Origin: The opposite of light; rays of light fade away.
Usage: *Lights out,* please. time to *turn off the lights.*
      It's time to *turn off the lights.*

LIGHTS ON, TURN ON THE LIGHT

The closed "AND" hands are opened to "FIVE" positions, palms forward.
Origin: Rays of light are seen.
Usage: The *lights are on.*
      Turn on the lights, please.

ALWAYS, EVER

Describe a clockwise circle in front of you with the index finger, palm facing up.
Origin: A circle is never ending.
Usage: *always* learning; *ever* present.

NEVER

Move the right open hand, palm down, in a circular movement in front of the body as follows: up-right-down-left; then move the hand abruptly off the right.
Origin: Adapted from the natural gesture.
Usage: *never* satisfied.

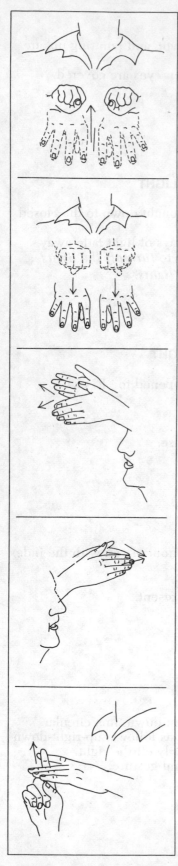

ADOPT, ASSUME, TAKE UP

Lift the open hands (palms down) and close them into "S" positions.
Origin: Taking hold of something.
Usage: *assume* responsibility.
adopt children.
take up where he left off.

DROP

Place the "S" hands in front of you (palms down) and open them as they suddenly drop.
Origin: Opening the hands as if dropping something.
Usage: The waiter *dropped* a tray.
I was angry and *dropped* my membership.

BROAD-MINDED, OPEN-MINDED

Place the open hands pointing forward in front of the forehead; move them forward and away from each other.
Origin: Indicating an open mind.
Usage: My friend is *broad-minded* and won't object.

NARROW-MINDED

Place open hands at side of forehead, fingers together and pointing forward, palms facing each other; move hands forward and toward each other.
Origin: Indicating the narrowness of the mind.
Usage: His conversation showed he was *narrow-minded*.

APPEAR, SHOW UP

Bring the right index up between the index and middle fingers of the left hand.
Origin: Suddenly appearing.
Usage: He seemed to *appear* from nowhere.
Jim finally *showed up*.

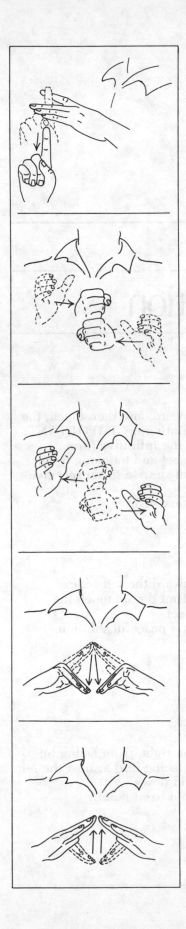

DISAPPEAR, DROP OUT

The right index finger pointing up is placed between the index and middle fingers of the left hand which has the palm facing down; the right index is then drawn down.
Origin: Dropping out of sight.
Usage: He *disappeared* suddenly.
dropped out of society.

CONDENSE, SUMMARIZE

Bring the "C" hands toward the center and close them into "S" positions as the right little-finger edge is placed on the forefinger-thumb edge of the left fist.
Origin: As if squeezing something together.
Usage: Your story is too long, *condense* it.
a *summary* of the news.

EXPAND, SWELL

Place the little-finger edge of the right "S" on the left "S" and draw them apart into a "C" position, left palm facing right and the right palm facing left.
Origin: Indicates enlargement.
Usage: Present your ideas and then *expand* on them.
Moisture causes wood to *swell*.

COLLAPSE, BREAKDOWN, CAVE-IN

Place the tips of the hands together; then let them suddenly move downward to a bent position.
Origin: From an upright to a collapsed position.
Usage: a nervous *breakdown*.
The building *collapsed*.
The coal mine *caved in*.

SET UP

Place the tips of both hands together, pointing down; then move them upward until tips, still together, point upward.
Usage: we *set up* the tent.

9

Location and Direction

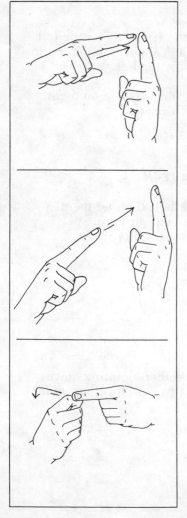

TO (As a preposition)

Direct the right index finger toward, and then touch, the left index fingertip which is pointing up. IMPORTANT: The sign for "to" is omitted in the infinitive form.
Origin: Heading toward the object and touching it.
Usage: going *to* California; from sunrise *to* sunset; give the book *to* him.
Note: like *to* walk (omit or fingerspell).

TOWARD

Direct the right index finger toward the left index fingertip which is pointing up, but do not touch it.
Origin: Heading toward an object.
Usage: We are working *toward* a peaceful solution.

FROM

Point the left index finger to the right, palm facing in; then place the right "X" (palm facing left) against the left index and pull it toward you and down.
Origin: As if moving away from a fixed point.
Usage: *from* east to west.

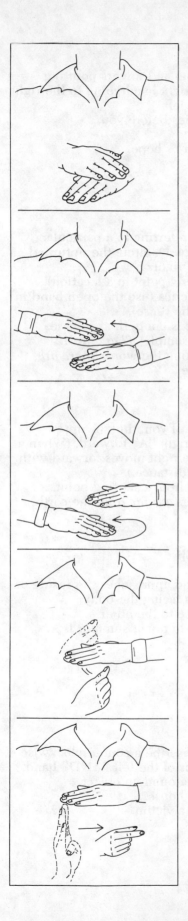

ON

Palm of the right open hand is placed on the back of the left open hand, both palms down.
Origin: One hand on top of the other.
Usage: The food is *on* the table.
Note: When "on" means "forward" sign it in that way.

ABOVE, OVER

Hold the right open hand above the left open hand, both palms down; move the right in a counterclockwise circle.
Origin: Indicating one thing above the other.
Usage: A family lives *above* us.
      a roof *over* their heads.

BELOW, BENEATH, UNDER, BASIC, UNDERLYING

Hold the right open hand under the left open hand, both palms down; move the right in a counterclockwise circle.
Origin: Indicating something beneath.
Usage: *below* the surface.
      beneath the ground.
      under the table.
      basic to your studies.
      the *underlying* cause.

UNDER

Move the right "A" (thumb pointing up) under the left down-turned palm (or circle the "A" under the left).
Origin: Representing that which is under or affected by someone or something.
Usage: *under* the law; *under* supervision; *under* obligation.

BACKGROUND

Form the right "B" and "G" under the left downturned palm.
Origin: Based on the sign for "below."
Usage: We need to know your *background* first.

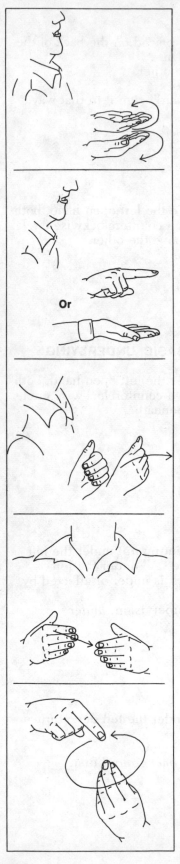

HERE, WHERE

With both open hands palms up and fingers pointing
forward, describe circles, the right hand going to the right
and the left hand going to the left.
Origin: Indicates that which lies before you.
Usage: *Here* I am.
Where there's life, there's hope.

THERE

Point with the index finger if referring to a particular
location. When used more vaguely, circle the upturned
open palm slightly toward the right.
Usage: The library is *over there* (point to a location).
There she is, Miss America (use the open hand in
a larger and more poetic sense).
Note: In many instances *there* is omitted, as in cases
where it precedes the verb. Example: *There* are 12
months in a year. While speaking the words *there are*,
only the sign for "are" is made.

FAR

Place both "A" hands in front of you, thumbs up,
knuckles touching; move the right "A" forward. (When a
great distance is indicated, the right moves forward with
more effort and also a greater distance.)
Origin: Indicates the distance from a starting point.
Usage: not *far* from home; stars are *far* from the earth.

NEAR, CLOSE TO, APPROACH

The back of the right bent hand approaches the inside of
the left bent hand, both palms facing the body.
Origin: One hand coming close to the other.
Usage: sit *near* me; live *close to* town; summer is
approaching.

AROUND, SURROUNDING

With the right index finger, describe a counterclockwise
circle around the upturned tips of the left "AND" hand.
Origin: Indicating movement around an object.
Usage: flowers all *around* the house.
people *surrounding* the victim.

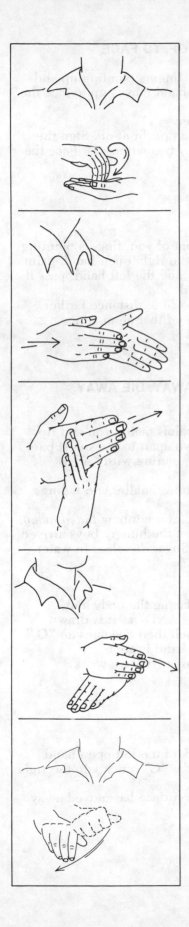

CENTER, MIDDLE

Describe a circle over the left palm with the right bent hand and then place the right fingertips in the center of the left palm.
Origin: In the center of the hand.
Usage: *center* of attention.
in the *middle* of the story.

AGAINST, SUE

Strike the tips of the right open hand, palm facing you, against the left palm which is facing to the right.
Origin: Coming against something.
Usage: *against* the law.
After the accident, she wanted to *sue* the driver.

THROUGH

Move the right open hand forward between the index and middle fingers of the left hand which is facing you.
Origin: Moving through the fingers.
Usage: driving *through* town.

ACROSS, CROSSING, OVER

The little-finger edge of the right open hand passes across the back of the left open hand which is facing palm down.
Origin: Indicates movement from one side over to the other.
Usage: *across* the country; *crossing* the river; *over* the mountain.

AWAY

Moving away from the body, the "A" hand opens and faces out.
Origin: Moving the hand away.
Usage: a vacation *away* from everybody.

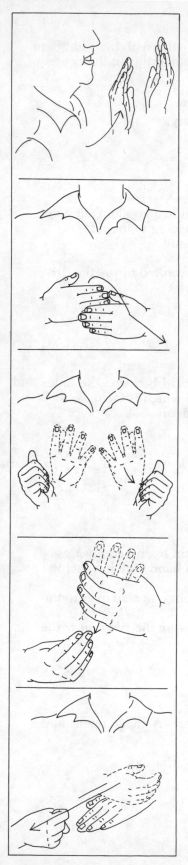

BEFORE, IN THE PRESENCE OF, TO FACE

The left open hand is held up, fingers pointing up and palm facing in; the right open hand moves up to face the left.

Origin: Hands facing each other.

Usage: He stood *before* the class (in front of). Sign the paper *in the presence of* two witnesses. *Face* the judge.

BEYOND

Place the left open hand in front of you, fingers pointing right, palm toward you. Place the right open hand, palm toward you, between the body and the left hand; pass it over the left, down and forward.

Origin: On the other side and a little distance farther.

Usage: The old man lives *beyond* that mountain.

DISAPPEAR, VANISH, FADE AWAY, DIE AWAY, DISSOLVE

Hold up both "AND" hands, palms facing you and tips pointing up. As hands are drawn apart to the sides, pass the thumb along the fingertips, ending with "A" positions.

Origin: Something large becoming smaller and fading away.

Usage: The snow *disappeared*. The rainbow *faded away*. The food *vanished* when the hungry boys arrived. The music *died away*. Sugar *dissolves* in water.

GONE, ABSENT

The right open "AND" hand, facing the body and pointing up, becomes a closed "AND" as it is drawn down through the left "C" which then becomes an "O."

Origin: That which was in the hand is gone.

Usage: *gone* with the wind; *absent* twice a week.

ALL GONE

Place the right "C" on the back of the left open hand which is pointing right; draw the "C" quickly to the right into an "A" position.

Origin: That which was on the surface has moved away.

Usage: the pie is *all gone*.

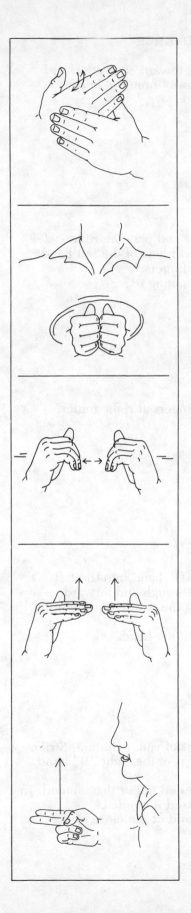

BETWEEN

Place the little-finger side of the right open hand between the thumb and fingers of the left open hand and move it back and forth between the thumb and index finger.
Origin: Between the thumb and fingers.
Usage: Let's keep it *between* us.

TOGETHER

Place the "A" hands together, palm to palm; move them right-forward-left in a semicircle.
Origin: Moving along with another.
Usage: We can accomplish a lot if we work *together*.

SEPARATE, APART

Both curved hands with fingers back to back, palms down, are pulled apart.
Origin: That which has been together is separated.
Usage: in *separate* groups.
    Keep them *apart*.

HIGH, ADVANCED, PROMOTION

Both bent hands, tips pointing toward each other and palms facing down, are moved upward in stages.

Origin: Being elevated.
Usage: a *high* position.
    advance to a better job.
    receive a *promotion*.

Note: The sign for "HIGH" is sometimes made by raising the right "H." This is the sign most often used for being *high* on drugs or alcohol.

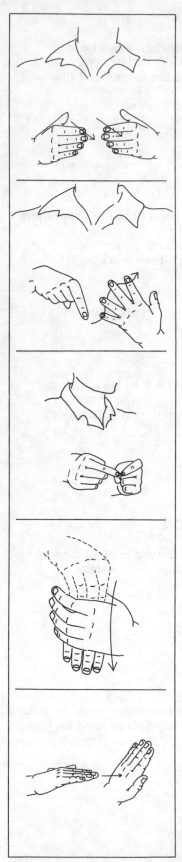

ONWARD, ON, FORWARD, ADVANCE

Both bent hands, tips pointing toward each other and palms facing you, are moved away from the body.
Origin: Natural motion forward.
Usage: *onward* to battle.
They marched *forward*.
We will go *on*.
The army *advanced*.

AMONG

Hold up the left "FIVE" hand and pass the right index finger in and out between the fingers of the left hand.
Origin: In and out among the fingers.
Usage: Are there any experts *among* us?

CORNER

Touch the tips of both index fingers at right angles.
Origin: Showing a corner.
Usage: the *corner* of a room.

INTO, ENTER

Place the tips of the right "AND" hand into the left "O" hand, pushing the right hand through and forward.
Origin: Indicates movement to the inside of something.
Usage: Come *into* the house.
That idea never *entered* my head.

AT

Hold the left "B" hand in front of you, palm out. Strike the back of the left with the tips of the right "B" hand, both hands pointing upward.
Note: This word is usually spelled rather than signed. In poetry and music the sign is used if needed.
Usage: *at* the end of the way and *at* the close of the day.

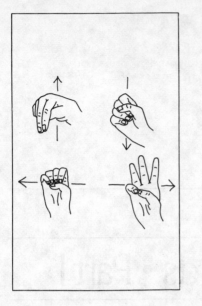

NORTH, SOUTH, EAST, WEST

Move the initial in the appropriate direction as if a map were before you.

Usage: the *north* pole; going *south* for the winter; wind is from the *east*; go *west*, young man.

Note: When giving directions, it is often better to use the initial in the direction of the compass. That is, if you are facing south and you tell someone to drive west, you would move the "W" to the right.

10

Verbs and Related Words • Part I

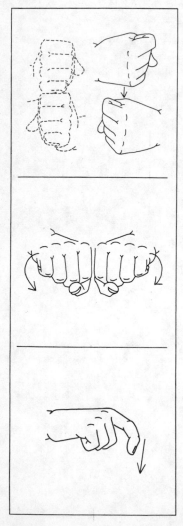

MAKE

Place the right "S" (palm facing left) on the left "S" (palm facing right). Turn them so the palms face you and strike them together again. Repeat several times.
Origin: Twisting and pounding.
Usage: He *made* the table and chairs in his shop.

BREAK

Hold the "S" hands side by side, palms down, and give them a sudden outward twist.
Origin: Holding an object in the hands and breaking it in two.
Usage: He didn't mean to *break* the window.

MUST, NECESSARY, NEED, OUGHT, SHOULD, HAVE TO

The crooked index finger, pointing down, moves downward forcefully.
Usage: I *must* take care of that today. Sleep is a *necessity*. What do you *need* now? Laws are *necessary*. We *should* obey them. We *ought to* investigate. Do you *have to* leave now? Ginger *has to* study tonight. Dan *had to* leave yesterday.

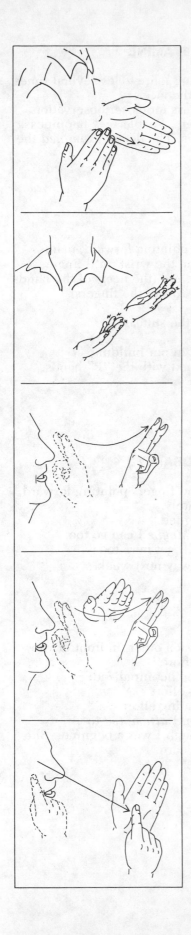

EXCUSE, FORGIVE, PARDON, EXEMPT, WAIVE

Stroke the edge of the left palm with the right fingertips.
Origin: Wiping off the guilt.
Usage: *Excuse* me please. He asked *forgiveness*. The
governor granted a *pardon*. Your course is *waived*.
The organization is tax *exempt*.

WAIT

Hold the left open hand, palm up, a little away from the
left side. Hold the right hand in the same position nearer
the body, fingers pointing toward the left wrist. Wiggle
the fingers of both hands.
Usage: Ray *waited* patiently for Joyce.

LOOK, WATCH, OBSERVE, SURVEY

Place the "V" in front of the face, palm in; turn the "V"
so the fingertips point forward. (Often made with both
hands.)
Origin: Fingertips represent the eyes looking out.
Usage: *Look*, it's raining. Astronomers *observe* the stars.
Watch the children for me. The principal
surveyed the situation. (Move the "V" hands back
and forth.)

PREDICT, FORECAST, FORESEE, PROPHESY

Make the sign for "LOOK," passing it under the left open
hand, palm down. For "prophet," add the "PERSON"
ending.
Origin: Looking into the future.
Usage: *predict* bad storms; weather *forecast; foresee* a
problem; to *prophesy* war.

NOTICE, OBSERVE

Point to the eye with the right index finger and then
touch the left palm.
Origin: To see and show.
Usage: *notice* the difference; *observed* a problem with
her behavior.

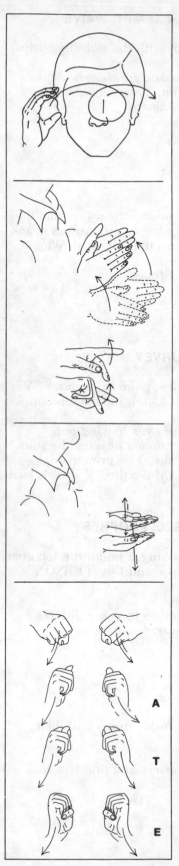

SEARCH, SEEK, LOOK FOR, EXAMINE

The "C" hand, with palm facing left, circles several times up-left-down-right in front of the face.
Origin: Using a magnifying glass for closer observation.
Usage: He *searched* everywhere. People *seek* happiness. She *looked for* her keys. The doctor *examined* the patient.

ALLOW, LET, MAY, PERMIT

Both open hands with fingers pointing forward, palms facing in, are bent upward from the wrist until fingers point slightly upward and outward (the heels of the hands being closer together than the tips of the fingers).
Usage: We don't *allow* that.
  Let me *help* you with the suitcase.
  You *may* go now.
  Pets are not *permitted* in our building.
Note: "PERMIT" is often signed with the "P" hands.

MAYBE, MAY, PERHAPS, PROBABLY

Both open hands, facing up and fingers pointing forward, are raised and lowered alternately.
Origin: The idea is being weighed.
Usage: It *may* rain tomorrow. *Maybe* I can go too.
  Perhaps your check will get here today.
  We will *probably* go away next week.

TRY, ATTEMPT, EFFORT

Place both "S" hands, facing each other, in front of you and push them forward with effort.
Note: The following words may be initialized:
"A"—attempt; "T"—try; "E"—effort
Origin: Pushing forward indicating effort.
Usage: It's not easy but I'll *try*. I *attempted* to communicate even though I was a beginner. She made a great *effort* to learn.

HELP, ASSIST, AID

Place the right open hand under the left "S" which is facing to the right; lift both hands together.
Origin: Offering a helping hand.
Usage: Please *help* me.
I need your *assistance*.
The Red Cross came to their *aid*.

REHABILITATION

Place the left open hand under the right "R"; lift them both.
Origin: Based on the sign for "help."
Usage: The client was ready for *rehabilitation*.
Note: The term "vocational rehabilitation" is often signed with the initial letters "V" and "R."

DO, DONE, DOES, ACTIVITY, CONDUCT, DEEDS

Place both "C" hands in front of you, palms down; move both hands to the right and left several times.
Origin: Hands in active motion.
Usage: What will you *do* now? Is that all he *does?* We've *done* a lot. Let's plan some *activities*. Claude is a man of *action*. His *conduct* is admirable. He is thoughtful in word and in *deed*.
Note: This sign should not be used when it does not refer to activity. In the following sentences it should either be omitted or spelled: *Do* you like chocolate? *Did* Mel leave Minnesota? *Does* Rita still live in Tennessee?

BEHAVIOR

Place the "B" hands in front of you, palms forward, and swing them back and forth.
Origin: The "do" sign is initialized.
Usage: The psychologist observed Andy's *behavior*.

USE, UTILIZE

Circle the right "U" in a small clockwise motion.
Usage: *Use* both signs and fingerspelling.
We *utilized* old lumber for the project.
studying word *usage*.

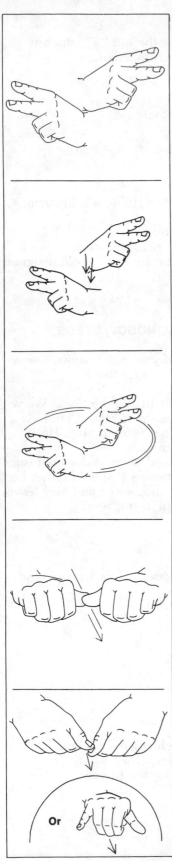

KEEP

Place the right "V" hand, palm leftward, on the wrist of the left "V" hand, palm rightward.
Origin: Hands in the position of "seeing," represented by four eyes watching.
Usage: Will you *keep* that car for a while?

CAREFUL

Make the sign for "KEEP" and strike together several times at the wrist.
Origin: A combination of watching and warning, represented by striking the wrist.
Usage: If you aren't *careful* you'll fall on the ice.

TAKE CARE OF, SUPERVISE

Make the sign for "KEEP" and circle it from right to left.
Origin: Four eyes watching over an area.
Usage: Virginia will *take care of* the children.
Grace is a good *supervisor*. (ADD the "person" ending.)

CONTINUE, ENDURE, LASTING, PERMANENT, PERSEVERE, KEEP ON

Place the thumb of the right "A" on the thumbnail of the left "A" and move both forward.
Origin: One thumb pushing the other forward.
Usage: The story will *continue*. Gold *endures* forever. Will the speech *last* long? He has no *permanent* address. *Persevere* until you succeed. *Keep on* trying!

STAY, REMAIN, STAND

Place the thumb of the right "A" on the thumbnail of the left "A" and push downward slightly. Or, direct the right "Y" hand downward in a short motion.
Origin: One thumb holds the other down.
Usage: *Stay* here, don't leave. His wife *remained* at home. The rule *stands*.

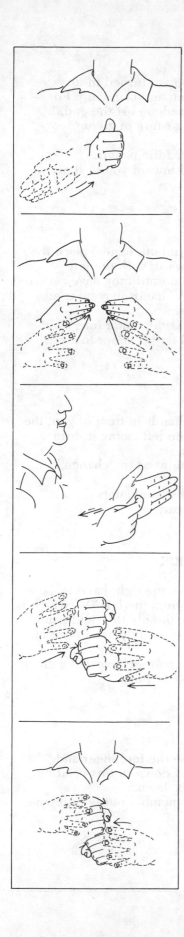

TAKE

Draw the open hand from right to left (palm facing left), ending in an "A" position.
Origin: Taking hold of something.
Usage: Can you *take* me home?

ACCEPT

The open "AND" hands point toward each other, palms facing the body. Move the hands toward the chest, closing them into the "AND" position, the fingers touching the body.
Origin: Taking it to oneself.
Usage: I am happy to *accept* your invitation.

DEMAND, REQUIRE

Place the tip of the bent, index finger in the left palm which is facing right; draw both hands toward the body. (The sign for "demand" is made more emphatically.)
Origin: As if demanding that something be placed in the palm.
Usage: The officer *demands* attention.
  The English class is *required*.

GET, OBTAIN

Both open "FIVE" hands, palms facing each other, close into "S" hands, the right on top of and touching the left.
Origin: Grasping hold.
Usage: How did you *get* that answer?
  We *obtain* knowledge through study and experience.

RECEIVE

Sign "GET" and draw it toward yourself.
Origin: Grasping something and taking it to yourself.
Usage: Joy *received* her M.A. degree in counseling.

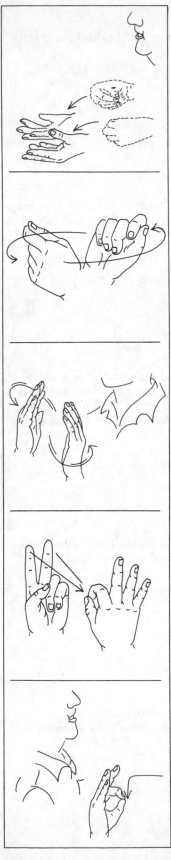

GIVE, DISTRIBUTE

Both "AND" hands facing down are turned in-up-forward, ending with palms open and facing up. For "DISTRIBUTE" the sign is broadened at the end.
Origin: Opening the hand in a gesture of giving.
Usage: I'll *give* what I can.

Miss Rumford *distributed* the papers.
Note: This sign can be directed toward you to show someone is giving to you.

CHANGE, ADJUST, ADAPT

Using a modified "A" position in both hands, place the right "A" so the palm faces forward, with the left "A" facing it. Twist the hands around until they have reversed positions. For "ADAPT" the "A" hands may be used.
Origin: Hands change positions.
Usage: *changed* my mind; *adjust* the motor (use short quick motions back and forth); *adapt* to a new environment.

BECOME, GROW, GET

Place the slightly curved open hands in front of you, the right palm facing forward and the left facing it; turn hands so they reverse positions.
Origin: The hands change positions as in "change."
Usage: Jerry *became* a father.

She *grew* weary of all the complaints.

Mike *got* sick after the party.

CHOOSE, CHOICE, SELECT, PICK

With the thumb and forefinger of the right hand make a motion as if picking something from the left "V" which is facing you. (Sometimes made with only the right hand.)
Origin: Making a choice between two items in front of you.
Usage: a wise *choice*; *pick* your partner; *selected* a green dress; *chose* her friends carefully.

APPOINT

Extend the right hand and close the forefinger and thumb; draw the hand back and down in this position.
Origin: Choosing and putting it down.
Usage: He was *appointed* as a member of the Supreme Court.

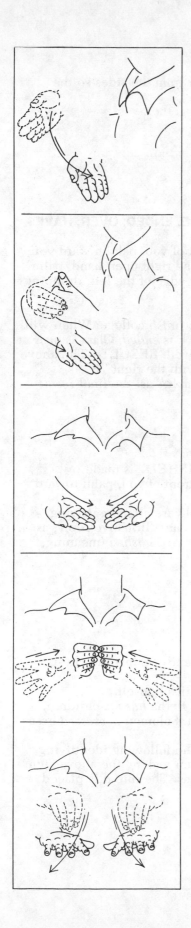

WELCOME

Bring the right open hand toward the body, palm facing up.
Origin: Extending the hand in an invitation to come.
Usage: Today we *welcome* our visitors from Japan.

INVITE

Touch the back of the left hand with the palm of the right and then bring the right toward the body, palm facing up.
Origin: A combination of the signs for "call" and "welcome."
Usage: *invited* to a party; The *invitation* arrived late.

INTRODUCE

Hold both open hands in front of you, somewhat apart with palms up; bring hands toward each other, tips pointing toward each other.
Origin: Bring two people together.
Usage: Let me *introduce* you.

MEETING, ASSEMBLE, GATHER

Bring both open "AND" hands together from the sides into closed "AND" positions so the fingertips are touching and the palms are facing each other.
Origin: Everyone coming together.
Usage: The *meeting* began at 8. We all *gathered* together.
    The students *assembled* early.

SCATTER, SPREAD

Place both "AND" hands together in front of you, palms down, and direct them forward and toward each side as fingers open.
Origin: Fingers spreading represent people scattering.
Usage: The meeting was over and the people *scattered*.
    The news *spread* rapidly.

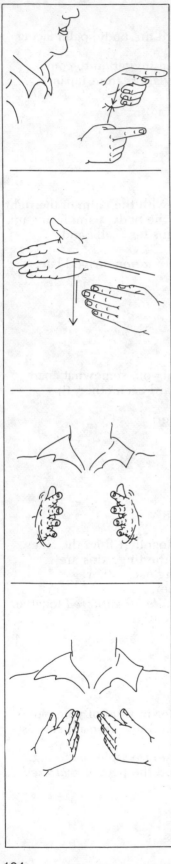

MEET

Bring both "G" hands together from the sides so the palms meet.
Origin: Two persons coming together.
Usage: Glad to *meet* you!

COMPLETED, FINISHED, DONE, ENDED, OVER, HAVE

Hold the left "B" hand in front of you, palm toward you; move the little-finger edge of the right open hand, palm facing left, along the forefinger edge of the left, dropping off at the edge.
Origin: Cut off at the end.
Usage: *completed* his program; *finish* college; When will you be *done?* The search is *ended.* Class is *over* at three. Visitors *have* arrived. RESULT—The above sign movement made with the right "R" is sometimes used for "result," as: the final *result.*

FINISHED, ALREADY

This less formal sign for "FINISHED" is made by holding the "FIVE" hands in front of you, palm toward palm, and shaking them.
Usage: *finished* working; people are *already* arriving.
Note: This sign is often used as an affirmative reply, as: Q: Have you been to the store? A: *Finished* (meaning, "Yes, I've already been there").

HAVE, HAS, HAD, POSSESS

Place fingertips of both bent hands against the chest, palms facing you.
Origin: Holding the object against oneself.
Usage: We *have* a large office. Retha *has* six children. Pete *had* a Volkswagen. Solomon *possessed* great wisdom.
Note: In educational settings the following identifying letters are sometimes used when making the above sign: "V"—have; "D"—had; "S"—has. The initial is placed against the chest.

PRAISE, APPLAUD, CLAP, OVATION

Clap the hands several times.
Origin: Natural sign.
Usage: People stood and *applauded* for the winner.
The basketball coach *praised* his team.
The students *clapped* for 5 minutes.
We gave the speaker a standing *ovation*.

CONGRATULATE

Sign "GOOD" and then clap the hands to indicate praise.
Or, clasp the hands as if in a handshake.
Usage: *Congratulations*, we're proud of you!

CELEBRATE, TRIUMPH, VICTORY, FESTIVAL, HAIL, HOORAY

Swing the right modified "A" above the side of the head.
The "V" hands are often used for "VICTORY."
Origin: Waving a banner.
Usage: *celebrate* a birthday; *triumph* over the enemy;
game ended in *victory*; cherry blossom *festival*;
Hail to the Chief! *Hooray*, we won!

WIN

Sign "GET" and "TRIUMPH."
Usage: Who will *win* today?

SUCCEED, EFFECTIVE, FINALLY

Point both index fingers toward each other, palms in.
Turn and raise both hands so the index fingers point up
with palms facing out; repeat several times, higher each
time.
Origin: Going higher and higher on the ladder.
Usage: a *successful* person.
effective training.
Finally! I found it!

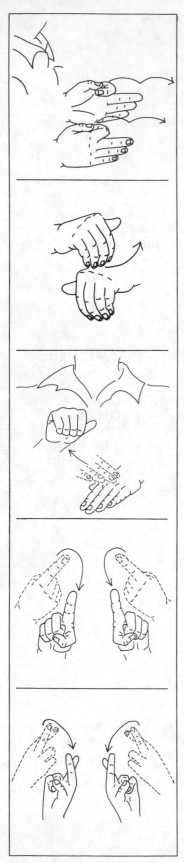

POSTPONE, PROCRASTINATE, DELAY, PUT OFF

Place both "F" hands in front of you, palms facing each other and fingers pointing forward; lift them up, forward, and down. Repeat and move farther away from you each time.
Origin: The decision is moved farther and farther away.
Usage: *postpone* the game; we *procrastinate*; *delay* a decision; Don't *put off* until tomorrow what you can do today.

SEND

Place the fingertips of the right bent hand on the back of the left and lift the right hand, straightening it into the open position, palm down.
Usage: Earl *sent* Betty some roses.

CALL

Place the palm of the right open hand on the back of the left open hand and draw the right up into an "A" position.
Origin: A deaf person is called by tapping him.
Usage: The meeting is now *called* to order.

HAPPEN, OCCUR

Point the index fingers up with the palms facing you, then twist them forward so the palms face forward.
Usage: Something interesting *happened* recently.
Eclipses do not *occur* often.

RESULT

Sign "HAPPEN" with the "R" hands.
Usage: What are the test *results?*

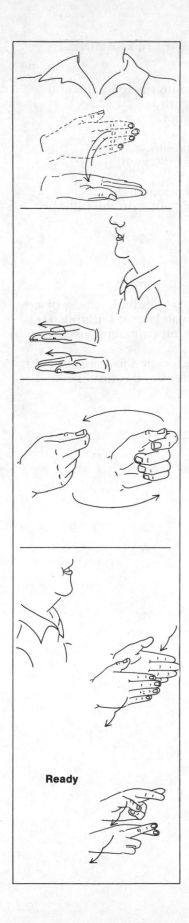

Ready

WILLING

Place the open palm on the chest; move it away from the body and turn the palm up.
Origin: My heart is extended to you.
Usage: Are you *willing* to assume responsibility?

OFFER, PRESENT, PROPOSE, SUGGEST, RECOMMEND, MOTION

Place the open hands in front of you, palms up and fingers pointing forward; move the hands up and forward in this position.
Origin: Lifted and offered.
Usage: *offered* a job; want to *present* an idea; *propose* a new plan; What can you *suggest?* Whom do you *recommend?* I make a *motion.*

EXCHANGE, TRADE, INSTEAD OF, SWITCH, REPLACE, SUBSTITUTE

Using the modified "A" position for both hands, place the right "A" behind the left; draw it under and place it in front of the left, while circling the left up and back, so that the hands have changed relative positions.
Origin: One hand changes places with the other.
Usage: *exchanged* the gift; *trade* stamps with me; coffee *instead of* tea; quickly *switched* places; men are *replaced* by machines; a *substitute* for sugar.

PLAN, ARRANGE, PREPARE, READY, IN ORDER

The open hands, facing each other and pointing forward, are moved toward the right in several short sweeping motions.
Origin: Everything in stacks, all arranged.
Usage: Make *plans* early.
Arrange to leave soon.
Prepare the food.
everything *in order*.
Are you *ready?*

Note: "READY" is often signed with the "R" hands.

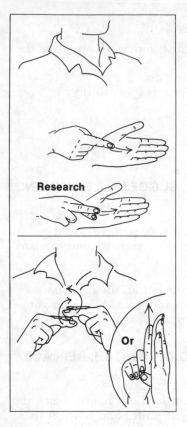

Research

Or

INVESTIGATE, INSPECT, RESEARCH, EXAMINE, CHECK

Place the tip of the right index into the left palm and move it forward toward the fingertips.
Origin: As if digging into the hand.
Usage: Let us *investigate*.
  inspected by the government.
  He *examined* the dollar bill carefully.
  a *research* project.
  They had to *check* my background.
Note: "RESEARCH" is often signed with the right "R."

DEVELOP

Using the index and middle fingers of both hands, place them on top of each other alternately as if building. Or, place the right "D" against the left palm and move the "D" upward.
Usage: *develop* a curriculum; a recent *development* (add the "MENT" ending after the upward "D").

11

Verbs and Related Words • Part II

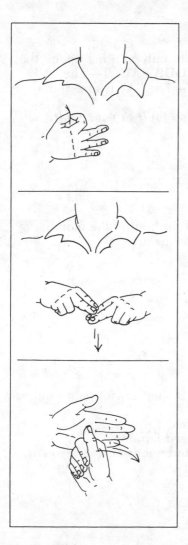

VOLUNTEER, APPLY

With the thumb and forefinger of the right hand grasp
your lapel (or clothing) and pull it forward.
Origin: Putting oneself forward.
Usage: Dennis *volunteered* to chair the committee.
   If you want a job you'll have to *apply* for one.

DEPEND, RELY

Place the right index and middle fingers on the back of
the left index and middle fingers, both palms down, and
push down slightly. (Can be made using only the index
fingers.)
Origin: One is leaning on the other.
Usage: It all *depends* on the weather.
   We *rely* on the newspaper for lots of information.

IMPRESS, EMPHASIZE

Press the thumb of the right "A" hand into the left open
palm and move the hands forward slightly.
Usage: *impressed* on my mind.
   emphasize the need for more cooperation.
   make a good *impression*.

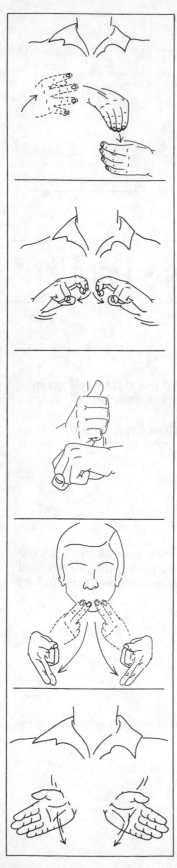

INCLUDE, INVOLVE

The right "FIVE" hand (palm up) is moved up, turns over with fingers coming together, and is placed into the left "C" hand.
Origin: As if taking something and placing it inside.
Usage: Please *include* me!
      Would you like to be *involved?*

ANALYZE

Place the bent "V" hands in front of you, facing each other with palms down; move them away from each other several times.
Origin: Taking things apart.
Usage: Let's try to *analyze* the problem.

BLAME, FAULT

Place the right "A" hand with thumb pointing up, on the back of the left closed hand. YOUR FAULT—The "A" is directed outward. MY FAULT—The "A" is directed toward self.
Usage: Who's to *blame?* Is it *my fault* or *your fault?*

INNOCENT

Place the "U" hands (palms in) in front of the mouth; move them toward the sides, palms up.
Usage: I'm *innocent!*

ENCOURAGE

Move the open hands forward in stages with palms out as if slightly pushing.
Origin: Gently pushing in stages.
Usage: The president *encouraged* farming.
      Sue seems depressed and needs *encouragement.*

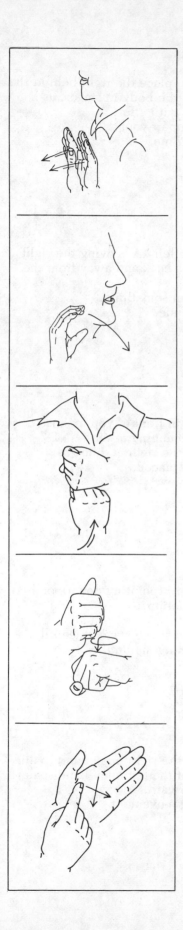

PUSH

Move the open hands forward, palms out, as if pushing an object.
Origin: Natural motion of pushing.
Usage: Three men *pushed* the car.

FORCE

Place the right "C" (pointing forward) below the cheek and push forward.
Usage: No one likes to be *forced*.

SUPPORT, IN FAVOR OF, ADVOCATE

Place the right "S" under the left "S" and push upward.
Origin: The right hand supports the left.
Usage: He *supports* a large family. All *in favor*, say aye.
The governor *advocates* building better roads.

ESTABLISH, FOUNDED, BASED, SET UP

Using the right "A" make a clockwise circle and then place the little-finger edge firmly on the back of the left fist.
Origin: Firmly planted on a rock.
Usage: *established* in 1864; *founded* in the 16th century;
a statement *based* on fact; *set up* a new program.

CANCEL, CRITICIZE, CORRECT

Draw an "X" in the left palm with the right index finger.
Origin: An "X" is used to cancel out something.
Usage: *Cancel* my appointment.
quick to *criticize*.
Correct test papers after school.

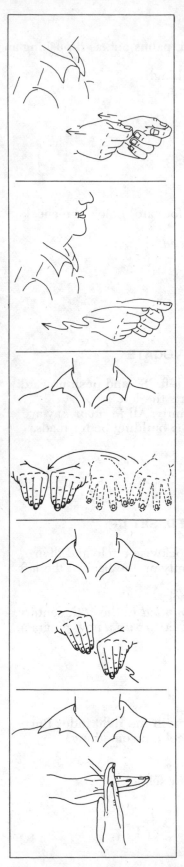

URGE, PERSUADE

Using the modified "A" hands, place the right behind the left and pull the hands toward the body in stages, as if pulling something toward you with effort.
Usage: *Urge* your friend to support you.
They almost *persuaded* me.

AVOID

Place the right "A" behind the left "A"; swing the right wrist back and forth as it draws back and away from the left.
Origin: Trying to get away from something.
Usage: He was trying to *avoid* me.

PUT, MOVE

Place the open "AND" hands in front of you, palms down, and lift them slightly, changing to the "AND" position as you move them to the right and down.
Origin: An object is lifted and placed.
Usage: *Put* the children's toys away.
Moving to Georgia?

MOVE, MOVEMENT

Move the "AND" hands forward (pointing down), one behind the other in a zigzag motion.
Origin: Moving things around.
Usage: The dancers *moved* across the stage gracefully.
I thought I saw something *moving!*

PREVENT, BLOCK

Place the little-finger edge of the right open hand (palm down) against the forefinger of the left open hand (palm right) and push both hands forward.
Origin: Something is blocking movement.
Usage: You can't *prevent* that.
He *blocked* my plans.

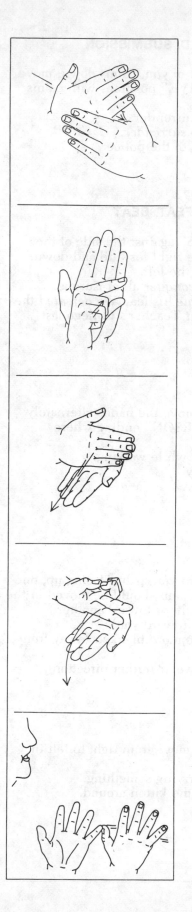

BOTHER, INTERFERE

Place the little-finger edge of the right open hand between the thumb and forefinger of the left open hand and strike it several times.
Origin: The right hand coming between.
Usage: Don't *bother* me?
       The police *interfered*.

FORBID

Throw the side of the right "G" hand against the left palm which is pointing up and facing right.
Usage: Smoking is *forbidden* in elevators.

REJECT

Place the little-finger side of the right hand on the open left palm; push the right hand out toward the fingertips.
Origin: Pushing something off the palm.
Usage: The army *rejected* Sue's brother.

FAIL

Place the back of the right "V" in the left open palm and slide it forward and off.
Origin: Falling over the edge.
Usage: If you *fail*, try again.
       Do you sometimes feel like a *failure?*

LINE UP

Place the "FIVE" hands in front of you, pointing up, right palm facing left and left palm facing right; the right thumbtip touches the tip of the little finger on the left hand.
Origin: The fingers represent people standing in line.
Usage: The children *lined up* for ice cream cones.
       Everyone please *get in line.*

SURRENDER, GIVE UP, YIELD, SUBMISSION

Place both "A" hands in front of you, palms down; move them forward and up into "FIVE" positions with palms facing out.
Origin: Hands thrown up in surrender.
Usage: The enemy refused to *surrender*.
The prisoners *yielded* to the police.
Why not *give up*?
Submit to authority.

CONQUER, OVERCOME, DEFEAT, BEAT

Place the wrist of the right "S" against the side of the wrist of the left "S"; push the right forward and down.
Origin: Right hand conquers the left.
Usage: Napoleon wanted to *conquer* all of Europe.
Brad couldn't *overcome* his fear. We *defeated* the enemy. Our team *beat* Teacher's College last year.

SERVE, SERVANT, WAITER

With both palms facing up, move the hands alternately back and forth. Add the "PERSON" ending where needed.
Origion: As if carrying a tray while walking.
Usage: He *served* his country.
a faithful *servant*.
call the *waiter*.

BRING

Bring both open hands toward you, palms facing up, one hand behind the other. (This sign should be moved in the intended direction; toward self, or toward another.)
Usage: *Bring* me some soap (toward you).
I will *bring* you some more blankets (away from you).
Who *brought* the flowers? (either direction).

CARRY

Both open hands, palms up, move from right to left in front of the body.
Origin: Hands move as if carrying something.
Usage: Jamie loves to *carry* the kitten around.

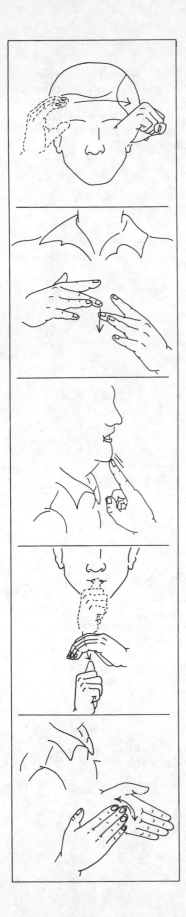

MISS (Fall to catch)

Place the right "C" near the right side of the forehead (palm left) and pass the hand quickly to the left, ending with the "S" position.
Origin: Something went by quickly.
Usage: *missed* the train.

MISS (Fail to meet)

The right middle finger strikes the tip of the left middle finger and passes it in a downward movement (both palms down).
Usage: *missed* classes often.
He *cut* classes every Friday afternoon.

MISS (Feel the absence of)

Touch the chin with the right index finger.
Origin: This sign is used for "disappointed"; if you miss someone you are disappointed he has not come.
Usage: I'll *miss* you when you move away.

HIDE

Place the thumb of the "A" hand against the lips and then move the "A" hand under the left palm, which is held in front of you.
Origin: A secret that is hidden.
Usage: Children enjoy playing "*Hide* and Seek."

RUB

Rub the tips of the right hand against the palm of the left.
Origin: Natural motion of rubbing.
Usage: My shoes are *rubbing* and my feet hurt.

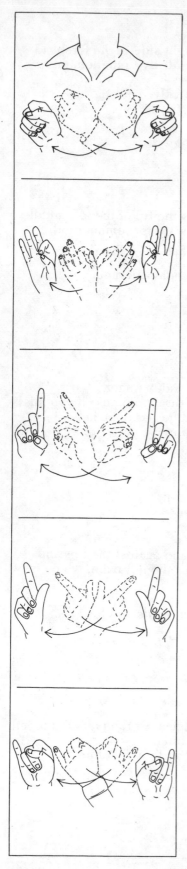

SAFE, SAVE, RESCUE

Cross the "S" hands in front of you, both hands facing you as if bound at the wrists; turn both hands so they are separated and facing forward.
Origin: First the hands are bound, then they are free.
Usage: We arrived *safely* after our long journey.
   The fireman *rescued* the baby.

FREE

Sign as for "SAVE," using the "F" hands.
Usage: President Lincoln will always be remembered for *freeing* the slaves.

DELIVER

Sign as for "SAVE," using the "D" hands.
Usage: *Deliver* us from evil.

LIBERTY

Sign as for "SAVE" using the "L" hands.
Usage: sweet land of *liberty*.

INDEPENDENT

Sign as for "SAVE," using the "I" hands.
Usage: a very *independent* young man.

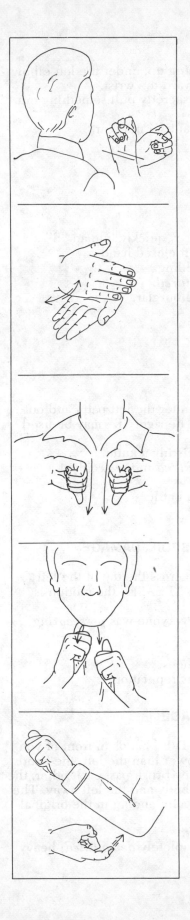

BOUND, BIND

Place the wrist of the right "A" (palm up) on the wrist of the left "S" (palm up) and push down slightly.
Origin: As if wrists are tied.
Usage: prisoners *bound* in chains.
Marriage vows are *binding*.

SHARE

Place the little-finger side of the right open hand crosswise on the left palm and move it back and forth between the left wrist and fingertips.
Origin: As if dividing something that is in the hand and saying, "Some for you and some for me."
Usage: Let's *share* the lunch.

DENY (Self-denial)

With both hands in the "A" position, thumbs pointing down, push the hands down the chest a short distance.
Origin: The inner feelings that would rise are pushed down.
Usage: She *denied* herself all candy during Lent.

DENY (To declare not to be true)

Place the thumb of the right "A" hand under the chin and push it forward; repeat with the left "A" and alternate several times.
Origin: Repeating the sign for "NOT" several times.
Usage: He *denied* everything when he was accused.

TEMPT

Tap the left forearm near the elbow with the right index finger.
Origin: Tapping someone to entice him.
Usage: Rich food is a great *temptation* to people on a diet.

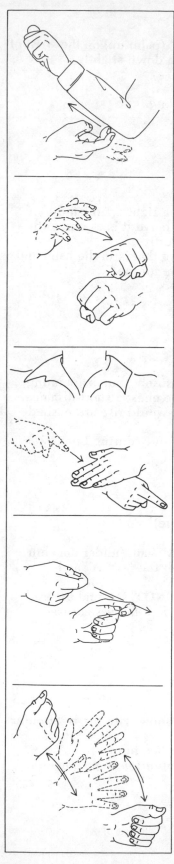

STEAL

Place the right "V," palm facing up, under the left elbow and bend it as it is drawn toward the wrist.
Origin: As if using a hook to secretly pull something out from underneath an object.
Usage: Someone *stole* my beautiful new car.

CAPTURED, CATCH

The right curved "FIVE" closes quickly into an "S" position on the back of the left closed hand.
Origin: As if grasping and holding.
Usage: The prisoner was *captured*.
The police *caught* the burglar.
Quick, *catch* him!

KILL, SLAY, MURDER

Slide the right index finger under the left palm and out toward the left with a twist. The right "K" may be used as an initial sign for "kill."
Origin: As if inserting and twisting a knife.
Usage: Several people were *killed* in the accident.
in jail for *murder*.
Soldiers were *slain* in battle.

PERSECUTE, TEASE, RUIN, SPOIL, DAMAGE

Slide the right modified "A" across the top of the left modified "A." When used for "TEASE" the motion is repeated several times.
Usage: The patient thought everyone was *persecuting* her.
teasing little girls.
The rain *ruined* my shoes.
That could *damage* his reputation.
The child is *spoiled*.

DESTROY, DEMOLISH, DAMAGE

Place both slightly curved "FIVE" hands in front of you facing each other, the right lower than the left; the hands change to "A" positions as they brush past each other, the right one moving toward the body and the left away. The hands then pass each other again, ending in the original position.
Origin: As if tearing up paper.
Usage: *destroyed* by fire; completely *demolished*; heavy *damage*.

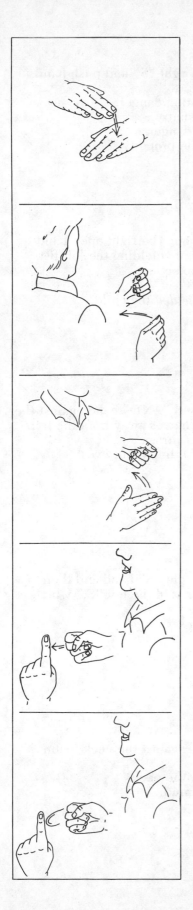

WARN

Tap the back of the left hand several times with the right open hand. Sometimes the right index finger is also raised as if in warning.
Origin: As if tapping someone quickly to give warning.
Usage: The policeman gave the driver a *warning*.

PUNISH, PENALTY

Hold the left "A" hand in front of you as if holding an imaginary culprit; move the right index finger down quickly just below the left arm.
Usage: The judge determined the *punishment*.
$10 *penalty* for speeding.

SPANK

Hold the left modified "A" in front of you; move the right open hand as if giving a spanking.
Origin: Natural motion of spanking a child.
Usage: He really needs a *spanking*.

HIT, IMPACT, STRIKE

Strike the left index finger (which is pointing upward) with the right "S" (palm-side left).
Origin: Striking an object.
Usage: His words really *hit* me hard. The president's speech had a strong *impact*. A car *struck* the pole.

BEATING

Strike the left index finger (which is pointing upward) with the right "S" from left to right several times.
Origin: As if beating on someone.
Usage: The gang gave him a *beating*.

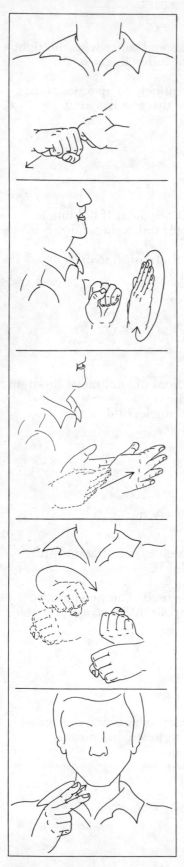

DEFEND, PROTECT, GUARD

Place the left "S" behind the right "S" and push hands out slightly.
Origin: Pushing away or resisting danger.
Usage: Soldiers *defend* our country.
　　　They *protect* us from danger.
　　　Men were *guarding* the property.

SHIELD, SHELTER

Place the left "S" in front of you. The right open hand (palm out) moves clockwise as if shielding the left fist.
Origin: Raising a shield for protection.
Usage: a *shelter* in the storm.
　　　The mother always *shielded* the child.

REFLECT

Place the tips of the right closed "AND" hand against the left palm; open the right as it moves away from the left.
Origin: Light reflecting from a surface.
Usage: The strong *reflection* bothered our eyes.

LOCK

Make a small circle with the right "S" hand and then place the right wrist on the wrist of the left "S," which is facing right.
Usage: All doors should be *locked*.

STUCK, TRAPPED

Place the tips of the right "V" against the neck (palm down).
Origin: As if sticking a fork in the neck.
Usage: We were *stuck* in the mud.
　　　The thief was *trapped*.

TURN

Hold up the left index finger; point the right index finger down and circle it around the left index in a counterclockwise motion, the left index turning slightly.
Origin: Shows turning away from the original position.
Usage: The men *turned* against their leader.

TURN takes on various meanings when combined with other words. It is then signed according to its meaning in the sentence. The following are a few examples:

turn off the motor (turn a key to the left).
turn off the light (the open "AND" position closes to show lights going off).
doing a *good turn* (a good deed).
take turns (twist the right "L" back and forth).
turn down an offer (thumbs down).
rain *turned to* snow (changed to).
it *turned* his stomach (sign "UPSET," hands flip over near stomach).
turned over in her sleep ("V" hand turns over from palm-down to palm-up).
turn loose (sign "CONNECT" and then open the fingers).
everyone *turned out* (came).
he *turned out to be* a successful doctor (became).
he *turned over* the business to his son (gave).
leaves *turned* in the fall (changed).
she *turned* pale (became).

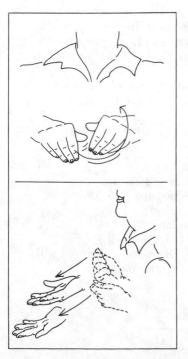

COVER

Slide the right curved hand over the back of the left curved hand from right to left, both palms facing down.
Origin: Covering the hand.
Usage: ground *covered* with snow.

CAUSE

Place the "A" hands in front of you, thumbs pointing up; throw the hands leftward as they open, palms up and open.
Origin: As if throwing something into the air or into existence.
Usage: Floods *cause* destruction.
The combination of sun and rain *caused* the rainbow.

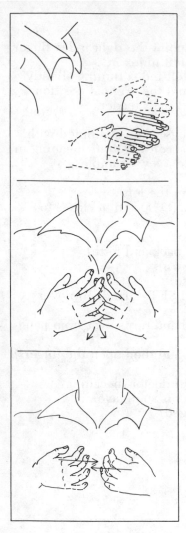

BET

Place the open hands in front of you several inches apart, palm facing palm; turn both palms down in a quick motion.
Origin: Placing the cards face down on the table.
Usage: He made a *bet* of $5.

MESH, FIT TOGETHER, FALL IN PLACE, MERGE, BLEND, MAINSTREAM, INTEGRATE

Place both curved "FIVE" hands in front of you, palms facing you, and interlock the fingers beginning with the little finger (as gears fit together).
Usage: We couldn't understand what happened but suddenly everything *fit together (meshed, fell in place)*. The colors *blended*. The school was *integrated*. The two businesses *merged*. The deaf children were *mainstreamed*.

MATCH, FIT

Bring the curved "FIVE" hands together so that the fingers interlock (palms facing self).
Usage: Joel's coat *matches* his pants.
The test included true-false, multiple choice, and *matching*.
Punishment should *fit* the crime.

MATCH and FIT take on various meanings depending on context. A few examples are listed here:

MATCH: You can't *match* his skill (come up to or meet).
The twins wore *matching* dresses (same).
The tennis *match* was exciting (game).
I never saw her *match* (never saw anyone her equal).
The young man is a good *match* for my daughter. (Fingerspell, or use the sign pictured above.)
Do you have a *match?* (Mime striking a match in the left palm.)

FIT: *fit* food for animals (right food).
It is *fit* that we give thanks (right, proper).
young men, *fit* for duty (prepared).
feeling *fit* now (well, healthy).
He had a *fit* about it (was angry).
The dress *fits* perfectly. (Fingerspell.)
a house not *fit* to live in. (Reword or fingerspell.)
having a *fit* (a seizure). (Fingerspell.)

12
Quality, Kind, and Condition

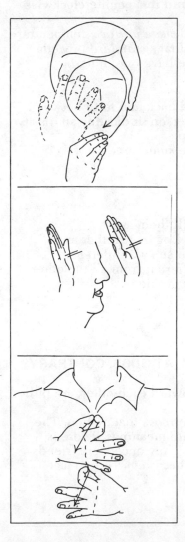

BEAUTIFUL, PRETTY, LOVELY

Place the right "AND" hand in front of the chin, palm
facing you; open the fingers and circle the hand in front
of the face from right to left, ending in the original
position.
Origin: Attention is drawn to the face.
Usage: a *beautiful* sunset; a *pretty* girl; a *lovely* smile.

WONDERFUL, MARVELOUS, GREAT, FANTASTIC

Throw both open hands up, palms facing forward.
Origin: Hands are thrown up in wonder.
Usage: The trip to Australia was *wonderful*.
     a *marvelous* invention.
     a *great* person.
     a *fantastic* place.
     the *wonders* of the world.

INTERESTING

Place the thumbs and index fingers against the chest,
with the other fingers extended, and draw the hands
away from the body, closing the indexes and thumbs.
Origin: The heart is drawn toward the object.
Usage: The speaker told an *interesting* story.
     People have different *interests*.

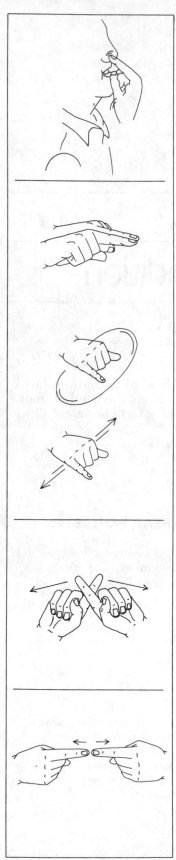

BORING, TEDIOUS, DULL

Place the tip of the index finger against the side of the
nose and twist the finger slightly.
Origin: Nose to the grindstone.
Usage: Students get *bored* with their studies.
       a long and *tedious* journey.
       a *dull* evening.

SAME, LIKE, SIMILAR, UNIFORM, STANDARD, IN COMMON

Place both index fingers side by side, touching each other
with palms down.
Origin: Both fingers are alike.
Usage: at the *same* time; he looks *like* his father; they
       have *similar* ideas (sign "same" twice).

Or, place the "Y" hand in front of you palm side
down and move it around in a counterclockwise
circle.
Usage: they all have *similar* ideas; a *uniform* temperature
       throughout the house; that's *standard* procedure
       in each department; we have one thing *in
       common.*

Or, move the "Y" hand back and forth between
yourself and another person, indicating similarity
between the two of you.
Usage: Look, we both have the *same* shoes.

DIFFERENT, DIFFER

Cross the index fingers and pull them apart.
Origin: Instead of keeping the fingers together as in
"same" they are pulled apart to show a difference.
Usage: The first house was *different* from all the others.
       You and I *differ* in our opinions.

OPPOSITE, OPPOSE, ENMITY, AT ODDS, CONTRARY

Both index fingers, pointing toward each other, are pulled
apart.
Usage: He sat *opposite* her. I *oppose* that motion. The
       two words have *opposite* meanings. There is
       enmity between them. They once were friends
       but now are *at odds*. That is *contrary* to fact.

PARALLEL

Place both index fingers side by side but not touching, palms down; move them forward.
Origin: Side by side.
Usage: His thinking *parallels* mine.

VARIETY, VARIOUS, DIVERSE

Place the index fingers in front of you, pointing straight ahead; move the fingers up and down several times as the hands move apart. (Or, sign as for "different.")
Usage: a great *variety* of things.
We wanted *various* people to give opinions.
a man of *diverse* interests.

KIND

Circle the right "K" around the left "K" while the left one also circles slightly.
Usage: What *kind* of food do you like?
Note: Some prefer to use the above sign for "variety" in this context.

EXACT, PRECISE

Bring the fingertips of the modified "A" hands together until the tips of the index fingers and thumbs touch (right hand facing out and left hand facing self).
Origin: Hitting the nail on the head.
Usage: Give me the *exact* word.
We need *precise* measurements.

PERFECT

Bring the middle fingertips of the "P" hands toward each other until they touch.
Origin: Using the initial letter and hitting the nail on the head.
Usage: a *perfect* plan.
That's *perfectly* clear.
striving for *perfection*.

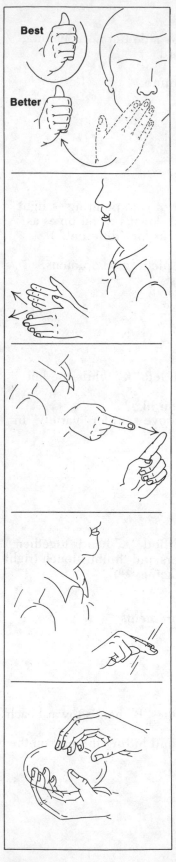

BETTER, BEST

Place the open hand in front of the mouth, palm facing in and fingers pointing left; draw it up into an "A" position. For "BEST" the "A" is moved higher than for "BETTER."
Origin: Good to a greater degree.
Usage: Your signs are *better* than mine.
  best in the world.

GENERAL

Place the tips of the open hands together; then move the hands apart, wrists bending back (hands point forward).
Origin: Broadening out the hands indicates the meaning.
Usage: This television program is of *general* interest.

SPECIFIC, POINT

Place the left index in front of you, palm side facing right; direct the right index toward the tip of the left and touch it.
Origin: The left index represents a specific item that is pointed out.
Usage: a *specific* requirement.
  That's a good *point*.

NEUTRAL

Shake the right "N" in front of you.
Note: This sign will usually only be understood in context.
Usage: I'm neither for nor against your idea; I'll remain *neutral*.

CONFUSION, MIXED UP

The left curved "FIVE" is held in front of you, palm facing up; the right curved "FIVE," with palm down, circles counterclockwise above it.
Origin: Everything going in circles.
Usage: There was a lot of *confusion* after the game.
  We couldn't find anything—everything was *mixed up*.

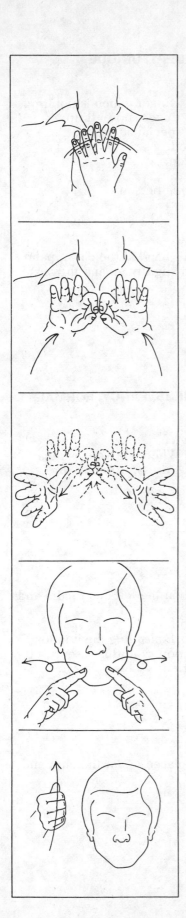

VAGUE, OBSCURE, BLURRY

Rub the right palm back and forth against the left palm, both hands in the "FIVE" position, the back of the right hand facing you.
Usage: Your explanation is *vague* and I don't understand.
Legal language is sometimes *obscure.*
The picture is *blurry.*

IMPORTANT, WORTH, WORTHY, PRECIOUS, VALUABLE, MERIT, SIGNIFICANT

Draw the "F" hands up from the sides toward the center until they touch.
Origin: Brought to the top.
Usage: *important* people; *worth* a hundred dollars; an action *worthy* of praise; gold is *precious;* a *valuable* old book; your plan has *merit.* a *significant* decision.

WORTHLESS

Sign "WORTH" (as above) and drop the open hands from the center to the sides.
Origin: Worth nothing.
Usage: We thought the old coin would be valuable but discovered it was *worthless.*

FAMOUS

Index fingers touch the lips and move away from the face, describing small circles in the air.
Origin: It has been told abroad.
Usage: a *famous* president.

PROMINENT, CHIEF, HIGH

Lift the right "A" hand, thumb pointing up.
Origin: High up.
Usage: a *prominent* lawyer ("FAMOUS" could be used here); *chief* of staff; *high* in government.

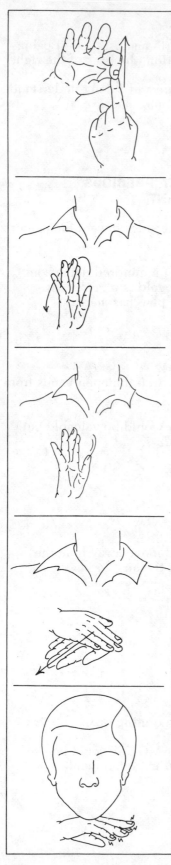

SPECIAL, EXCEPTIONAL, EXCEPT, UNIQUE, OUTSTANDING

Grasp the end of the left index finger which is pointing up, with the thumb and index finger and pull up.
Origin: One is singled out for special attention.
Usage: He requires *special* food.
 All were here *except* Joe.
 an *exceptional* child.
 an intelligent and *unique* person.
 outstanding skills.

FINE

Place the thumb of the "FIVE" hand at the chest, palm facing left, and move the hand slightly up and forward.
Origin: Representing ruffles.
Usage: a *fine* man.
 feeling *fine*, thank you.

POLITE, COURTEOUS, MANNERS, FANCY, FORMAL, ELEGANT

Repeat the sign for "FINE" twice.
Usage: a *polite* young woman; Where are your *manners?*
 courteous answer; *fancy* dress; *formal* party;
 elegant drapes.

CLEAN, NICE

The right open palm is placed on the left open palm and is passed across it.
Origin: All the dirt is rubbed off.
Usage: a *clean* house; a *nice* girl; *cleaning* the window
 (when used to show action as in this case, rub the
 hands in a circular motion).

DIRTY, FILTHY

The back of the right hand is placed under the chin and the fingers wiggle.
Origin: Similar to the sign for "pig."
Usage: *dirty* hands.
 The street was *filthy*.

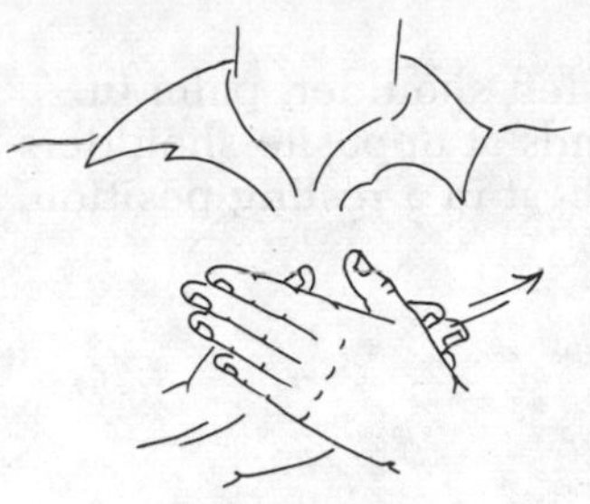

NEW

The left open hand faces up; the back of the right open hand brushes across the heel of the left from right to left.
Usage: a *new* town and *new* friends.

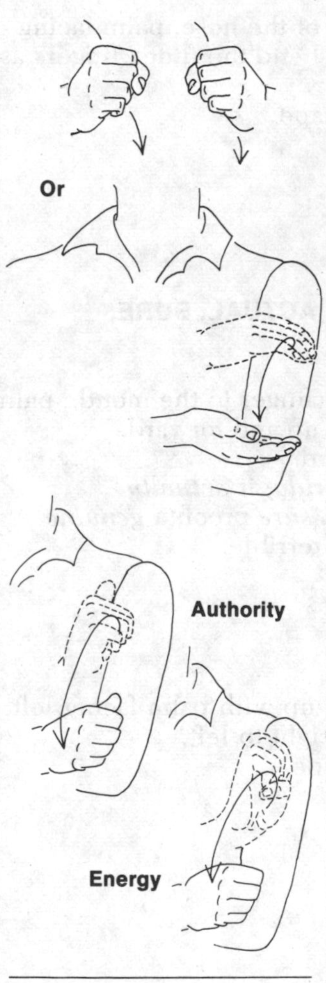

STRONG, POWERFUL, MIGHTY, AUTHORITY, ENERGY

Bring the "S" hands down with force. Or, use the right open hand to indicate the size of the left arm muscle.
Note: Sometimes "authority" and "energy" are initialed over the muscle as in the second description.
Origin: The fists and muscles represent power.
Usage: a *strong* wind.
      a *mighty* army.
      a *powerful* nation.
      authority to sign the paper.
      an *energy* program.

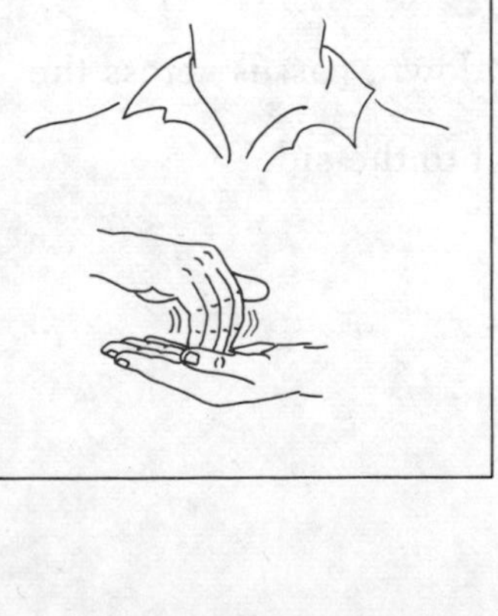

Or

Authority

Energy

WEAK, FEEBLE

Place the four fingertips of the right hand in the left palm; then bend the fingers of the right hand.
Origin: Weak in the knees.
Usage: a *weak* foundation.
      old and *feeble*.

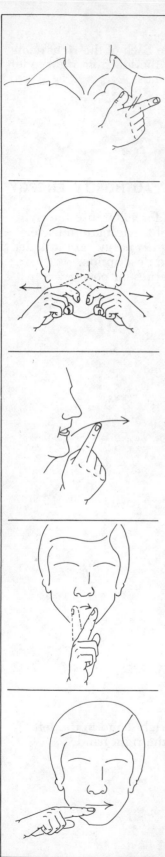

LAZY

Strike the right "L" against the left shoulder, palm in. (Sometimes made with both hands at opposite shoulders.)
Origin: Hands crossed on the chest in a resting position.
Usage: It was a *lazy* afternoon.

UGLY

Cross the index fingers in front of the nose, palm facing palm; then pull them apart and bend the index fingers as they cross the face.
Origin: Face is pulled out of shape.
Usage: an *ugly* duckling.

TRUE, TRULY, REAL, REALLY, ACTUAL, SURE, GENUINE, INDEED

Touch the tip of the right index finger to the mouth, palm facing left, and move it slightly up and forward.
Origin: Speaking straight forward.
Usage: a *true* friend; love you *truly*; it *actually* happened; Oh, *really*? a *sure* proof; a *genuine* diamond; war is *indeed* terrible.

FALSE, ARTIFICIAL, FAKE

The right index finger, pointing up with palm facing left, is brushed across the lips from right to left.
Origin: The truth is brushed aside.
Usage: *false* teeth.
artificial flowers.
The painting was a *fake*.

LIE

Right index finger, palm facing down, passes across the lips from right to left.
Origin: Not straight forward, but to the side.
Usage: He *lied* in the courtroom.

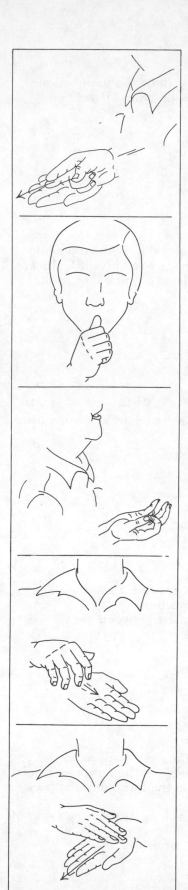

HONEST, TRUTH

Place the middle finger of the right "H" on the left palm near the wrist and move it forward toward the fingertips.
Origin: Divided in half honestly.
Usage: an *honest* man.
       tell the *truth*.

SECRET, PRIVATE, CONFIDENTIAL

Place the thumbnail of the right "A" against the lips.
Origin: The lips are sealed.
Usage: hidden in a *secret* place.
       private conversation.
       confidential papers.

FINE (in small particles)

Rub the thumb and index finger together, while the other fingers are extended.
Origin: Rubbing a grain of sand between the fingertips.
Usage: very *fine* sand; *fine* dust.

ROUGH, SCRATCH, RUGGED

Place the fingertips of the right curved hand against the left palm and move it forward with a wavy motion.
Origin: Indicating the surface is rough.
Usage: The wood is *rough*.
       Shoes *scratched* the floor.
       a *rugged* path.

SMOOTH

Place the open hands palm to palm at right angles and draw the right one across the left slowly.
Origin: Showing a smooth surface.
Usage: a *smooth* board.

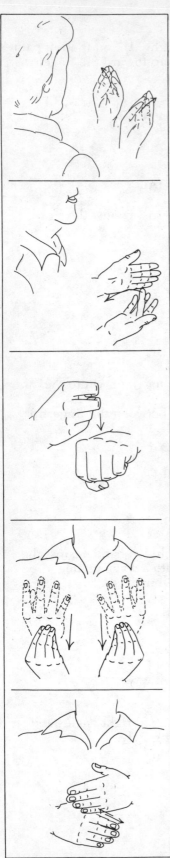

SMOOTH, FLUENT

Hold out both "AND" hands and draw the thumb along the tips of the fingers, moving both hands slightly away from each other.
Origin: Fingers feel smooth.
Usage: Robin uses signs *fluently*.
Everything went *smoothly*.

SHARP

Pass the tip of the middle finger of the right hand along the little-finger edge of the left open hand (as if feeling a sharp edge) and give the right hand a quick turn so the palm faces down.
Origin: As if feeling the edge of a knife.
Usage: need a *sharp* knife.

HARD

Strike the middle finger of the right bent "V" on the back of the left "S."
Origin: Back of the hand is hard.
Usage: *hard* as a rock.

SOFT

Both open "AND" hands point upward; then draw them down into the closed "AND" position.
Origin: As if feeling something soft between the fingers.
Usage: a *soft* bed; *soft*-hearted.

MEDIUM

Place the little-finger edge of the right open hand crosswise on the index-finger edge of the left open hand. Move the right toward the tip of the left index and back several times.
Origin: Indicating an area not as long as the finger, sort of medium in length.
Usage: boiled eggs—hard, soft, or *medium?*

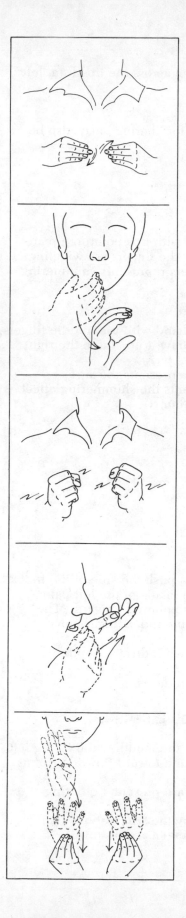

FLEXIBLE

Place the closed "AND" hands in front of you, tips pointing toward each other; move them in and out alternately.
Origin: As if showing that something can be bent.
Usage: easy to work with and *flexible*.

HOT, HEAT

Place the right "C" at the mouth, palm facing in; give the wrist a quick twist so that the palm faces out.
Origin: Something hot quickly taken from the mouth.
Usage: *hot* water.
       Can you feel the *heat?*

COLD

Shake both "S" hands, palms facing each other.
Origin: As if shivering.
Usage: A *cold* day in January.

WARM

Place the "A" hand in front of the mouth, palm in, and open the hand gradually as it moves slightly up and out.
Origin: Blowing into the hand to warm it.
Usage: *Warm* yourself at the fireplace.

WET

Sign "WATER" ("W" at right side of mouth) and "SOFT."
Origin: Feeling the water between the fingers.
Usage: We had a leak and everything was *wet*.

DRY

Bent right index finger is drawn across the lips from left to right.
Origin: The lips are dry.
Usage: The ground was *dry*.
      a *dry* lecture (the sign for "boring" may also be used in this instance).

SHINING

Open palms facing each other with tips pointing up are drawn apart to the sides while the fingers are wiggling.
Origin: Movement of the fingers represents shimmering light.
Usage: Susan's eyes *shone*.

Or, touch the back of the left hand with the middle finger of the right open hand; then draw it up and to the right with a shaking motion from the wrist.
Origin: Back of the left hand represents the surface; movement of the right represents the shimmering effect.
Usage: The kitchen floor is *shiny*.

DEEP

Using the right index position, push the side of the index finger straight down along the inside of the left palm, which is facing right with tips pointing forward. (The greater the depth, the farther the index finger moves downward.)
Origin: The finger moving down indicates depth.
Usage: The ocean is *deep*.
      I studied the subject in *depth*.

QUIET, CALM, STILL, TRANQUIL, SERENE

Place the index finger against the mouth, palm facing left; draw both open hands down and toward the side, palms facing down.
Origin: Hands moved downward present a quieting effect.
Usage: a *calm*, sweet voice; by the *still* waters; a *quiet* man; a *tranquil* morning; a *serene* spirit.

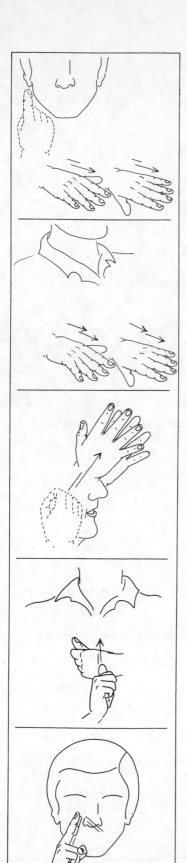

NOISY, SOUND, LOUD

Touch the tip of the ear with the index finger; direct both "FIVE" hands toward the left, right behind left, palms down.
Origin: The ear and the vibrations.
Usage: What was that *noise?*
       I hear the *sound* of singing.
       very *loud* talking.

VIBRATION

Place the "FIVE" hands in front of you, palms down, and move them back and forth alternately.
Origin: Indicating movement.
Usage: I felt the *vibration* in the floor.

AWFUL, FEARFUL, TERRIBLE, DREADFUL, HORRIBLE

Hold the "O" hands at the sides of the face and direct them upward while opening the hands into "FIVE" positions, the palms facing in.
Origin: Hair standing on end.
Usage: an *awful* storm; a *fearful* animal; *terrible* suffering; a *dreadful* place; a *horrible* crime.

DANGER

Place the thumb of the right "A" hand at the back of the left hand; brush the right "A" hand upward several times.
Usage: a *dangerous* stunt.

FUNNY, HUMOROUS

Brush the tips of the "N" fingers off the end of the nose.
Usage: That's not *funny*.
       a *humorous* story.

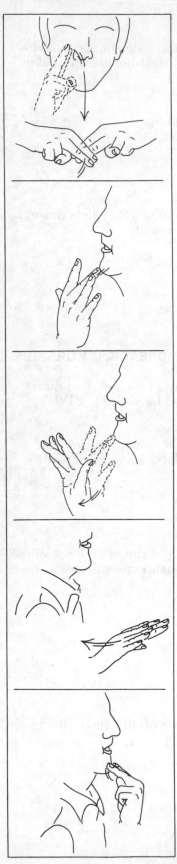

FUN

Brush the tip of the nose with the tips of the "N" fingers; then brush off the tips of the left "N" with the tips of the right "N" and reverse.
Usage: all in *fun*.

FAVORITE

Touch the chin several times with the right middle finger.
Usage: What is your *favorite* dessert?

LUCKY

Touch the chin with the middle finger; then the hand is quickly turned with the palm facing out.
Usage: You're a *lucky* person!

PET

Stroke the back of the left hand with the palm of the right hand.
Origin: As if petting an animal.
Usage: *Petting* a child too much may not do him any good.
This is my *pet*.

CUTE

Draw the tips of the "U" fingers down the chin once or twice.
Usage: That's a *cute* little girl.

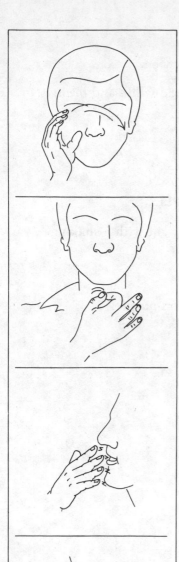

ODD, QUEER, STRANGE

Place the right "C" in front of the face; then give the wrist a quick downward twist.
Usage: a very *odd* fellow; a *queer* person; a *strange* thing happened.

CURIOUS

Grasp a bit of skin at the neck with the right index and thumb, other fingers extended; twist back and forth slightly.
Origin: The neck is extended in curiosity.
Usage: *curious* about other people's business.
   satisfy your *curiosity*.

COLOR

Place the "FIVE" hand in front of the mouth and wiggle the fingers as the hand moves away very slightly.
Usage: The *colors* of our flag are red, white, and blue.

RED

Draw the inside tip of the right index finger down across the lips (sometimes made with an "R").
Origin: Red as the lips.
Usage: Joy has a new *red* Cutlass.

PINK

Draw the middle finger of the "P" hand down across the lips.
Origin: Pink as the lips.
Usage: The bride carried *pink* roses.

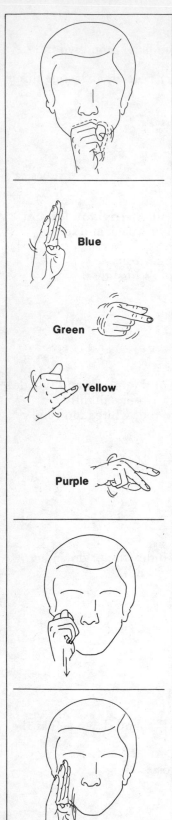

ORANGE

Squeeze the "S" hand once or twice.
Origin: As if squeezing an orange.
Usage: The playroom was painted white and *orange*.

BLUE, GREEN, YELLOW, PURPLE

Draw the initialed hand to the right with a shaking motion.
Usage: *blue* sky.
      green field.
      bright *yellow* moon.
      a combination of pink and *purple*.

TAN

Draw a "T" down the cheek.
Usage: came home from Florida with a nice *tan*.
      a *tan* raincoat.

BROWN

Draw the index-finger side of the "B" hand down the right cheek.
Usage: a *brown* dog.

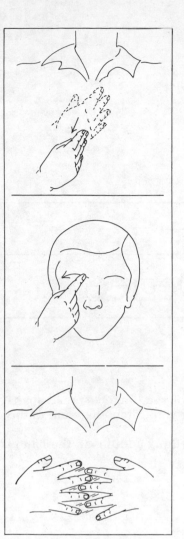

WHITE

Place fingertips of the open "AND" hand against the chest and draw the hand forward into the "AND" position.
Usage: *white* elephant sale.

BLACK

Draw the index finger across the right eyebrow from left to right.
Usage: a *black* cat sitting in the window.

GREY

Place the "FIVE" hands in front of you, palms in; pass them back and forth through the open fingers.
Origin: Showing a mixture.
Usage: a *grey* flannel suit.
Note: This word is usually fingerspelled.

13

Quantity, Size, and Degree

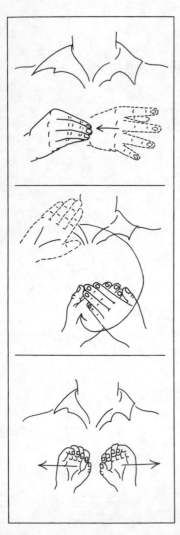

AND

Place the right hand in front of you, fingers spread apart and pointing left (palm facing you); draw the hand to the right, closing the tips.
Origin: "And" indicates something additional; the hand is preparing for the "add" sign.
Usage: bread *and* butter.

ALL, WHOLE

The left open hand faces the body; make a circle with the right hand, going out and around the left hand, ending with the back of the right hand in the palm of the left.
Origin: The sweeping movement of the right hand includes everything.
Usage: *all* the world; the *whole* school.

NONE, NO

Place the "O" hands in front of you, palms facing out; bring both hands to the sides, still in the "O" position.
Origin: Two zeros indicate the absence of any quantity.
Usage: We have *none*.
We have *no* money for a new car.

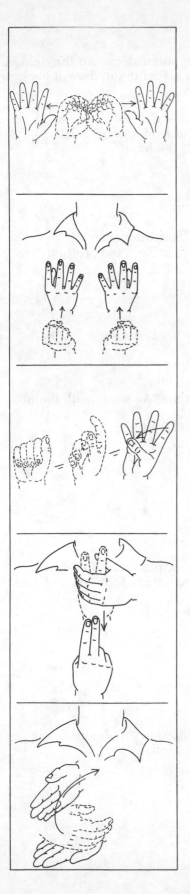

NOTHING

Place the "O" hands in front of you, palms facing out; bring both hands to the sides, opening into the "FIVE" position, palms forward.
Origin: Hands open completely to indicate there is nothing in them.
Usage: I have *nothing* to hide.

MANY, LOTS

Hold both "S" hands in front of you, palms facing up, and open them quickly several times.
Origin: All the fingers opening up indicate a great number.
Usage: *many* paintings in the museum.
lots of people watched the parade.

FEW, SEVERAL

The right "A" hand, with palm facing up, opens slowly as the thumb passes along the inside of the opening fingers.
Origin: A small number is indicated by opening the fingers one by one.
Usage: a man of *few* words.
Several days passed.

BOTH

Pass the right "TWO" hand down through the left "C"; right hand ending with the two fingers coming together (both palms facing self).
Origin: Indicates two becoming one unit.
Usage: *both* are in college.

SOME, PART, PORTION

Place the little-finger side of the right curved hand into the left palm; draw the right hand toward self and straighten it.
Origin: Indicating a part of the whole.
Usage: *some* of the books.
part-time work.
a *portion* of my time.

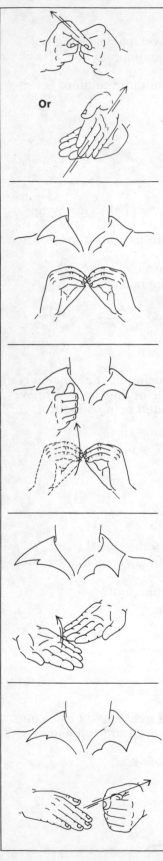

HALF

Hold out the left index finger, pointing toward the right, palm in; place the right index across it and draw it back toward self.

Or, place the little-finger edge of the right open hand across the left palm and draw it back toward self.
Origin: Half the finger, or half the hand.
Usage: *Half* is enough.
    half the pie.

MORE

Bring the tips of both "AND" hands together.
Origin: Adding to a quantity. (Similar hand positions are used for "add.")
Usage: *more* than enough.

MOST

Sign "MORE"; then lift the right "A" hand, with thumb pointing up.
Origin: "MORE" plus the "EST" ending.
Usage: *Most* plants require sun.

ALMOST, NEARLY

With both open palms facing up, place the little-finger edge of the right under the fingertips of the left and draw up.
Origin: Barely touching the fingertips.
Usage: *almost* fell.
    nearly missed the plane.

FULL, FILL

Place the right open hand on the left "S" (palm facing right) and brush across it to the left.
Origin: Filled to the brim.
Usage: The elevator was *full*.
    People *filled* the room.

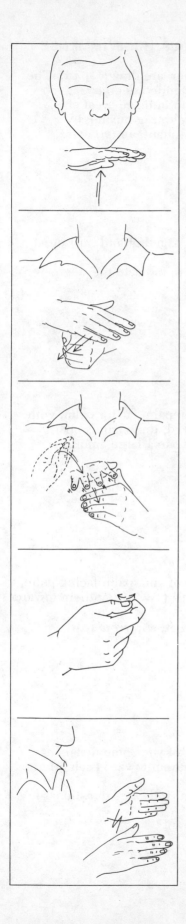

FULL, FED UP

Place the top of the right open hand under the chin.
Origin: Filled up to the chin.
Usage: I'm *full* and can't eat any more.
   I'm *fed up* with her gossip.
Note: In the slang usage the sign is made with great emphasis.

ENOUGH, PLENTY, SUFFICIENT, ADEQUATE

Place the right open hand on the left "S" which is facing right; brush across it to the right several times.
Origin: Filled to the brim and starting to run over.
Usage: money *enough* for everything.
   sufficient proof.
   plenty of time.
   His wages are *adequate*.

OVERFLOW, RUNNING OVER

Place the right "AND" hand against the left palm; move the right hand up to the index-finger edge and then over the side, fingers wiggling.
Origin: Running over the edge.
Usage: My heart is *overflowing*.
   The tub is *running over*.

LITTLE, BIT, SLIGHTLY

Using an "X" position, rub the end of the thumb against the end of the index finger, palm facing up.
Origin: As little as might be on a fingertip.
Usage: feel a *little* hungry.
   a *bit* doubtful.
   felt *slightly* dizzy.

SMALL, LITTLE

Hold both slightly curved hands in front of you, palm facing palm, and push hands toward each other several times.
Origin: Hands pushed toward each other indicate smallness.
Usage: a *small* country; a *small* animal; a *small* house; a *little* baby; a *little* kitten.

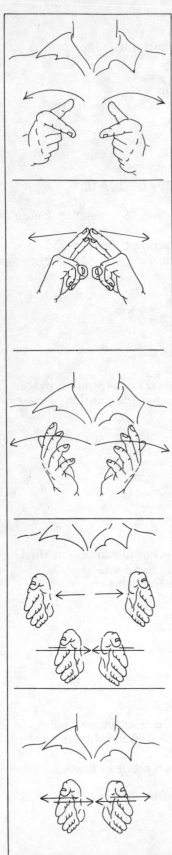

LARGE, GREAT, BIG, ENORMOUS, HUGE, IMMENSE

The "L" hands, facing each other, are drawn apart. (The size of the sign indicates the intended degree.)
Origin: Hands are drawn apart to indicate great size.
Usage: a *large* house; a *great* field; *big* business; *enormous* ship; *huge* elephant; an *immense* national debt.

VERY

Place the tips of the "V" hands together and pull them apart.
Origin: Hands are drawn apart to indicate the degree.
Usage: *very* good work.

MUCH, A LOT, LOTS

Hold both hands in front of you, palm facing palm, with fingers slightly spread and curved; draw hands apart.
Origin: Hands drawn apart indicate a large amount.
Usage: *much* confusion.
heard *a lot* about that.
lots of trouble.

WIDE, BROAD—NARROW

Place both open hands in front of you, palm facing palm, and draw them apart. For "NARROW" bring them toward each other.
Usage: 3 feet *wide;* a *broad* street; a *narrow* road.

WIDTH

Place both open hands in front of you some distance apart, palm facing palm; move them toward each other and out again several times.
Origin: The in-out-in movement indicates questionable width.
Usage: Is that the *width* you want?

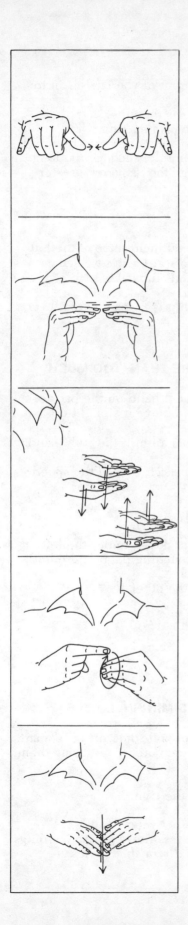

MEASURE

Place the "Y" hands in front of you, palms facing down, and touch the thumb tips together several times.
Origin: Using the thumb and little finger to measure.
Usage: *Measure* your windows before buying drapes. The *measurements* of the living room are 15' x 18'.

EQUAL, FAIR

Place bent hands in front of you, palm sides down; bring tips together several times.
Origin: One is on the same level with the other.
Usage: *equal* work, *equal* pay.
The judge was *fair*.

HEAVY—LIGHT

Place both open hands in front of you, palms facing up, and drop the arms slightly as if holding too heavy an object. For "LIGHT" raise the hands slightly as if bouncing a light object.
Usage: He's not *heavy*, he's my brother.
My suitcase was very *light*.

ABOUT

Place the left "AND" hand in front of you pointing right, and use the right index to circle around the tips up-forward-down-in.
Usage: a book *about* animals.
something different *about* her.

THAN

Place the left open hand in front of you, palm down, and brush the index-finger edge of the right open hand off the fingertips of the left and down.
Origin: This word is used in a comparative sense and the sign shows that what follows is of a lower degree.
Usage: older *than* I am.

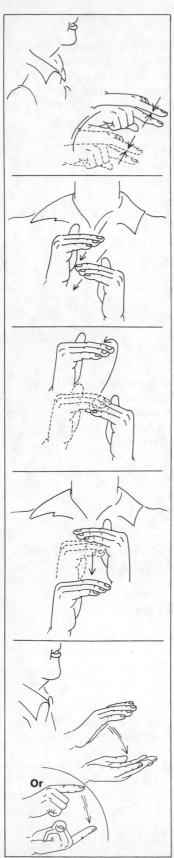

TOO, ALSO

Sign "SAME" twice, once in front of you and again to the left.
Origin: Something is the same as the other.
Usage: Are you going *too?* I'm *also* making plans.
Note: There is no sign for "too" when it refers to something beyond what is desirable, such as: *too* long. In such a case the word following "too" is given greater emphasis.

LIMIT, RESTRICT

Place the right bent hand several inches above the left bent hand; bring both hands forward a short distance.
Origin: The position of the hands indicates how high one can go.
Usage: a time *limit;* membership is *restricted* to 20.

ABOVE, OVER, EXCEED, MORE THAN, TOO MUCH

Place the fingers of the right bent hand on the back of the left bent hand; lift the right and move it straight up, palm still facing down.
Origin: The left hand represents a limit; the right hand goes beyond the limit.
Usage: *above* the fifth floor; *over* 21; *exceed* the speed limit; ate too much.

BELOW, UNDER, LESS THAN

Place the right bent hand, palm down, under the left open hand (top of right hand touching palm of the left); lower the right hand a few inches.
Origin: One hand lower than the other.
Usage: 30° *below* zero.
boys *under* 18.
less than $5.

DECREASE, LESS, REDUCE, DIMINISH, LOWER

Hold the open hands in front of you some distance apart, right above left, palms facing each other, and bring them toward each other.

Or, use index fingers to make the sign.

Origin: Less and less distance between hands.
Usage: cars *decrease* in value; *less* noise please; earnings were *reduced;* savings *diminished;* taxes are *lower.*

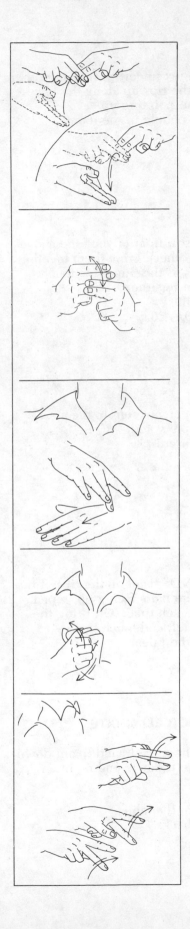

INCREASE, GAIN WEIGHT—TAKE OFF WEIGHT

Hold the left "H" in front of you, palm facing down; bring the right "H" from a palm-up to a palm-down position on the left "H"; repeat several times. For "TAKE OFF WEIGHT" make the sign in reverse (move the right "H" off the left).
Usage: an *increase* in pay; an *increase* in the number present; *gained* another pound; *took off* 5 pounds.

WEIGH

Place the middle finger of the right "H" across the index of the left "H" and balance the right "H" on the left, similar to the motion of a seesaw.
Origin: Indicating a scale balancing.
Usage: turkey *weighed* 18 pounds.
illness caused a *weight* loss.

EMPTY, VACANT, BARE, BALD

Move the middle fingertip of the right "FIVE" hand along the back of the left open hand.
Origin: As bare as the back of your hand.
Usage: *empty* closet; house is *vacant; bald* head; room is *bare.*

CROWDED, CRUSHED

Place the "A" hands together, palm to palm; while they are touching, twist the right hand toward you and the left hand away from you.
Origin: Squeezed together.
Usage: The room was *crowded.*
My clothes were *crushed.*

AS

Place the index fingers side by side several inches apart, palms down, and move them over to the left in this position.
Origin: Similar to the sign for "SAME."
Usage: white *as* snow.

PROPORTION

Sign as above using the "P" hands.
Usage: pay is in *proportion* to work done.

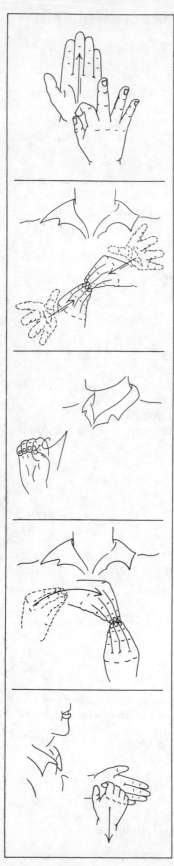

COUNT

Close the right thumb and index fingertips (leaving other fingers extended) and move the tips up along the left palm which is facing right and pointing up.
Usage: *Count* the number of people in the room.

TOTAL, SUM

Hold the open "AND" hands in front of you, one above the other (palms facing each other); bring them together, closing into "AND" positions as the fingertips touch.
Origin: Everything is brought together.
Usage: The *total* cost is $24.50.
       The *sum* of 10 and 10 is 20.

PERCENT, INTEREST

Using the "O" hand, draw a percent sign in the air.
Usage: 60 *percent* of the people voted.
       The bank pays high *interest*.

ADD

Place the tips of the right "AND" hand on the tips of the left "AND" hand which has the palm facing up; repeat, bringing the left hand higher each time. (Or, bring the right "AND" hand under the left and touch tips.)
Origin: Adding something to the pile.
Usage: *add* to your knowledge.

SUBTRACT, REMOVE, DEDUCT, ELIMINATE

Place the fingertips of the right curved hand (palm down) against the left palm and move it down, ending in an "A" position.
Origin: *subtract* 3 from 10.
       Remove the paper from the table.
       deductions from paychecks.
       eliminate several names.

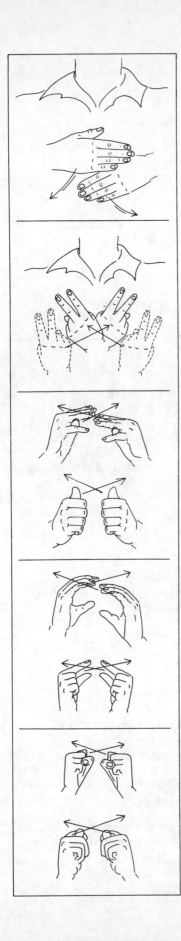

DIVIDE

Place the little-finger edge of the right open hand crosswise on the index-finger edge of the left open hand; draw both hands to the sides, ending with palms down.
Origin: As if splitting something.
Usage: *Divide* 40 by 5.
   Divide the class in half.

FIGURE, ARITHMETIC, MULTIPLY, WORSE

Place both "V" hands in front of you, palms facing you, and cross them so that the back of the right "V" passes across the palm of the left.
Usage: *figure up* the bill; *multiply* 5 x 6; traffic problems are *worse*.

MATHEMATICS

Sign as for "FIGURE" using the "M" hands.

ALGEBRA

Sign as for "FIGURE" using the "A" hands.

CALCULUS

Sign as for "FIGURE" using the "C" hands.

GEOMETRY

Sign as for "FIGURE" using the "G" hands.

STATISTICS

Sign as for "FIGURE" using the "S" hands.

TRIGONOMETRY

Sign as for "FIGURE" using the "T" hands.

14

Communication and Government

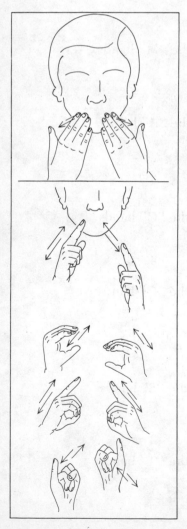

THANK, THANK YOU, YOU'RE WELCOME

Place the tips of the open hands against the mouth and throw them forward, similar to throwing a kiss. (May be made with one hand.)

Usage: *Thank you* for the birthday card. *You're welcome.*
Esther *thanked* Will for the flowers.

CONVERSATION, TALK

Place the tips of the index fingers on the lips and move them forward and backward alternately.

Origin: Talking back and forth.

Usage: Their *conversation* is about sports.
Let's *talk* for a while.

COMMUNICATE—Make the above sign with "C" hands.

Usage: Good *communication* is important.

DIALOGUE—Make the above sign with the "D" hands.

Usage: It was an interesting *dialogue*.

INTERVIEW—Make the above sign with the "I" hands.

Usage: Make an appointment for the *interview* at three.

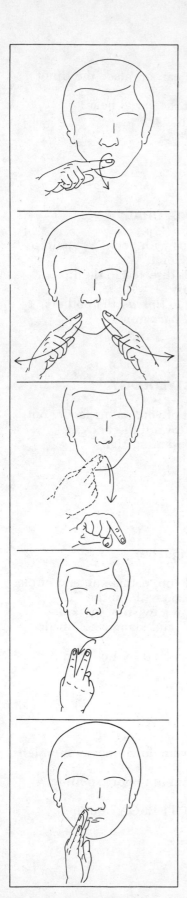

SPEAK, SAY, TELL, SPEECH

The index finger, pointing to the left, is held in front of the mouth and rolls forward in a circular movement.
Origin: Words proceeding from the mouth.
Usage: Actions *speak* louder than words.
What did you *say?*
Tell me about it. She has good *speech.*

ANNOUNCE, PROCLAIM, DECLARE

Index fingers touch the lips and are drawn forward and out, away from the face.
Origin: The sign for "tell" is enlarged.
Usage: *Announce* the winner.
He *proclaimed* a holiday.
The president *declared* an emergency.

COMMAND, ORDER

Point the right index finger toward the mouth; turn it outward and down in a strong motion.
Origin: Telling with force.
Usage: The captain gave a *command*. He *ordered* his men to march.

VOICE, VOCAL

Place the tips of the "V" at the throat and draw them up towards the chin.
Origin: Indicating the throat with the initial.
Usage: a high *voice;* your *vocal* cords.

WHISPER

Place the right curved hand at the right side of the mouth, palm facing left.
Origin: Hiding the mouth while talking.
Usage: She *whispered* her secret.

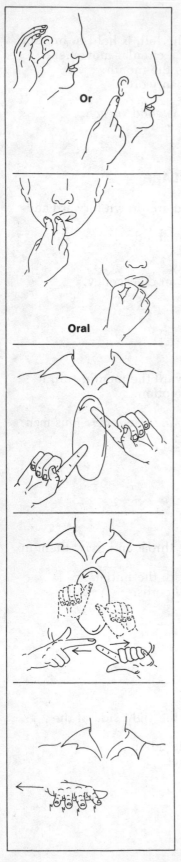

Or

Oral

LISTEN, HEAR

Place the "C" against the right ear; or, place the tip of the index finger at the ear.
Origin: Cupping the hand over the ear to hear.
Usage: *Listen*, the birds are singing.
Do you *hear* what I *hear?*

SPEECHREADING, LIPREADING, ORAL

Describe a circle around the lips with bent "V," palm facing in. Some use an "O" for "oral."
Origin: The sign for "READ" is directed to the lips.
Usage: *Speechreading* is not easy.
Some people are easier to *lipread* than others.
She comes from an *oral* background.

SIGNS (the language of), DACTYLOLOGY

Cross the index fingers in front of you, palms facing out, and circle the arms alternately toward the body.
Origin: Hands are moved, representing signs.
Usage: *Signs* represent concepts.
Study *dactylology.*

AMESLAN (American Sign Language)

Place the "A" hands in front of you, palms out, and circle the arms alternately toward the body; form the "L" positions and draw them apart in a twisting motion.
Origin: Signs made with an "A" and "language" made with an "L."
Usage: The term *Ameslan* was coined by Lou Fant.

FINGERSPELLING, SPELL

The right "FIVE" hand with palm down moves from left to right, fingers wiggling.
Origin: Indicating the movement of fingers spelling.
Usage: *Fingerspell* your name.
a poor *speller* (add the "PERSON" ending).

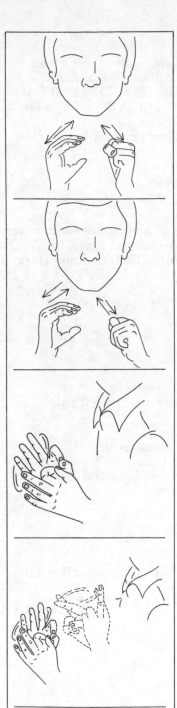

SIMULTANEOUS COMMUNICATION

Make an "S" with one hand and a "C" with the other; move them forward and backward alternately, just below the mouth.
Usage: All of our teachers use *simultaneous communication.*
Note: Use the "S" and "M" hands for SIMULTANEOUS METHOD.

TOTAL COMMUNICATION

Make a "T" with one hand and a "C" with the other; move them forward and backward alternately, just below the mouth.
Usage: *Total communication* helps deaf children.

INTERPRET

Make the sign for "CHANGE" using "F" hands.
Origin: Hands in the original "language" position make the sign for "change." (In other words, interpreting is language that is changed.)
Usage: *Interpreting* requires great skill.
   Good *interpreters* are in demand. (Add the "PERSON" ending.)

REVERSE INTERPRET

Sign "REVERSE" by using the "R" hands to sign "CHANGE" backwards; then sign "INTERPRET."
Origin: Making the sign in a reverse motion.
Usage: *Reverse interpreting* is most difficult.

TRANSLATE

Make the sign for "CHANGE" using "T" hands.
Origin: Translating refers to changing.
Usage: We *translate* word for word.

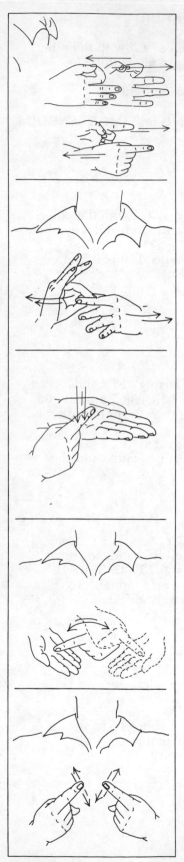

EXPLAIN, DESCRIBE, DEFINE

Place the "F" hands in front of you, palms facing each other and fingers pointing forward; move the hands forward and backward alternately. (The "D" hands may be used for "DESCRIBE" and "DEFINE," with index fingers pointing forward.)
Usage: *explain* your problem; *describe* the place; a clear *definition*.

STORY

The thumb and index fingertips of both hands (with other fingers extended) are pulled apart several times.
Usage: Our children look forward to their bedtime *story*.

DISCUSS, ARGUE

Strike the side of the index finger into the left palm several times.
Usage: a *discussion* about politics.
The Senator *argued* for a new policy. (Used in this sense the index can remain on the left palm while both hands are moved back and forth.)

DEBATE

Make the sign for "DISCUSS" alternately with the right and left hands.
Usage: a *debate* about capital punishment.

QUARREL

Point both index fingers toward each other, palms facing you, and shake the hands up and down from the wrists simultaneously.
Origin: Imitation of roosters fighting.
Usage: stop *quarreling*.

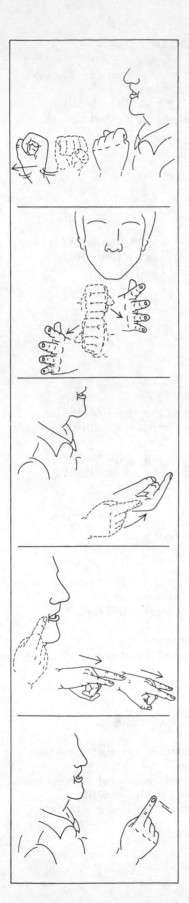

EXAGGERATE

Place the right "S" in front of the left "S" (both palms down) and move the right "S" away in a twisting motion, as if stretching and pulling.
Origin: Stretching the story.
Usage: That story seems *exaggerated*.

BAWL OUT

One "S" hand above the other, palm sides out; hands snap open as they move forward.
Usage: She *bawled out* the student.

INSULT

The index finger twists as it moves forward and slightly up.
Origin: Piercing with a knife and twisting it.
Usage: That's an *insult* to my intelligence!

MOCK, SCORN, RIDICULE

Draw the right index finger back from the mouth and direct both hands forward (right behind left), with the index and little fingers extended.
Origin: Laughing and pointing fingers in derision.
Usage: The children *mocked* Jimmy.
They *scorned* the traitor.
The little boys *ridiculed* Fern.

SCOLD

Shake the index finger in a natural motion of scolding.
Origin: A natural sign.
Usage: Mrs. Robertson *scolded* the boys.

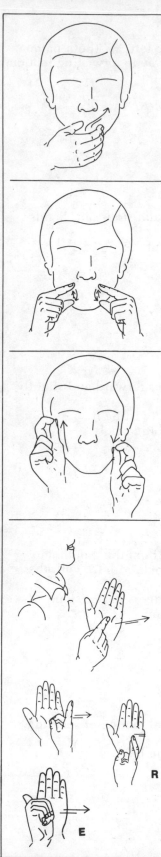

SCREAM, SHOUT, CRY OUT, ROAR

Place the right "C" hand at the mouth, palm facing you, and move it upward in a wavy motion.
Origin: Indicating the cry coming from the mouth.
Usage: girls *scream;* boys *shout;* people *cried out;* the lion *roared.*

GOSSIP

The thumb and index fingertips of both hands (with other fingers closed) face each other and open and close.
Origin: Two mouths opening and closing.
Usage: spreading *gossip.*

EXPRESSION (Facial)

Place both modified "A" hands at the sides of the face, palms facing each other; hands alternate in short up-and-down movements.
Origin: The face is pulled into various expressions.
Usage: Facial *expression* is important when signing.

SHOW, REVEAL, FOR EXAMPLE

Place the tip of the right index into the left open hand, which is facing out, and move both hands forward.
Origin: As if pointing to something in the hand.
Usage: *Show* me how to do it.
Her words *revealed* her ignorance.
One word can have several meanings, *for example* . . . .

DEMONSTRATE, REPRESENT, EXPRESS

These words may be signed "SHOW" as above, or they may be initialed as shown here.
Usage: The teacher *demonstrated* the use of the machine.
Sue *represented* her class in the meeting.
Some people find it difficult to *express* their feelings.

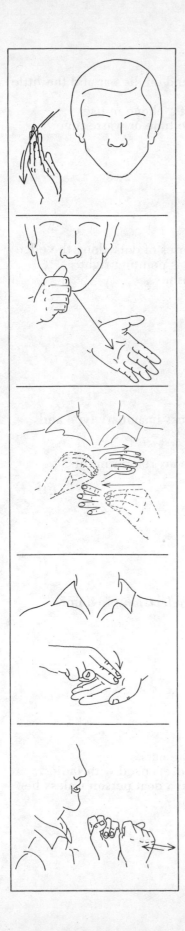

LECTURE, SPEECH, TESTIMONY

Hold the right open hand to the side with palm facing left and fingers pointing up; move the hand from the wrist forward and backward several times.
Origin: A gesture made in public speaking.
Usage: the *lecture* was boring; a very interesting *speech*; a *testimony* in court.

LETTER, MAIL

Place the thumb of the right "A" hand against the mouth and then into the left palm.
Origin: Stamping a letter.
Usage: I received a *letter* from Bea and Hal.
Any *mail* today?

CORRESPONDENCE

The right closed "AND" hand opens as it moves to the left; at the same time the left closed "AND" hand opens as it moves to the right, both hands passing each other.
Origin: Sending in both directions.
Usage: It took a lot of *correspondence* to solve the problem.

STAMPS

Place the right index and middle fingers on the palm of the left.
Origin: Affixing the stamp.
Usage: a collection of over 5,000 *stamps*.

ADVERTISE, PUBLICIZE

Place the right "S" in front of the left "S" (palm sides down) and move the right "S" away and back again several times.
Origin: As if blowing a horn.
Usage: *Advertise* in the newspaper.
Actors receive a lot of *publicity*.

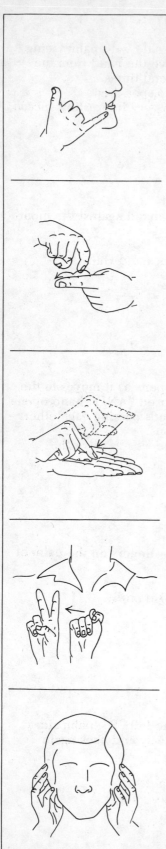

TELEPHONE, CALL

Place the thumb of the "Y" hand on the ear and the little finger at the mouth.
Origin: The natural position of a phone in use.
Usage: The *telephone* can save time or waste time.
    Call me at home.

TELEGRAM

Using the right "X" make a series of dots along the edge of the left index finger, which is pointing right.
Origin: Indicating dots and dashes.
Usage: send a *telegram*.

NEWSPAPER

The right "G" (palm down) picks imaginary type and places it in the left palm.
Origin: Old-style typesetting.
Usage: Did you read about the tax reform in the *newspaper?*

TELEVISION

Spell TV.
Usage: Which is your favorite *television* program?

RADIO

Hold the cupped hands over the ears.
Origin: The old-fashioned headsets used with radios.
Usage: *Radio* means nothing to a deaf person unless he has an interpreter.

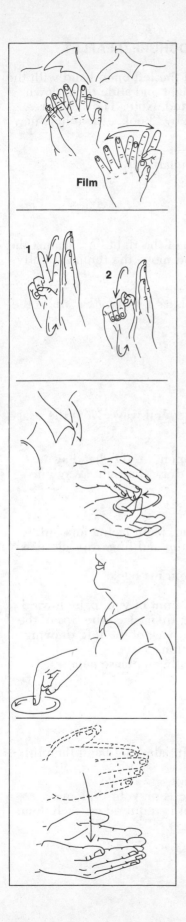

Film

MOVIE

Place the palm of the right "FIVE" hand against the palm of the left "FIVE" hand and move it back and forth slightly.
Origin: The shimmering effect of the screen.
Usage: an old *movie* with captions.
Note: "Film" is sometimes signed with the right "F."

VIDEOTAPE

Place the side of the right "V" against the left open palm, which is pointing up and facing right; move the "V" forward-down-back-up in a circle. Repeat with the right "T."
Origin: Indicating the movement of the reel.
Usage: A *videotape* of yourself signing is helpful.

RECORD PLAYER

Left hand palm up, right hand above it, palm down; point the middle fingers toward each other (leaving hands in the "FIVE" position); move right hand in a counterclockwise direction.
Origin: Left middle finger represents the spindle and right represents the record going around.
Usage: I hear a *record player* in the next room.

TAPE RECORDING

Using the index finger pointing down, describe a counterclockwise circle.
Origin: Indicating the tape going around.
Usage: We used *tapes* for practicing our signs.

BOOK

Place the open hands palm to palm; then open them as if opening a book.
Origin: Indicating the closed and then the open book.
Usage: *book* of the month.

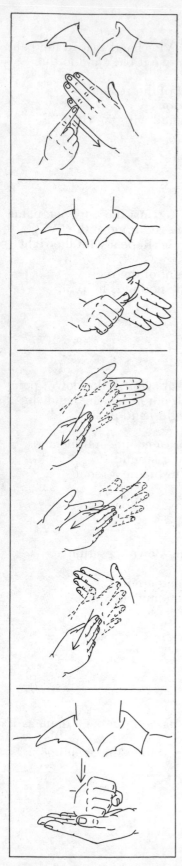

MAGAZINE, PAMPHLET, BROCHURE, LEAFLET

Grasp the little-finger edge of the left open hand with the thumb and forefinger of the right and slide them down the outside edge of the left hand. Note: The sign for "magazine" may be preceded by "book"; the others may be preceded by "paper."
Origin: A book that is thin.
Usage: Subscribe to several *magazines.*
  pamphlets in the mail.

PAGE, LOOK IT UP

Place the inside of the thumb of the right "A" against the palm of the open left hand and move the thumb slightly to the left several times.
Origin: Paging through a book.
Usage: What is the *page* number? I will *look it up* in the dictionary.

COPY

This word may be signed in several ways. Note the usage in each one.

1) Place the tips of the right open "AND" hand against the palm of the left hand and draw the right away into the closed "AND" position.
Usage: Make a *copy* for me.

2) The right open "AND" hand, palm facing forward, is drawn toward the left open palm and fingertips close as they touch the left palm.
Usage: *Copy* the paragraph from his book.

3) Place the left open hand in front of you, palm toward you and fingers pointing right; then place the tips of the open "AND" hand against the back of the left, drawing away into closed "AND" position.
Usage: Let's sing in signs together—please *copy.*

SEAL, STAMP

Strike the right "S" on the left palm, hold and then lift quickly.
Origin: As if making an imprint.
Usage: The *seal* of the college is on your diploma.
  The *stamp* of approval is required on each item.

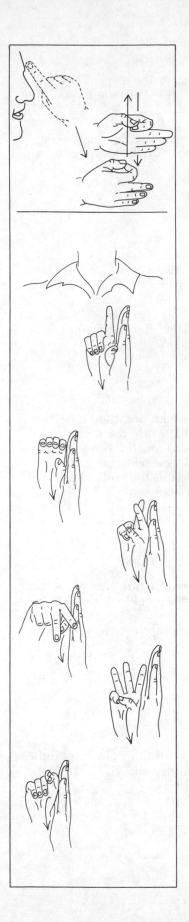

JUDGE, TRIAL, COURT

Touch the forehead with index finger; then move both "F" hands up and down alternately (palms facing each other and fingers pointing forward).
Origin: Thoughts are being weighed in a balance.
Usage: *judge* and jury; the *trial* is postponed; he will be *tried* in New York; *court* begins at nine.

LAW, LEGISLATION, LAWYER, ATTORNEY

Place the right "L," with palm facing forward, against the palm of the left hand. Add the "PERSON" ending as needed.
Origin: "L" representing the law is on the books.
Usage: the *law* of the land; better see your *lawyer;* a tax *attorney* can help you; new *legislation* requires interpreters.

Initial signs are used for the following:

COMMANDMENTS, CONSTITUTION

Usage: Ten *Commandments.*
Constitution of the U.S.

RULES, REGULATIONS

Usage: *rules* of the game.
regulations of the institution.

PRINCIPLES, PARLIAMENTARY

Usage: a man of high *principles.*
parliamentary procedure.

WILL

Usage: his last *will* and testament.

TESTAMENT

Usage: the Old *Testament.*

Note: Often the letter is placed against the palm twice, the second time lower than the first.

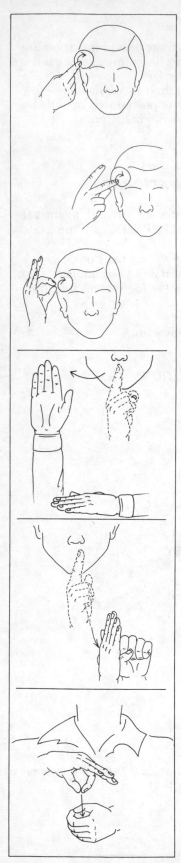

GOVERNMENT, GOVERNOR

Using the right index finger, describe a small circle at the right side of the temple and end by placing the point against the temple.
Origin: Authority is indicated at the head.
Usage: "...*government* of the people, by the people, and for the people, shall not perish from the earth" (Abraham Lincoln).

Initial signs are used for the following:

POLITICS, POLITICAL

Usage: involved in *politics*.
studying *political* science.

FEDERAL

Usage: Washington is often called the *federal* city.

VOW, SWEAR, OATH, LOYAL

Place the index finger at the mouth and then raise the right hand, palm facing forward, while the fingertips of the left hand (palm facing down) touch the right elbow.
Origin: Raising the right hand as if taking an oath.
Usage: made a *vow;* I *swear* to tell the truth; President's *oath* of office; *loyal* to his party.

PROMISE

Place the index finger at the mouth and then place the right open palm on the index-finger side of the left "S" hand.
Usage: If you make a *promise*, keep it.

VOTE, ELECTION

Touch the thumb and forefinger of the right hand (other fingers extended) and place in the left "O."
Origin: Dropping a ballot in the box.
Usage: We *vote* for our president.
Election Day is in November.

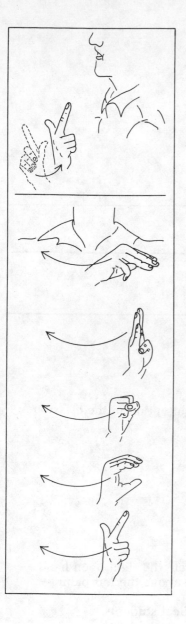

SECOND (As, a motion)

Twist the right "L" in an inward motion.
Usage: A motion was made and *seconded*.

MEMBER

Place the right "M" at the left shoulder; then at the right.
Usage: a *member* of our club.

Initial signs are also used for the following:

BOARD—"B"

Usage: *board* of directors.

SENATE—"S"

Usage: attending a meeting of the *senate*.

CONGRESS—"C"

Usage: listened to a speech by a *congress*woman.

LEGISLATURE—"L"

Usage: The state *legislature* meets today.

NOTES:

DEMOCRAT, REPUBLICAN—Shake the right "D" or "R." These are understood in context. Since shaking the right "D" could also mean "dictionary" it would have to be lipread or used within a context that would clearly identify the intended word.
AMEND—Sign "CHANGE" using "A" hands; or, use the sign for "ADD" as the case may be.
ALL IN FAVOR—Sign "SUPPORT" since this is the meaning of the phrase ("All supporting the issue say aye").
CAPTIONS—Use the sign for "STORY" or "SENTENCE." Since the term "captioned films" is used frequently by deaf people, this sign has been generally adopted as being appropriate.

15
Education

SCHOOL

Clap the hands twice.
Origin: The teacher claps for attention in the classroom.
Usage: *School* days are over.

COLLEGE

Clap the hands once, then circle the right open hand, palm down, counterclockwise above the left palm.
Origin: A school that is higher.
Usage: a *college* program for deaf students.

INSTITUTION, INSTITUTE

Make a small clockwise circle with the right "I" and place it on the back of the left closed hand.
Origin: The sign for "establish" made with the letter "I."
Usage: a well-known *institution*.
Note: This sign is commonly used to refer to residential schools for the deaf.

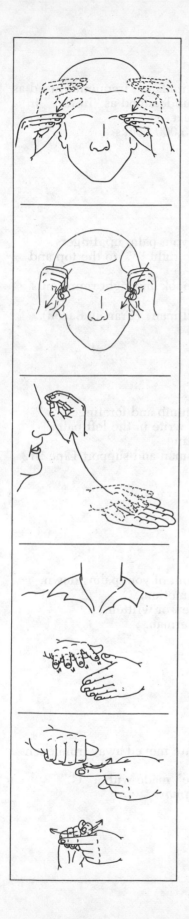

TEACH, INSTRUCT, EDUCATE

Place both open "AND" hands in front of the forehead facing each other; bring them forward, away from the head, into closed "AND" positions.
Origin: Taking something from the mind to pass to others.
Usage: *teach* me to sign well; *instruct* me to play tennis; *educate* people in college.

EDUCATION

Place both "E" hands in front of the forehead, facing each other; move them away from the head and back several times.
Origin: Derived from the sign for "teach."
Usage: received my *education* in England.

LEARN, STUDENTS

Hold out the left hand, palm facing up, and with the right hand make a motion as if taking something out of the left hand and placing it on the forehead.
Origin: From the book into the mind.
Usage: always interested in *learning* more.
a fine *student* (sign "LEARN" + "PERSON" ending).

STUDY

Point the fingers of the right hand, palm down, at the left open hand; wiggle the fingers of the right hand as it is moved toward and away from the left hand.
Origin: Poring over a book.
Usage: Success in college requires *study*.
Note: "Student" may be signed: "STUDY" + "PERSON" ending.

PRACTICE, TRAINING

Rub the "A" hand back and forth along the outside edge of the left index finger. (Sometimes the "T" is used for "training.")
Origin: As if polishing something.
Usage: *Practice* your interpreting.
a valuable *training* program.

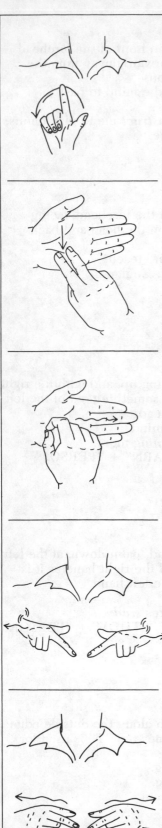

LIBRARY

The right "L" is circled.
Note: In particular settings, initials are frequently used as shortcuts. The "L" would be understood as "library" in an educational setting or context.
Usage: The *library* contains 75,000 books.

READ

Hold the left hand in front of you, palm up, fingers pointing to the right; point the right "V" to the top and move downward.
Origin: Left hand represents book and right represents eyes scanning the page.
Usage: "*Reading* maketh a full man" (Francis Bacon).

WRITE

Pressing the tip of the right thumb and forefinger together, other fingers closed, write in the left palm.
Origin: Natural motion of writing.
Usage: *Write* to your congressman and support Line 21.

LANGUAGE, TONGUE

Place the two "L" hands in front of you, palms down; draw them apart in a twisting motion.
Usage: *Language* can be spoken or written.
My native *tongue* is German.

GRAMMAR

Both hands in "G" positions are moved away from each other in a twisting motion.
Origin: The sign for "sentence" made with a "G."
Usage: studying English *grammar*.

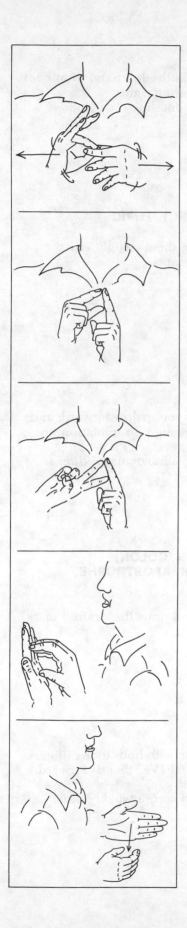

SENTENCE

The thumb and index fingertips of both hands (with other fingers extended) are pulled apart in a twisting motion.
Origin: The sign originated with the word *chain* and was used to indicate words linked together.
Usage: several *sentences* in a paragraph.

WORD

Place the right index and thumb (with other fingers closed) against the left index which is pointing up, palm facing right. Note: Sometimes "vocabulary" is signed by repeating "WORD" several times.
Origin: One segment of a sentence.
Usage: a man of few *words*.

VOCABULARY

Place the right "V" (palm out) against the left index which is pointing up, palm facing right.
Origin: Initialed sign for "word."
Usage: Deaf children often have a limited *vocabulary*.

PARAGRAPH

Place the curved right "FIVE" hand against the left open palm which is facing right and pointing upward.
Origin: The left hand represents a page and the right indicates the paragraph that is a portion of that page.
Usage: Read the first *paragraph*.

CHAPTER

Place the tips of the right "C" hand against the left palm and draw down.
Origin: Indicating a long passage.
Usage: Read the third *chapter*.

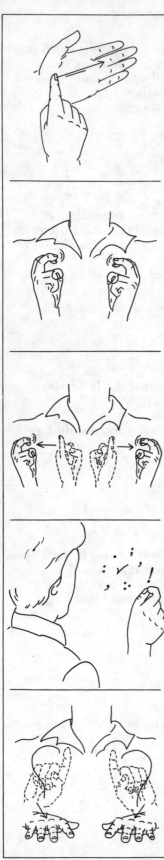

LINE

Run the right index finger across the left palm from heel to fingertips (left fingertips pointing right).
Origin: The finger underlining one line on a page.
Usage: The fifth *line* is not clear.

QUOTE, THEME, TITLE, SUBJECT, TOPIC

Use the bent "V" hands, giving them a slight twist inward to make the quotation marks.
Usage: and I *quote*.
 theme of our play.
 title of the song.
 our *subject* today.
 the *topic* of conversation.

IDIOM

Place the "I" hands in front of you, palms forward, and draw them apart; then make the sign for quotation marks, as above.
Usage: We must also learn the sign language *idioms*.

PERIOD, COMMA, SEMICOLON, COLON, EXCLAMATION, CHECK MARK, APOSTROPHE, THEREFORE

Use a modified "A" position and draw the desired mark in the air.

EXAMINATION, TEST QUIZ

Draw question marks in the air with both index fingers; then direct the fingers of both "FIVE" hands forward.
Origin: All questions coming at you.
Usage: a difficult *exam*; a short *test*; a weekly *quiz*.

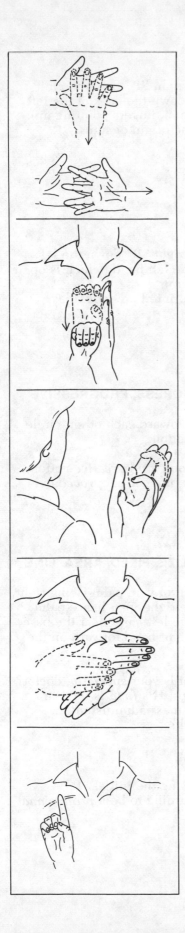

SCHEDULE

Move the right fingertips (fingers slightly spread) downward across the left palm which is pointing rightward; then turn the right palm inward the brush back of fingertips to the right across the left palm.
Origin: Showing the paper rules for a schedule.
Usage: Prepare a *schedule* and follow it.

CURRICULUM

Hold the left palm in front of you; place the right "C" against it, lower the right hand slightly, form an "M" and place it against the left.
Usage: The *curriculum* includes math, English, and history.

COURSE

Hold the left palm in front of you; place the little-finger edge of the right "C" on the left hand near the fingertips, then in the center of the palm.
Origin: The sign for "lesson" made with a "C."
Usage: I'm taking four *courses* this semester.

LESSON

Hold the left palm in front of you; strike the little-finger edge of the right open hand across the fingers of the left and then again across the lower palm.
Origin: Representing the portion of the page to be studied.
Usage: Our *lesson* for tomorrow will be short.

DICTIONARY

Shake the right "D" slightly.
Note: The "D" would only be understood in context. (Shaking the "D" could mean Democrat when used in another setting.)
Usage: We cannot do without *dictionaries*.

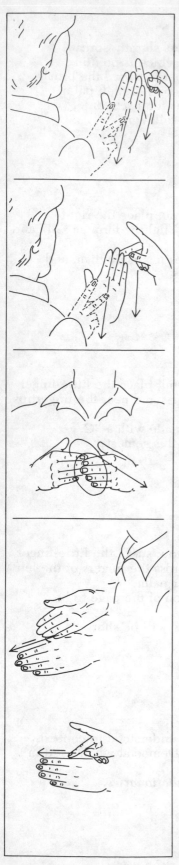

PROJECT

Draw the middle finger of the right "P" down the left palm; then draw the right "J" down the back of the left hand (which is open with palm in, fingers pointing up). **Usage:** a research *project* on the origin of signs.

PROGRAM

Draw the middle finger of the right "P" down the left palm, then down the back of the left hand (which is open with palm in, fingers pointing up).
Origin: Represents a program printed on both sides.
Usage: planning a full *program*.

PROCESS, PROCEDURE, PROGRESS, PROGRESSIVE

Both bent hands, tips pointing toward each other, circle over each other in a forward motion.
Origin: Wheels of progress.
Usage: making *progress* in school; a *progressive* nation; the educational *process*; the correct *procedure*.

MAJOR, SPECIALTY, SPECIALIZE, FIELD, AREA, LINE

Hold the left open hand in front of you, palm facing right, tips pointing forward; place the right open hand (palm left and pointing forward) on the left hand near the base of the index finger. Move the right hand forward on the left index.
Origin: Following a specific line.
Usage: My *major* is math. What is your *specialty*, doctor? *specializing* in pediatrics; His *field* is nuclear physics. My *area* is business administration. What's your *line* of work?

PROFESSION, PROFESSIONAL

Make the sign for "MAJOR" using the initial "P."
Usage: the legal *profession*; learning to be a *professional* interpreter.

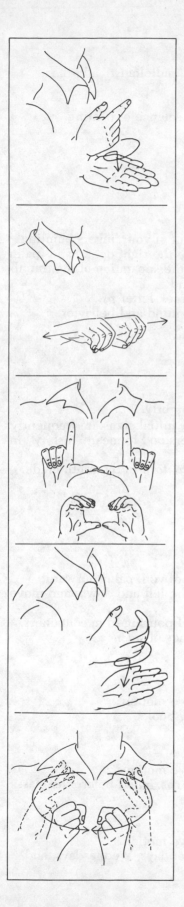

GRADUATE

Describe a small clockwise circle with the right "G" hand and place it in the left palm.
Origin: Placing the seal on the diploma.
Usage: Carol will *graduate* from New York University.
    Margaret Meade was our *graduation* speaker.

DIPLOMA, DEGREE

Place both "O" hands in front of you, palms down, and draw them apart.
Origin: Indicating the shape of the rolled diploma.
Usage: received a *diploma* from high school.
    Working for a college *degree*.

LICENSE, CERTIFICATE

Place both "L" hands in front of you, palms out. For "certificate" use the "C" hands.
Origin: Indicates the shape of a license or certificate.
Usage: driver's *license*.
    R.I.D. *certificate*.

CERTIFY

Describe a small clockwise circle with the right "C" hand and place it in the left palm.
Origin: Placing the seal on the certificate.
Usage: A *certified* interpreter is used in the courts.

WORKSHOP

Place the "W" hands in front of you, draw them apart to the sides and around, changing to an "S" hand, ending with the little fingers of the "S" hands touching.
Origin: The "group" sign initialized.
Usage: a *workshop* for vocational rehabilitation counselors.

AUDIOLOGY

Circle an "A" at the ear. (For "audiologist" add the "PERSON" ending.)
Usage: His field is *audiology*.
Audiologists study the science of hearing.

PSYCHOLOGY

Hold the left open hand in front of you, fingers pointing up and palm facing right; place the right open hand (palm left, fingertips pointing up) at the separation of the thumb and index finger of the left hand.
Origin: The hands form the Greek letter *psi*.
Usage: *Psychology* studies the mind and behavior.

HISTORY

Move the "H" up and down slightly.
Note: In the area of education, initial signs are frequently used. The "H" would be understood to mean "history" in this setting.
Usage: We studied American *history* in the ninth grade.

SCIENCE

Place both "A" hands in front of you, palms forward; alternately move the right to the left and down, and move the left to the right and down.
Origin: Imitating the motion of pouring from containers.
Usage: There are many branches of *science*.

CHEMISTRY

Use the "C" hands in the above motion.
Usage: Where is my *chemistry* book?

EXPERIMENT

Use the "E" hands in the above motion.
Usage: He demonstrated the *experiment* before the class.

BIOLOGY

Use the "B" hands in the above motion.
Usage: *Biology* class meets Mondays, Wednesdays, and Fridays.

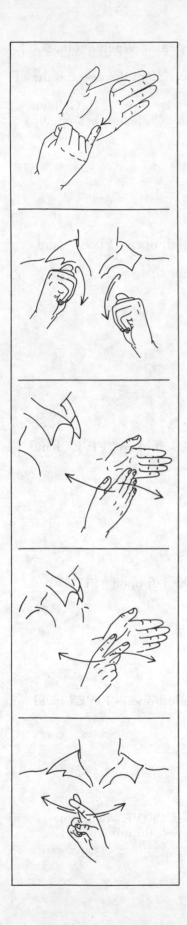

ART, DRAWING, DESIGN

Using the right "I" as an imaginary brush, draw a wavy line down the left palm. ("Design" can be initialized.)
Origin: As if drawing a picture.
Usage: *drawing* pictures.
      a skilled *artist* (add the "PERSON" ending).
      a modern *design*.

DRAMA, PERFORMANCE, ACTING, PLAY, THEATRE

Place the "A" hands in front of you (palm side out) near the chest and circle them toward the body alternately.
Origin: Going through the motion of acting.
Usage: a student of *drama*; a good *performance*; well
      known for her *acting*; a Shakespearean *play*;
      National *Theatre* of the Deaf.

SING, SONG, MUSIC

Extend the left arm; pointing the fingertips of the right hand to the left palm, wave the right arm back and forth.
Origin: Directing the music.
Usage: Let's *sing* in signs.
      an old *song* from the sixties.
      the sound of *music*.

POETRY

Extend the left arm; pointing the fingertips of the right "P" toward the left palm, wave the right back and forth.
Origin: The sign for "music" is initialed.
Usage: "I think that I shall never see a *poem* lovely as a
      tree...."

RHYTHM

Using the right "R" swing the arm back and forth in front of you in a rhythmic motion.
Origin: Indicating the rhythm or beat.
Usage: I've got *rhythm*.

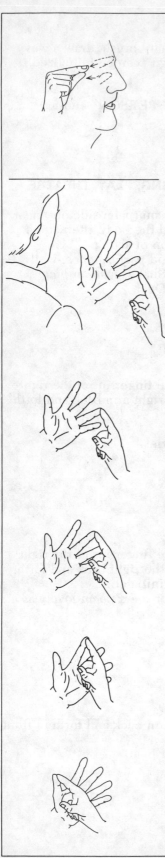

GALLAUDET (College for the deaf in Washington, D.C.)

Place the right "G" hand at the side of the eye and draw back, closing the fingers.
Origin: Represents glasses worn by Rev. T. H. Gallaudet.
Usage: The charter for *Gallaudet* College was signed by Abraham Lincoln.

PREPARATORY STUDENT

Point to the little finger of the left open "FIVE" hand.

FRESHMAN

Point to the fourth finger of the left open "FIVE" hand.

SOPHOMORE

Point to the middle finger of the left open "FIVE" hand.

JUNIOR

Point to the index finger of the left open "FIVE" hand.

SENIOR

Point to the thumb of the left open "FIVE" hand, or, place the open right hand on the left thumb which is facing you.

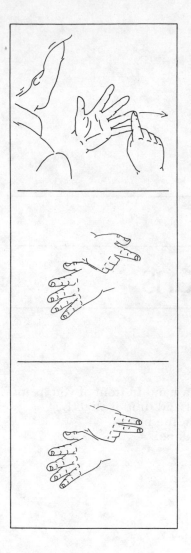

LEAVING COLLEGE

Leaving college during a particular year is indicated by using the index finger to touch and move away from the left-hand finger that represents the year in which the student left. The illustration shows that a student left during his freshman year.

FIRST-YEAR GRADUATE STUDENT

Place the right "G" on the left wrist.

SECOND-YEAR GRADUATE STUDENT

Place the side of the "TWO" hand on the left wrist.

COLLEGES

The names of colleges are usually signed as they are spoken: U.C.L.A.—Each letter is circled slightly. New York University—"New York" + "U" (circled). University of Illinois—"U" (circled) + Ill.(fingerspelled). George Washington University—G. W. U. (all are circled).

DEGREES

B.A., M.A., M.S., Ed.D., Ph.D., etc.—Fingerspell.
DOCTOR—When referring to a person who has a doctorate in a field other than medicine, "doctor" is abbreviated "Dr."
Examples: my teacher, Dr. Williams (fingerspell "Dr."); our family doctor (use the medical-doctor sign, placing the "D" on the wrist).

16
Miscellaneous Nouns

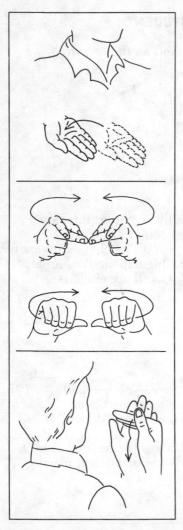

THING

Place the slightly curved open hand in front of you, palm
facing up; move it to the right and drop it slightly.
Origin: An imaginary object in the hand.
Usage: many *things* must be done.

PLACE

Touch the tips of the middle fingers of the "P" hands;
draw them apart; circle toward self and touch the
fingertips again. "Area" may be made with the "A"
hands.
Origin: Drawing a circle to indicate the limits of an area.
Usage: Have you traveled to many *places*? a small *area*
(use the "A" hands).

LIST

Hold the left palm in front of you, tips pointing up; strike
the little-finger edge of the right open hand several times
across the open left palm, slightly lower each time.
Origin: Showing a list from the top to the bottom of a
page.
Usage: a long *list* of groceries.

NAME

Place the middle finger of the right "H" across the index finger of the left "H."
Origin: Crossing the fingers to form an X represents the place where the name is to be signed.
Usage: Your *name* may have an interesting meaning.

NAMED, CALLED

Sign "NAME" and move the hands in this position slightly up-forward-down.
Usage: a man *named* Robertson.
They always *called* her Penny.

SIGNATURE

Hold the right "U" in front of you, palm in, turn it and place it face down on the left palm which is facing up.
Origin: Left hand represents the paper, right represents signature.
Usage: I need your *signature*.
Please *sign* your name.

SIGN, POSTER

Draw a square in front of you with both index fingers.
Usage: We followed the *signs*.
a large, colorful *poster*.

POSTING A NOTICE

Direct both "A" hands forward as if placing thumbtacks in a wall.
Usage: We wanted to inform everyone so we *posted a notice*.
We *put it up* on the bulletin board.

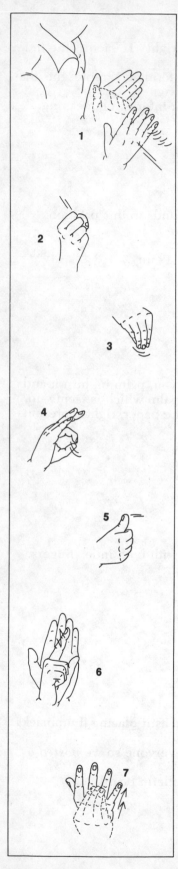

BELLS

Bells are signed by imitating the motion associated with them as described below:

1) CLAPPER STRIKING A BELL
Strike the left open hand with the inside of the right "A"; then opening the right to a "FIVE" position, shake it from the wrist while moving it away from the left.
Origin: Represents the striking and the vibration.
Usage: "I heard the *bells* on Christmas day . . . ."

2) A BELL RUNG BY PULLING A ROPE
Hold the rope of an imaginary church bell and pull down once or twice.
Usage: The war was over and they *rang the bells* everywhere.

3) HANDBELLS
Hold the bell with the tips of the "AND" and shake it.
Usage: The teacher had a *bell* on her desk.

4) DINNER BELL
Hold the bell with the thumb and index fingers, other fingers open.
Usage: The gift was a beautiful china *dinner bell*.

5) DOORBELL
Using the thumb of the "A" hand, push an imaginary doorbell.
Usage: I think our friends are here, I hear the *doorbell*.

6) ALARM CLOCK, FIRE ALARM
Strike the side of the right index finger against the left palm several times.
Usage: My *alarm* rang but I didn't get up. We heard the *fire alarm* and left the building.

7) LIGHT FLASHING
In the homes of many deaf people a flashing light is used as a doorbell and as an alarm clock. The sign is made by starting with the closed "AND" position, opening it and closing it again; repeat several times.

ELEVATOR

Move the right "E" up and down.
Origin: Indicates the movement of the elevator.
Usage: Take the *elevator* to the 13th floor.

FLAG

Place the right elbow in the left palm and wave the right hand.
Origin: The flag waving in the wind.
Usage: Salute the American *flag*.

JAIL, PRISON, BARS, CAGE

Place the back of the right "FOUR" hand crosswise against the palm of the left "FOUR."
Origin: Showing the prison bars.
Usage: 3 days in *jail*.
to *prison* for life.
The man is behind *bars*.
animals in a *cage*.

FIRE, BURN

Place the bent hands in front of the body, palms facing up; with the fingers wiggling, move first one hand upward, then the other.
Origin: Flames rising.
Usage: a five-alarm *fire*.
a cozy *fire*place.
Paper *burns* easily.

INSURANCE

Move the "I" hand back and forth in front of you, palm out.
Usage: My car *insurance* payment is due.

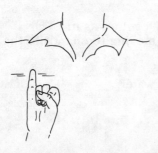

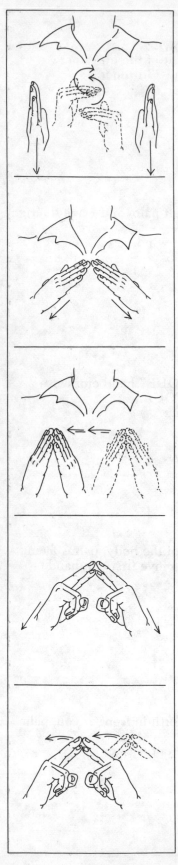

BUILDING

Place one hand on the other; reverse and repeat several times, raising the hands a little higher each time. Finish by outlining the top and sides of a building. (For the verb form use the first part of this sign only.)
Origin: Placing one brick upon another.
Usage: The Empire State *Building* is in New York City.

HOUSE

Place the tips of the open hands together and then trace the form of a roof.
Origin: A natural sign showing the roof of a house.
Usage: What makes a *house* a home?

CITY, TOWN, VILLAGE, COMMUNITY

Touch the tips of the open hands together as for "HOUSE," and repeat several times, moving to the right.
Origin: Showing a row of houses.
Usage: Our *city* has a new mayor.
We live in a small *town*.
People have lived in the old *village* for years.
Hillside is a small *community*.

TENT

Place the tips of the "V" hands together and draw them down and apart to indicate the shape of a tent.
Origin: The shape of the tent beginning at the center pole.
Usage: It was windy and our *tent* collapsed.

CAMP

Place the tips of the "V" hands together as in "TENT" and repeat several times while moving the hands to the right.
Origin: A row of tents.
Usage: Our *camp* was near the water.

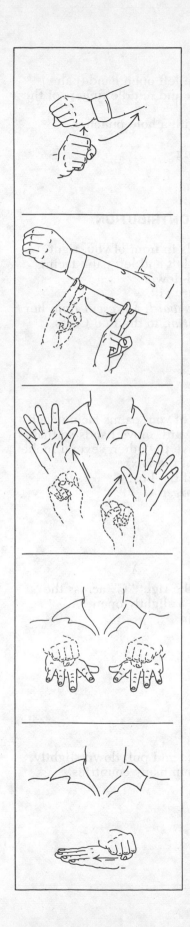

FOUNDATION

Place the right "S" under the left "S" and then under the left forearm.
Origin: Showing the support under a building.
Usage: first the *foundation*, then the house.

BRIDGE

Place the tips of the right "V" under the left wrist and again against the arm farther to the left.
Origin: Indicating the supports of a bridge.
Usage: The Golden Gate *Bridge* is in northern California.

FIREWORKS

Place "S" hands in front of you, palm sides forward. Move hands upward alternately, opening them into "FIVE" positions.
Origin: Picturing sudden bursts of fireworks.
Usage: Did you see the fantastic *fireworks* on the Fourth of July?

MAGIC

Place the "S" hands in front of you, palms down; move them forward and open them to "FIVE" positions, fingers pointing forward; repeat several times.
Usage: We always enjoy a *magic* show.

STAGE

Move the right "S" rightward across the top of the left open hand, which is in a palm-down position.
Origin: Indicating the surface of the stage.
Usage: star of *stage* and screen.

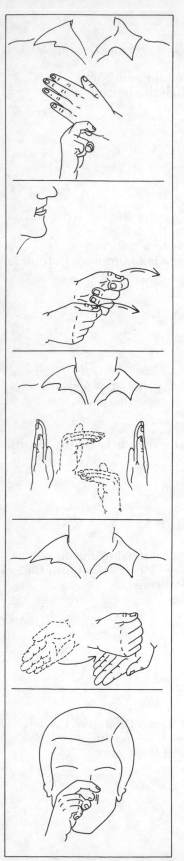

TICKET

Squeeze the lower edge of the left open hand (palm facing self) between the index and middle fingers of the right bent "V" hand.
Origin: Punching the ticket with a hole puncher.
Usage: *tickets* for the play.
got a *ticket* for speeding.

GIFT, REWARD, PRESENT, CONTRIBUTION

Place both modified "A" hands in front of you, right behind left (right palm facing left and left palm facing right); move hands up-forward-down.
Origin: Presenting an imaginary gift.
Usage: a birthday *gift;* a $10 *reward;* a *present* from her
co-workers; a *contribution* to the Red Cross.

BOX

Place the open hands in front of you, palms facing each other and fingers pointing upward; move hands so that both are palms down, one above the other, several inches apart (depending on the size of the box).
Origin: Indicating the shape of the box.
Usage: Pack books in small *boxes.*

COLLECTION

Draw the little-finger side of the right "C" across the palm toward you, and close to a slightly open "A."
Origin: Gathering something in.
Usage: a stamp *collection.*

DOLL

Place the right "X" on the nose and pull down slightly.
Usage: A collection of *dolls* from many countries.

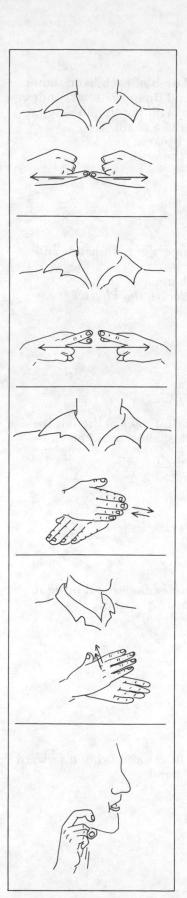

STRING, THREAD, LINE

Place the tips of the "I" fingers together and draw them apart.
Origin: As if string is pulled from a spool.
Usage: *string* for a kite.
use blue *thread*.
My fishing *line* is tangled.

ROPE

Place the fingertips of the "R" hands together and draw them apart.
Origin: Indicates the length and twisting of a rope.
Usage: a strong *rope* for the tug-of-war.

WOOD

Place the little-finger side of the right open hand on the back of the left open hand and make a sawing motion.
Origin: As if sawing wood.
Usage: *wooden* shelves.

PAPER

The left open hand faces up; the heel of the right palm brushes leftward across the heel of the left palm twice.
Usage: *Paper* is becoming expensive.

RUBBER

Stroke the side of the right "X" down along the side of the chin.
Origin: Indicating the gum.
Usage: Much of our *rubber* comes from South America.

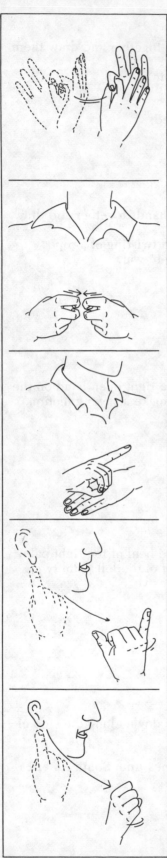

CHAIN

Link together the index and thumb of each hand (other fingers extended); repeat several times, first with index side of the right hand up, then with the thumb side up.
Origin: Fingers joined as links of a chain.
Usage: The *chain* couldn't be broken.
    Chain your bicycle to the post.

ELECTRICITY, PHYSICS

Bend the index and middle fingers of both hands and strike the joints together.
Origin: Indicating electrical charge.
Usage: Lightning cut off our *electricity*. *Physics* is a science.

DIAMOND

Place the right "D" on the fourth finger of the left hand.
Usage: *Diamonds* are the hardest substance known to man.

GOLD

Touch the right ear with the index finger and bring it forward with a quick twist into a "Y" hand.
Origin: Worn on the ear and yellow.
Usage: the *gold* rush of 1849.

SILVER

Touch the ear with the index finger and bring it forward with a quick twist into an "S" hand.
Origin: Worn on the ear.
Usage: *Silver* dollars are rare.

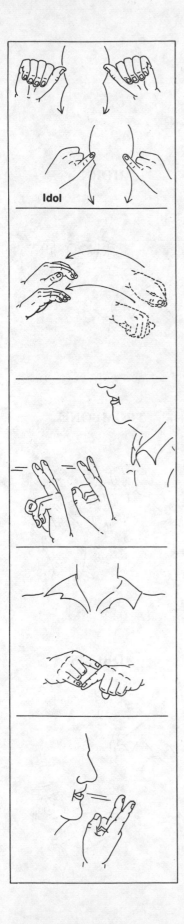

Idol

IMAGE, FORM, STATUE, IDOL

Trace an imaginary form in front of you with the "A" hands. The "I" hands are often used for "IDOL."
Usage: The ancient Greeks made *images* of their gods.
　　　Some were in the *form* of animals.
　　　the famous *Statue* of Liberty.
　　　idols of wood and stone.

BURY, GRAVE

Place both "A" hands in front of you, palms facing down; draw hands back toward the body into a curved-hand position, palms still down.
Origin: Showing the mound of earth.
Usage: In New Orleans the dead are *buried* above the ground.
　　　Kennedy's *grave* is visited by thousands of people.

FUNERAL

Place the right "V" behind the left "V," with both palms facing forward, and move them forward, tips pointing up.
Origin: A procession moving forward slowly.
Usage: His *funeral* service will be tomorrow.

CIGARETTE

Place the index and little finger of the right hand against the left index.
Origin: Showing the size of the cigarette.
Usage: Do you have any *cigarettes*?

SMOKING

Place the right "V" at the lips.
Origin: The natural motion of smoking a cigarette.
Usage: *Smoking* in bed often causes fires.

MUSICAL INSTRUMENTS

Musical instruments are signed by imitating the
movement associated with them. Pictured here are a few
examples:

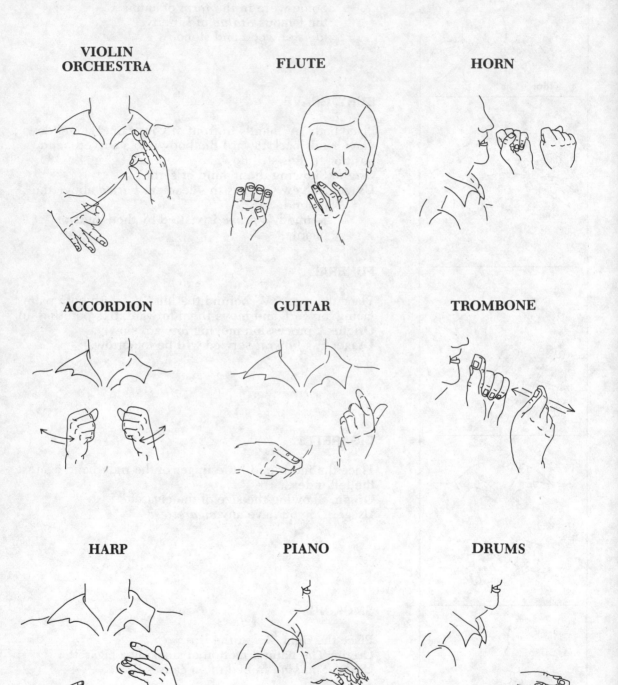

VIOLIN
ORCHESTRA   FLUTE   HORN

ACCORDION   GUITAR   TROMBONE

HARP   PIANO   DRUMS

17

Nature

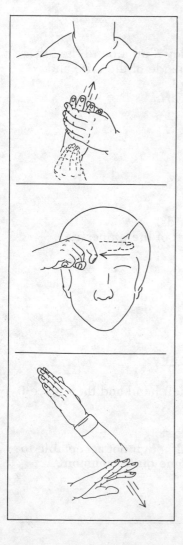

SPRING, GROW

The right "AND" hand opens as it comes up through the left "C," which is held in front of you with the palm facing right.
Origin: Right hand indicates that which is coming up out of the ground.
Usage: *Spring* begins in March.
      Flowers are *growing* everywhere.

SUMMER

The right index finger is crooked and wiped across the forehead.
Origin: Wiping the perspiration from the forehead.
Usage: a long, hot *summer*.

FALL, AUTUMN

The left open hand points upward toward the right. The right open hand brushes downward along the left forearm with the edge of the right index.
Origin: Leaves falling off a tree.
Usage: back to school in the *fall*.
      Autumn leaves are colorful.

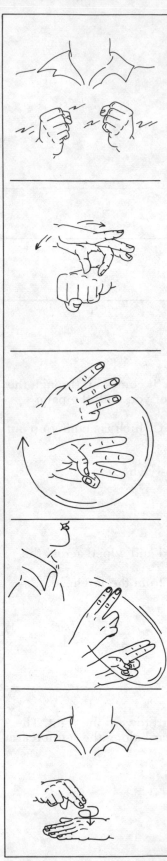

WINTER, COLD, CHILLY

Shake both "S" hands, palms facing each other.
Origin: Shivering from the cold.
Usage: in the middle of *winter;* sleeping in a *cold* room;
      feel *chilly* without a coat.

EARTH, TERRESTRIAL

Place the thumb and middle finger of the right hand on
the back of the left hand near the wrist and rock the right
back and forth.
Origin: The earth rotating on its axis.
Usage: The *earth* is 8,000 miles in diameter.
      on this *terrestrial* ball.

WORLD

Circle the right "W" forward-down-up around the left
"W" and place it on the thumb side of the left hand.
Origin: The world going around.
Usage: He sailed around the *world.*

UNIVERSE

Sign "WORLD" using "U" hands.
Usage: The earth is a small part of the *universe.*

NATURE, NATURAL, NATURALLY

Circle the right "N" over the left hand and then place it
on the back of the left hand.
Usage: the laws of *nature.*
      natural beauty.
      Naturally that's true (although not acceptable to
      all, this usage has become quite common).

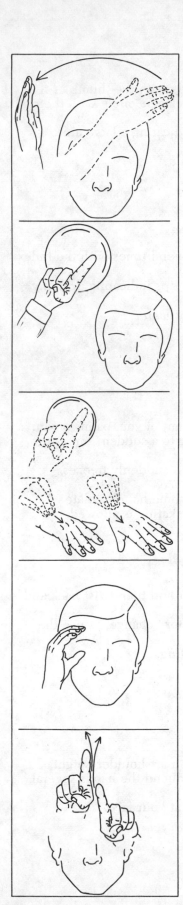

SKY, HEAVENS

Make a sweeping motion with the open hand from left to right, above eye level.
Origin: Indicating the vast expanse of the skies.
Usage: a starry *sky;* the blue *heavens.*

SUN

Draw a clockwise circle in the air.
Origin: Indicates the sun by a round circle overhead.
Usage: The *sun* is bright.

SUNSHINE

Sign "SUN"; then place both "AND" hands high, right behind the left, and open the fingers as the hands are moved forward, palms facing down and fingers pointing forward.
Origin: The rays of the sun
Usage: The warm *sunshine* felt good.

MOON

Place the "C" hand over the right eye, palm facing left.
Origin: The "C" represents the crescent.
Usage: by the light of the *moon.*

STAR

Using both index positions, palms facing forward and fingers pointing up, move the right index up along the side of the left index, alternating hands, and repeat several times.
Origin: Index fingers striking each other like a flint to represent both the light and the twinkling.
Usage: 50 *stars* in our flag.

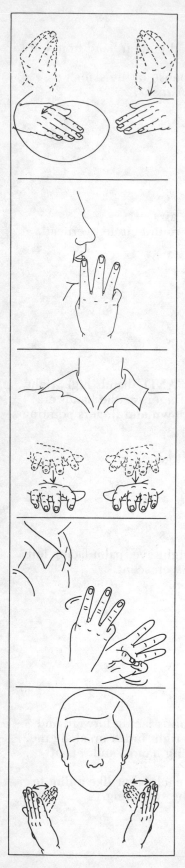

LAND, FIELD

Rub the fingertips of both hands with the thumb as if feeling soil; make a counterclockwise circle with the right open hand, palm down.
Origin: Feeling the soil and indicating a large area.
Usage: This is good farm *land*.
　　　walking through the *field*.

WATER

Strike the side of the mouth several times with the index finger of the "W" hand.
Origin: The initial letter at the lips indicating drinking water.
Usage: Man cannot live without *water*.

ICE, FREEZE

Place both "FIVE" hands in front of you, palms down, and drop them slightly, coming to a sudden stop as the fingers bend.
Origin: The water coming down suddenly freezes.
Usage: The rain is changing to *ice*.
　　　I'm *freezing* and want some hot chocolate.
　　　The lake is *frozen* and skating is allowed.

WEATHER

The "W" hands face each other and then twist back and forth.
Origin: Adapted from the sign for "change," since the weather is subject to change.
Usage: good *weather* for bicycling.

PLEASANT, COOL

Place open hands in front of you at shoulder height, palms toward you; bend and unbend the hands several times.
Origin: The breeze is blowing at your face.
Usage: a *pleasant* day.
　　　cool and comfortable.

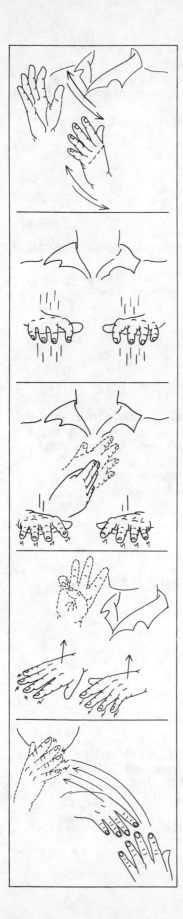

BREEZE

Place the open hands in front of you, tips pointing
forward with palms in; wave them gently back and forth.
Origin: Indicating a moving breeze.
Usage: Without an occasional *breeze* we couldn't bear the
heat.

RAIN

Sign "WATER"; then let both curved "FIVE" hands
(palms down) drop down several times in short, quick
motions. (The sign for "water" is sometimes omitted.)
Usage: Everything was dry and we needed *rain*.

SNOW

Sign "WHITE"; then lower both "FIVE" hands with
palms down and fingers gently wiggling.
Origin: White flakes gently falling.
Usage: Everyone wanted *snow* for Christmas.

FLOOD

Sign "WATER"; then place both "FIVE" hands in front
of you, palms down and fingers pointing forward; wiggle
the fingers as hands are raised.
Origin: The water level is rising.
Usage: The *flood* caused much damage.

RAINBOW

Sign "COLOR" (by placing the tips of the wiggling
"FIVE" hand at the mouth and moving it away); then
make a large arc from left to right with the right "FOUR"
hand.
Origin: Indicating the arch of colors in the sky.
Usage: A *rainbow* has seven beautiful colors.

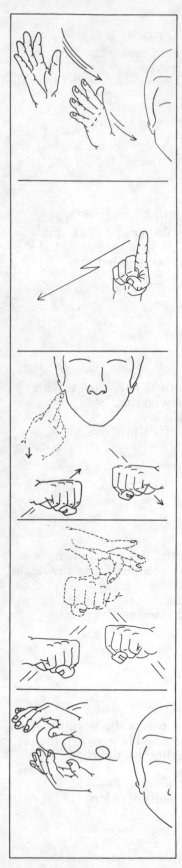

WIND

Hold the hands high, palms toward each other, the left slightly lower than the right; move them towards the left in several short sweeping motions.
Origin: Sweeping movement of the wind.
Usage: a cold northeast *wind*.

LIGHTNING

Use the index finger pointing up and make a quick zigzag motion in the air.
Origin: The quick flash of lightning in the skies.
Usage: The *lightning* struck a house.

THUNDER

Point to the ear, then place the "S" hands in front of you, palms down, bringing the right hand toward you and the left hand toward the side; reverse and repeat several times.
Origin: Movement of the fists represents vibrations.
Usage: That sounded like *thunder!*

EARTHQUAKE

Sign "EARTH" and finish with the "S" hands as in "THUNDER."
Origin: A natural combination of signs.
Usage: *Earthquakes* are frightening.

CLOUD, STORM

Place the slightly curved "FIVE" hand, palm down, above the left upturned slightly curved "FIVE" hand; swirl the hands around toward the left.
Origin: Indicating billows of clouds.
Usage: not a *cloud* in the sky.
Note: The sign for "storm" is made in a large swirling motion.

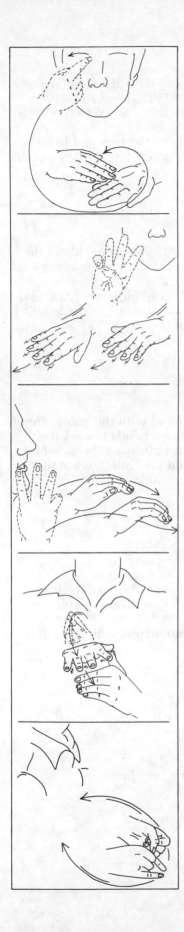

SHADOW

Sign "BLACK"; then make a counterclockwise circle with the right open hand, palm down, over the upturned left hand.
Origin: Indicating something black overshadowing an object.
Usage: We sat in the *shadow* of a large tree.

RIVER

Sign "WATER"; then place the left hand behind the right, palms down, and wiggle the fingers as the hands are moved toward the right.
Origin: Water that flows.
Usage: The Amazon is the largest *river* in the world.

OCEAN, SEA

Sign "WATER"; then place the left hand behind the right, palms down, and move the hands up and down to indicate the waves of the ocean.
Origin: Water and waves.
Usage: The ship crossed the *ocean* in 3½ days.
across the *sea*.

FOUNTAIN, SPRING

Push up the right "AND" hand (with palm facing left and fingers pointing up) through the left "C," opening it and wiggling the fingers as it is moved up, over, and down.
Origin: Water rising from its source and flowing over.
Usage: Watch the *fountain* change colors.
a health spa with mineral *springs*.

ISLAND

Touch the tips of the "I" hands and move them away from each other, then toward you.
Origin: The "I" hands draw a circle to indicate the limits of an area.
Usage: No treasure was found on the *island*.

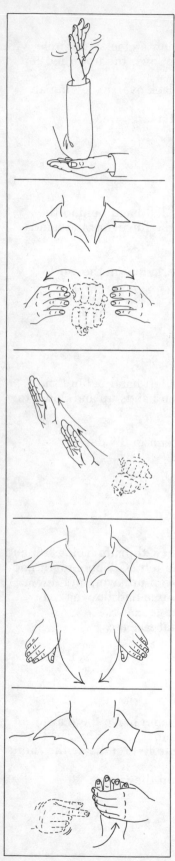

TREE, FOREST, WOODS

Hold the right arm up in front of you with the elbow in the left palm; shake the right "FIVE" hand in and out rapidly several times. For "FOREST" or "WOODS" the right "F" or "W" is sometimes used.
Origin: The arm and hand indicate the tree and branches.
Usage: a poem lovely as a *tree*; green *forest*; dark *woods*.

ROCK, STONE

Strike the back of the left "S" with the palm side of the right "A"; place the "C" hands in front of you facing each other, forming the shape of a rock.
Origin: Fist represents rock; striking indicates hardness.
Usage: a large *rock*; several small *stones* (for the latter, use only the first part of the sign).

MOUNTAIN, HILL

Strike the back of the left "S" hand with the palm side of the right "A"; then raise both open hands toward the side, one behind the other, as if indicating the side of a mountain. The same sign is used for "hill" except that the hands are not raised quite as high.
Usage: Climb every *mountain*.

VALLEY

Place both open hands high on each side, palms down, and bring them down and together with index sides touching.
Origin: Indicates sides of the mountains with the valley in the center.
Usage: a green *valley*.

GRASS

Sign "GREEN" and "GROW."
Usage: sitting on the *grass* eating our lunch.

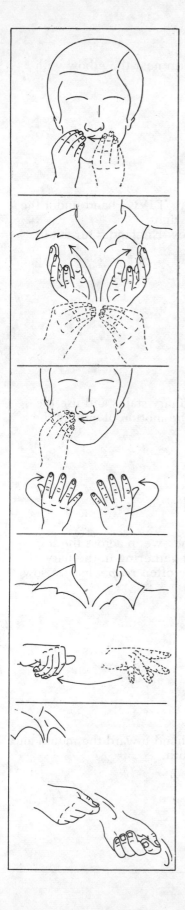

FLOWER

Place the tips of the "AND" hand first under one nostril, then under the other.
Origin: Smelling the flowers.
Usage: a variety of *flowers*.

BLOOM, BLOSSOM

Place the tips of the "AND" hands together; then open them upward slowly, fingers slightly separated.
Origin: Indicates the flower slowly opening.
Usage: flowers in *bloom*; The cherry trees *blossomed* overnight.

GARDEN

Place the "FOUR" hands in front of you, palms in; move them away from each other toward the sides and then toward you. Add the sign for "FLOWERS" if this is appropriate.
Origin: Indicating the fence and the flowers.
Usage: Come and see my flower *garden*.

PLANT, SOW

With the fingers pointing down, pass the thumb across the inside of the fingertips from the little finger to the forefinger and move the hand across from left to right as if planting seeds.
Origin: Planting seeds in a row.
Usage: *plant* corn; *sow* wheat.

HOEING, GARDENING

Using both "A" hands as if holding a hoe, go through the motion of hoeing.
Origin: Indicating the natural movement of hoeing.
Usage: They finished *hoeing* and then hoped for rain. *Gardening* can be hard work.

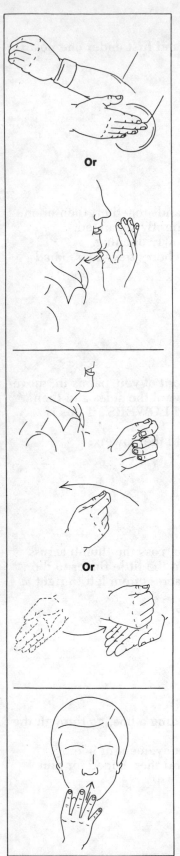

FARM, COUNTRY (Rural)

Rub the underside of the left arm near the elbow with the right open hand.

Or

Or, place the thumb of the right "FIVE" hand under the chin and move the hand to the right.
Usage: many small *farms* in New England; Our family lived in the *country*.

HARVEST, REAP

Use the left hand to hold imaginary stalks and use the right modified "A" to imitate the motion of cutting the stalks.

Or, use the right open hand and sweep across the left palm into an "A" position as if gathering in the harvest.
Usage: time for *harvesting*; We often *reap* what we sow.

Or

HAY

Point the tips of the "FOUR" hand toward the mouth and move the hand toward the mouth.
Usage: *hay* for the animals.

18

Body, Medicine, and Health

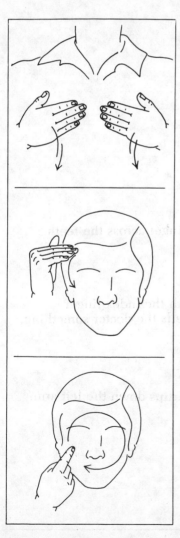

BODY, PHYSICAL

Place the flat hands on the chest; repeat slightly lower.
Origin: Indicating the body area.
Usage: Keep your *body* in good condition.
a *physical* examination.

HEAD

Place the fingertips of the bent hand at the side of the head near the temple and then slightly lower.
Origin: Indicating the temple area.
Usage: My *head* feels hot.

FACE, LOOK

Using the index finger, trace a circle in front of the face.
Origin: Indicating the whole face.
Usage: a pretty *face;* You *look* good today.

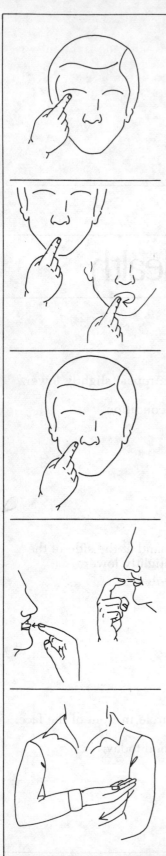

EYE

Point to the eye (or to both for the plural).
Usage: sparkling blue *eyes*.

MOUTH

Point to the mouth.
Usage: The dentist looked into my *mouth*.

LIPS

Trace the lips with the index finger.
Usage: Your *lips* are easy to read.

NOSE

Point to the nose.
Usage: My nose is *cold*.

TEETH

Run the tip of the bent index finger across the teeth.
Usage: strong white *teeth*.

TONGUE

Touch the tip of the tongue with the index finger.
Usage: A look at your *tongue* tells the doctor something.

ARM

Pass the back of the right fingertips down the left arm.
Usage: a baby in my *arms*.

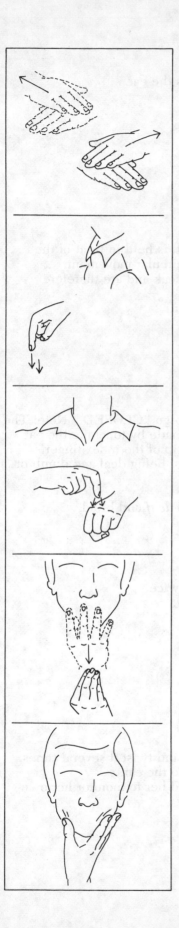

HANDS

Stroke the back of the left hand with the right and reverse.
Origin: Indicating the hands up to the wrist.
Usage: You have good *hands* for signing.

FEET

Point down twice.
Origin: Indicating both feet.
Usage: My *feet* hurt.

BONES

Tap the knuckles of the left hand with the curved index finger.
Origin: Indicating the bones of the hand.
Usage: a large-*boned* person.

BEARD (Long)

Place the open "AND" hand under the chin and draw it down to a closed position, back of the hand down.
Origin: Indicating the length of the beard.
Usage: Uncle Sam has a long *beard*.

BEARD

Place the tips of the right curved hand at the right cheek and draw down the side of the cheek.
Origin: Shows the heavy growth on the cheek and chin.
Usage: a red *beard*.

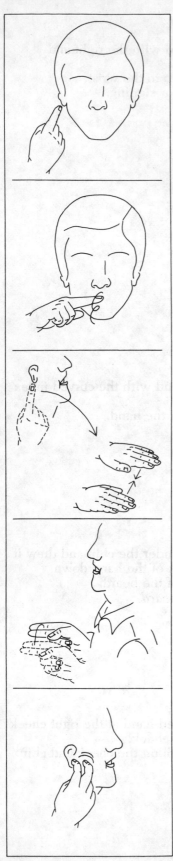

EAR, HEAR, SOUND

The right index finger touches the ear.
Usage: My *ear* aches.
I *hear* you.
Two words *sound* alike.

HEARING (A hearing person)

The index finger, pointing left, is held in front of the mouth and rolls forward in a circular movement.
Origin: Hearing people can speak and are therefore called speaking people.
Usage: Are you *hearing* or deaf?

DEAF

Touch the right ear and then sign "CLOSED." Note: The sign for "deaf" was formerly made by touching the ear and then the mouth with the tip of the index finger, representing the old concept of being deaf and dumb or deaf-mute.
Origin: Ears are closed.
Usage: Helen Keller was both *deaf* and blind.

HARD-OF-HEARING

Make an "H" in front of you twice.
Usage: Ann is *hard-of-hearing*.

HEARING AID

Place the bent "V" at the ear and twist it several times.
Origin: Place the ear mold into the ear.
Usage: The *hearing aid* helped her to monitor her own voice.

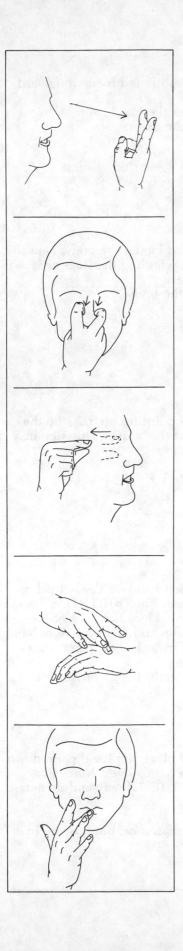

SEE, SIGHT, VISION

Place the "V" in front of the face, fingertips near the eyes, and move the hand forward.
Origin: Fingertips pointing to the eyes looking out.
Usage: Oh, say can you *see?*
  Sight is most important to deaf people.
  We *saw* the football game on television.
  He has poor *vision* (or eyesight) and
  needs glasses.

BLIND

Place the bent "V" in front of the eyes, palm in, and draw it down slightly.
Origin: Eyes pulled shut.
Usage: *Blind* people read Braille.

GLASSES

Draw the index finger and thumb together and back to show the frame of the glasses.
Origin: Represents the frame from lens to ear.
Usage: need new *glasses* soon.

TOUCH

Touch the back of the left hand with the right middle finger, other fingers extended.
Origin: The natural motion of touching.
Usage: Billy *touched* the hot stove and was burned.
  Keep in *touch* with me.

TASTE

Place the middle fingertip on the tip of the tongue, other fingers extended.
Origin: The finger placing something on the tongue to be tasted.
Usage: That homemade soup surely *tastes* good.

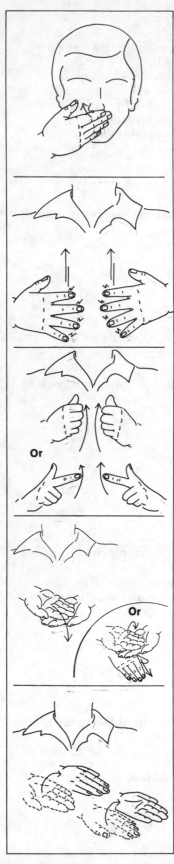

SMELL, FRAGRANCE

Place the palm in front of the nose and move it upward slightly several times.
Origin: Smelling something on the hand.
Usage: the *smell* of bread in the oven.
the *fragrance* of roses.

LIFE

Place the "FIVE" hands, palms facing the body, near the waist and draw the hands up, wiggling the fingers slightly. Or, use the "L" hands.
Origin: Life surging through the body.
Usage: full of *life*.
Life is short.

LIVE, ADDRESS

Both "A" hands, with thumbs pointing up, pass up the sides of the chest beginning at the waist. (This sign may also be made with "L" hands.)
Usage: Where do you *live*?
What is your new *address*?

BORN, BIRTH, BIRTHDAY

Place the back of the right open hand on the left palm; bring the hands up and forward. For "BIRTHDAY" add the "DAY" sign. Alternate sign: Place the back of the right open hand on the left palm and slide the right hand toward the body, down, and forward; right palm is now facing down.
Usage: *born* in 1958; date of *birth;* happy *birthday* to you.

DIE, DEATH, PERISH

Place right hand palm up and place left hand palm down in front of the right; turn both hands over. Note: For "DYING" make the sign for "DIE" slowly and do not turn the hands completely over.
Origin: To turn over and die.
Usage: "It matters not how a man *dies,* but how he lives" (Samuel Johnson).
Many people *perished.*
dying of starvation.

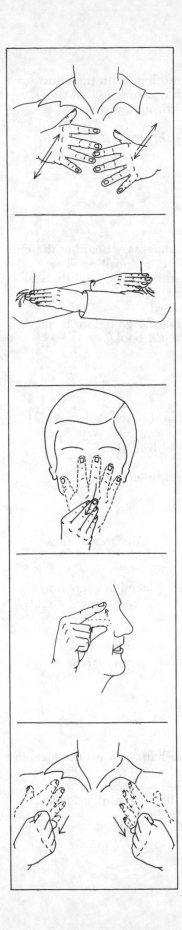

BREATHE

Place both palms on the chest, palms in, and move them in and out to indicate breathing.
Origin: Movement of the chest in breathing.
Usage: *"Breathes* there a man with soul so dead, who never to himself has said, 'This is my own my native land'"* (Sir Walter Scott).
She ran until she was out of *breath.*

REST

Fold the arms in front of the chest, one on top of the other.
Origin: Hands in a position of rest.
Usage: feel tired and need *rest.*

SLEEP

Draw the open fingers down over the face into an "AND" position near the chin, bowing the head slightly. (Repeat this twice for "sleepy.")
Origin: Hand draws down to represent eyes closing.
Usage: hard to get 8 hours of *sleep.*
Baby looks *sleepy.*

AWAKEN, WAKE UP

Place both "Q" hands at the sides of the eyes, forefinger and thumb touching; then separate the thumb and index.
Origin: Eyes opening.
Usage: We couldn't seem to *awaken* her.
Wake up, it's time to go to work.

HEALTHY, WELL, HEAL, WHOLE

The "FIVE" hands are placed on the chest near the shoulders and brought forward into "S" positions.
Origin: The body is strong.
Usage: *healthy* body.
in sickness and in *health.*
He looks and feels *well.*
The broken bone *healed* quickly.
Archaic use: He was *whole* (well) again.

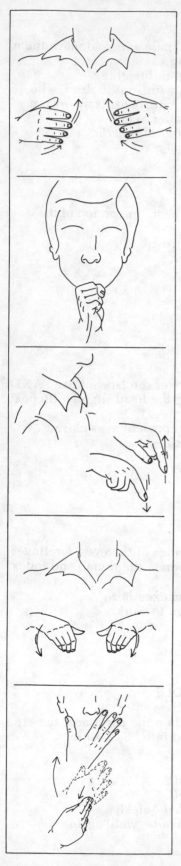

YOUNG, YOUTHFUL

Place the fingertips of both open hands on the chest, several inches apart, and brush upward several times.
Origin: Blood flowing quickly through the body.
Usage: Feel *young* again.
　　　That teacher seems *youthful*.

OLD, AGE

The right "C" hand grasps an imaginary beard at the chin and moves slightly down into an "S" position. To indicate great age, the "S" hand is moved slightly back and forth as it moves downward.
Origin: Age is signified by a beard.
Usage: How *old* is that gentleman? *Age* before beauty!
　　　We have a collection of *old* books.

CRIPPLED, LAME

Point both index fingers down and move them up and down alternately.
Origin: Represents two legs hobbling along.
Usage: a *lame* boy.
　　　The accident left him *crippled*.

TIRED, WEARY, EXHAUSTED

Fingertips of the bent hands are placed at each side of the body just above the waist and then dropped slightly.
Origin: The body is bent forward.
Usage: *tired* after working all day.
　　　My brain is *weary* after studying so much.
　　　The man seemed completely *exhausted*.

PALE

Sign "WHITE"; then direct the hand toward the face and open it.
Origin: Having a white face.
Usage: After a long illness she looked thin and *pale*.

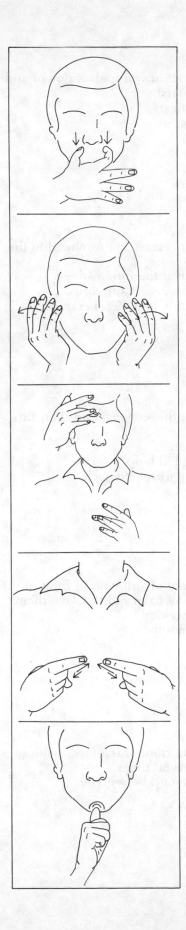

THIN, LEAN, GAUNT

Touch the right cheek with the right thumb and the left cheek with the right index finger; draw the hand in this position down the cheek.
Origin: Showing the hollow cheeks.
Usage: a *thin* face.
       a *lean* and strong young man.
       gaunt and starved.

FAT, OBESE, CHUBBY, PLUMP

The curved "FIVE" hands face the cheeks and are then drawn slightly away from the face to indicate puffy cheeks.
Origin: The face is fleshy.
Usage: a *fat* cat; a strong woman but not *obese*; a *chubby* baby; cheeks rosy and *plump*.

SICK, ILL, DISEASE

Touch the forehead with the middle finger of the right hand and the stomach with the middle finger of the left hand.
Origin: Both head and stomach are not well.
Usage: became *sick* after eating; *ill* and in the hospital; childhood *disease*; *sick* of studying (in this idiomatic usage both hands are given a twist).

PAIN, ACHE, HURT

The index fingers are jabbed toward each other several times.
Note: This sign is generally made in front of the body but may be placed at the location of the pain, as: headache, toothache, heartache, etc.
Usage: suffered *pain* after the accident; *aching* all over; my knee *hurts*; have an *earache*.

SORENESS

Place the tip of the thumb of the "A" hand at the chin and twist it back and forth.
Usage: After exercising I felt *sore* all over.

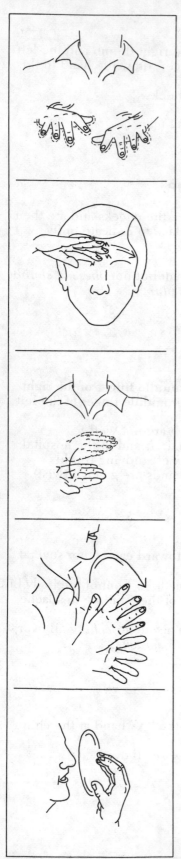

NERVOUS

Place the "FIVE" hands in front of you (palms down) and shake them slightly from the wrist.
Origin: Shaking with nervousness.
Usage: The new driver is *nervous*.

SWEAT, PERSPIRE

Pass the open, wiggling fingers across the forehead to the left (palm down).
Origin: Indicating perspiration at the forehead.
Usage: "Blood, *sweat*, and tears . . ." (Churchill).
"Genius is 1% inspiration and 99% *perspiration*" (Thomas A. Edison).

UPSET

Place the palm of the hand on the stomach and then flip it forward, palm up.
Origin: The stomach turns over.
Usage: She felt *upset* and needed help.
After eating she had an *upset* stomach.

VOMIT

Place the "FIVE" hands in front of you, one in front of the other (one palm left and one palm right); move them away from the mouth and downward.
Origin: Proceeding from the mouth.
Usage: a reason for *vomiting*.

DIZZY

Place the bent "FIVE" hand in front of the face, palm facing in, and circle slowly several times.
Origin: Everything is going around before you.
Usage: felt weak and *dizzy*.

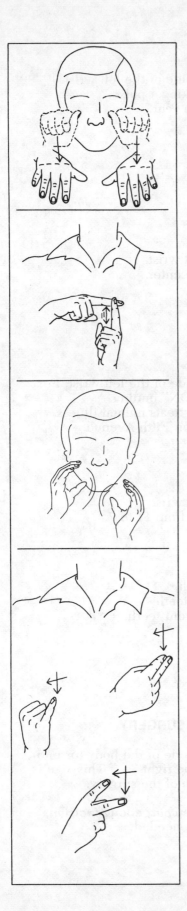

FAINT

Place the "A" hands in front of the face and drop them to "FIVE" positions.
Usage: became ill and *fainted*.

TEMPERATURE, THERMOMETER

Hold up the left index, palm facing right. Move the right index (palm down) up and down between the first and second joints of the left index finger.
Origin: Indicating the degrees on the thermometer.
Usage: What is the *temperature* today? The *thermometer* shows you have a fever.

EXAMINATION (Physical), CHECK-UP

Place both "C" hands in front of the face and move them alternately toward the center in circular motions. Or, use the sign for "INVESTIGATE" (right index in left palm).
Usage: an annual physical *examination*.
My doctor advises a yearly *check-up*.

HOSPITAL

Make a small cross on the left upper arm with the right index and middle fingers.
Origin: A cross on the sleeve.
Usage: a large 300-bed *hospital*.

INFIRMARY

Make the sign for "hospital" using an "I."
Usage: Our school *infirmary* was moved to a new building.

PATIENT

Make the sign for "hospital" using a "P."
Usage: The deaf *patient* needed an interpreter.

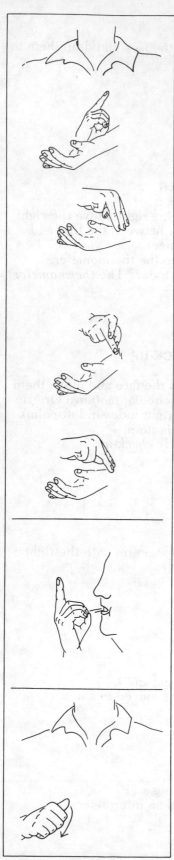

DOCTOR, PHYSICIAN

Place the right "D" on the inside of the left wrist.
Origin: The medical doctor taking a pulse.
Usage: See your *doctor* once a year.

MEDICAL

Place the right "M" on the left wrist.
Usage: a well-known *medical* center.

PSYCHIATRY

Place the right "P" on the inside of the left wrist. For "psychiatrist" add the "PERSON" ending.
Usage: *Psychiatry* studies and treats mental illness.
His *psychiatrist* lives on Fifth Avenue.

NURSE

Place the right "N" on the left wrist.
Usage: The night *nurse* works from 11 to 7.

DENTIST

Place the right "D" at the teeth.
Origin: The initial sign at the teeth.
Usage: Let the *dentist* check your teeth.

OPERATION, CUT, INCISION, SURGERY

Make a short stroke along the side of the body (or into the left palm) with the tip of the right "A." This sign is sometimes made at the location of the surgery.
Origin: Showing the incision.
Usage: a short *operation;* a deep *cut;* a long *incision;*
Immediate *surgery* was needed.

MEDICINE

Rub the tip of the right middle finger in the left palm.
Origin: Mixing the medicine in the palm.
Usage: Take the *medicine* at mealtime.

POISON

Rub the tip of the right middle finger of the "P" in the left palm.
Usage: What is the antidote for that kind of *poison?*

INJECTION, SHOT

With the right hand in the "L" position, place the tip of the index finger against the left upper arm and crook the right thumb.
Origin: The action of injecting the needle.
Usage: *injection* for allergy; a typhoid *shot;* The doctor gave him a *hypodermic.*

PILLS, TAKING A PILL

Place the thumb against the index finger and open them as you move the hand quickly toward the mouth.
Origin: As if popping a pill into the mouth.
Usage: Time for your *pills.*
   Have you *taken your pills?*

BLOOD, BLEED, HEMORRHAGE

Touch the lips with the right index finger; then let the wiggling fingertips move downward across the back of the left hand (or across the palm).
Origin: Red and flowing.
Usage: lost a lot of *blood;* the *bleeding* stopped; *hemorrhaging* from the nose.

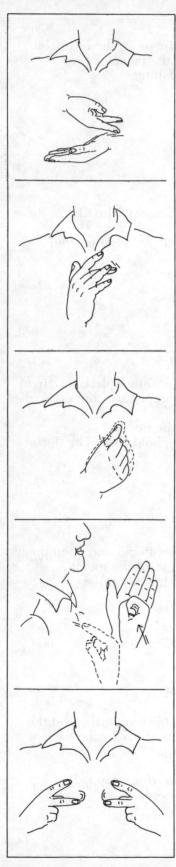

VEIN

Place the middle fingertip of the right "V" (palm up) on the inside of the left wrist.
Origin: Indicating the vein of the wrist.
Usage: suffering with enlarged *veins*.

HEART

Touch the area of the heart with the right middle finger.
Usage: She is physically weak but her *heart* is strong.

HEARTBEAT

Strike the inside of the right "A" against the chest several times.
Origin: Indicating the beating heart.
Usage: The doctor listens to your *heartbeat*.

HEART ATTACK

Point to the heart with the middle finger; strike the left open palm with the right fist.
Origin: Indicates the heart and then the action of an attack.
Usage: How can you prevent having a *heart attack?*

PNEUMONIA

Place the middle fingertips of the "P" hands against the chest and rock the hands back and forth with the tips still resting on the chest.
Origin: Initial finger and breathing motion of the lungs.
Usage: *Pneumonia* can be serious.

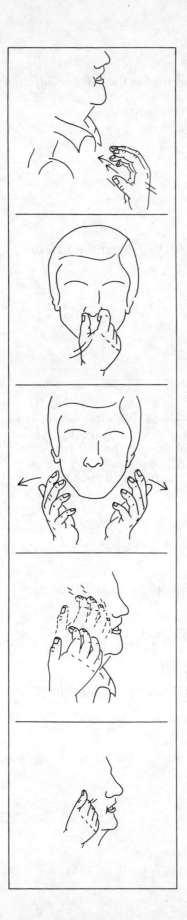

COUGH

Strike the tips of the curved "FIVE" against the upper chest several times.
Origin: Action of coughing.
Usage: How long have you had that *cough?*

A COLD

Place the bent index finger and thumb at the nose and draw down.
Origin: Using the handkerchief.
Usage: A bad *cold* kept me home several days.
Note: This sign is also used for "handkerchief."

MUMPS

Place the curved "FIVE" hands at the sides of the neck and move them away slightly.
Origin: Indicating the swollen glands just below the ear.
Usage: a severe case of *mumps.*

MEASLES

Place the tips of the curved "FIVE" hand against the face at several places.
Origin: Representing the spots on the skin.
Usage: *Measles* can cause deafness.

MENSTRUATION, PERIOD

Place the right "A" hand against the cheek and strike the cheek twice.
Usage: *Menstruation* started at the age of 12.
Are your *periods* regular?

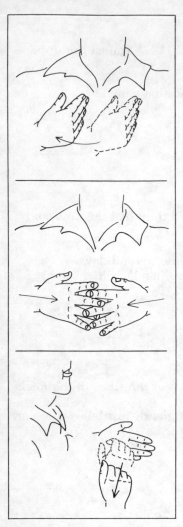

BREAST

Place the tips of the bent hand first at the left breast, then at the right.
Usage: A *breast* examination is important.

PREGNANT

Place the fingers of the right "FIVE" hand through the left "FIVE."
Usage: 3 months *pregnant*.

ABORTION

Use the sign for "REMOVE"—hold the left open hand in front of you, palm facing right; place the fingertips of the right curved hand (palm down) against the left palm and move it down, ending in an "A" position.
Usage: People are discussing the pros and cons of *abortion*.

NOTES

MENTALLY RETARDED—Spell "M" and "R" at the forehead.
HANDICAPPED—Spell "H" and "C."
CEREBRAL PALSY—Spell "C" and "P."
MULTIPLE SCLEROSIS—Spell "M" and "S."
CANCER—Fingerspell the word.
X RAY—Fingerspell the word.
CHICKEN POX—Sign "CHICKEN" and spell "POX" or add the sign for "MEASLES."

19
Home, Furniture, and Clothing

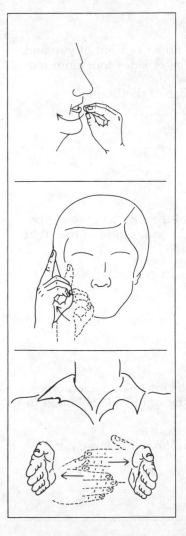

HOME

Place the tips of the "AND" hand against the mouth and then on the cheek. (Or, place the flat hand on the cheek.)
Origin: Home is the place where you eat and sleep.
Usage: "The land of the free and the *home* of the brave" (Francis Scott Key).

DORMITORY

Place the right "D" on the chin and then low on the cheek.
Origin: The sign for "home" made with a "D."
Usage: Living in a *dormitory* was a new experience.

ROOM

Place the open hands in front of you, palms toward you, left hand closest to the body; place open hands a distance apart, palms facing each other. May also be made with "R" hands.
Origin: Indicates the four sides of a room.
Usage: How many *rooms* do you have?
Note: "Office" is sometimes made as above using "O" hands.

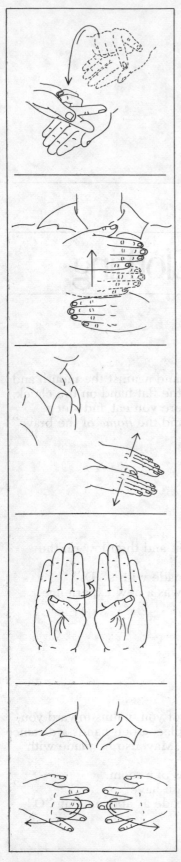

KITCHEN

Place the palm side of the right "K" into the left open palm; then turn over the "K" and place the back on the palm.
Origin: The sign for "cook" made with a "K."
Usage: Our *kitchen* is very small.

WINDOW

Place the left open hand in front of you, pointing right, and place the right hand on the edge of it, pointing left. Move the right hand up a few inches.
Origin: Indicates a window being opened.
Usage: The living room has four *windows*.

FLOOR

Place both open hands palms down in front of you and pointing forward with index-finger sides touching; move them apart.
Origin: Indicates the flat surface of the floor.
Usage: The new *floor* is shiny.

DOOR

Place the index-finger edges of the "B" hands together, palms facing forward; swing the index side of the right hand back and forth.
Origin: A door swinging open.
Usage: The *door* was painted red.

GATE

Point the tips of the "FIVE" hands toward each other, palms facing you, and swing the right "FIVE" hand in and out.
Origin: The swinging of the gates.
Usage: We entered the garden through a large *gate*.

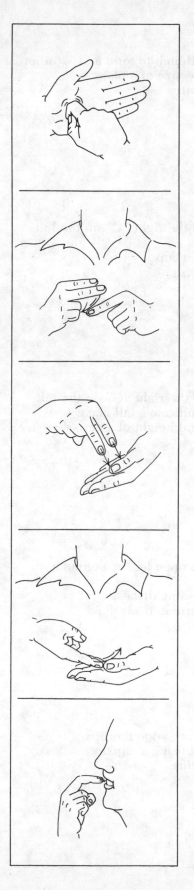

KEY

Place the knuckle of the crooked right index finger into the left palm and turn.
Origin: Turning the key in the lock.
Usage: Jim lost his car *key*.
What is the *key* to success?

KNIFE

Place the middle finger of the right "H" on the left index and slide it off the edge several times.
Usage: a sharp *knife*.

FORK

Place the tips of the right "V" against the left palm.
Origin: As if piercing food with the prongs of a fork.
Usage: The child couldn't use a *fork* yet.

SPOON

Place the tips of the right "H" against the left palm and lift; repeat several times.
Origin: As if placing a spoon in a dish and taking food.
Usage: We bought a special *spoon* for the baby.

PORCELAIN, CHINA, GLASS, DISHES

Strike the front teeth with the fingernail of the right curved index finger.
Origin: Hard as the teeth.
Usage: *porcelain* from Germany; English *china; glass* door; set of *dishes*.

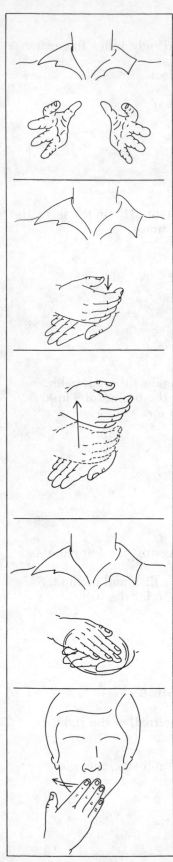

PLATE

Using the middle finger and thumb to form a "C" (other fingers extended), indicate the size of a plate.
Usage: We will need eight *plates*.

CUP

Place the little-finger edge of the right "C" on the left palm.
Origin: Indicate the shape of a cup.
Usage: a large collection of *cups*.

GLASS

Place the little-finger edge of the right "C" on the left palm; raise the right "C" to indicate a tall glass.
Origin: Indicates the shape and height of a glass.
Usage: a *glass* of water.

WASH DISHES

The open right hand rubs the open left in a circular motion.
Origin: Natural motion of washing dishes.
Usage: Have you finished *washing dishes?*

NAPKIN

Using the fingertips as a napkin, wipe the lips.
Origin: The natural motion of using a napkin.
Usage: special wedding *napkins*.

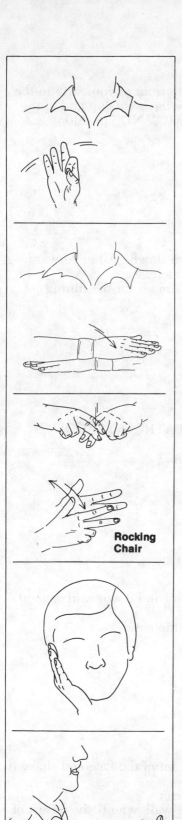

FURNITURE

Shake the "F" hand. (This sign may not be understood unless used in context.)
Usage: We moved all our *furniture* into the new house.

TABLE

Place the right forearm on the left forearm in front of you.
Origin: Indicates the top of the table.
Usage: The kitchen *table* is too small for us.

CHAIR

Sign "SIT" (the right curved index and middle fingers are placed crosswise on the left curved index and middle fingers, both palms facing down.)
Usage: a comfortable *chair*.
Note: For "rocking chair" make the above sign and rock it back and forth.

Rocking Chair

BED

Place the right open hand on the right cheek, bending the head slightly to the right.
Origin: Head on a pillow.
Usage: a king-size *bed*.

DRAWER

Hold the right "C" in front of you, palm up; draw it toward you.
Origin: Pulling out a drawer.
Usage: I use all three *drawers*.

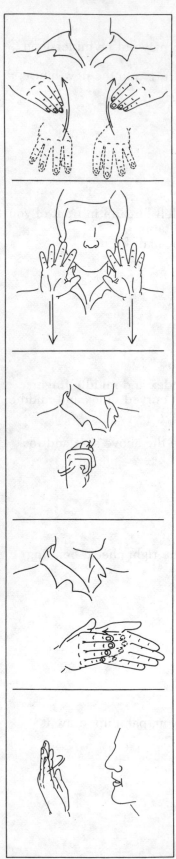

BLANKET

Place the open "AND" hands in front of you close to the body, tips pointing down; draw the hands up and to the neck, closing them as in the final "AND" position.
Usage: blue wool *blanket*.

DRAPES

Draw both "FIVE" hands down slowly, palms forward.
Origin: Indicating the drape panels.
Usage: We ordered lined gold *drapes* for the dining room.

TOILET, BATHROOM

Shake the right "T" (or sign "BATH" and "ROOM.")
Usage: The *toilet* needs repair.
    new rug in the *bathroom*.

SOAP

Draw the end of the right open hand downward several times in the palm of the left.
Origin: As if lathering soap in the hand.
Usage: a mild *soap*.

MIRROR

Hold the right open hand in front of the face and shake it slightly.
Origin: As if looking into a mirror.
Usage: "*Mirror, mirror*, on the wall, who is the fairest of them all?"

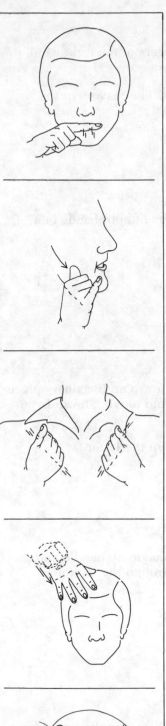

TOOTHBRUSH

Using the index finger as a brush, imitate the motion of brushing the teeth.
Usage: *brushing teeth* twice a day.

SHAVE

Draw the outside edge of the thumb of the right "Y" hand down the cheek as if shaving.
Origin: Using a razor.
Usage: *Shave* every morning.

BATH

Rub the "A" hands on the chest near the shoulder.
Origin: As if washing the body.
Usage: *Bathe* every day.
    Do you prefer a *bath* or a shower?

SHOWER

Snap open the "S" hand over the head several times, palm side down.
Origin: Coming down over the head.
Usage: A morning *shower* feels good.

SHAMPOO

Use the "A" hands and rub against the head (or use the slightly curved "FIVE" hands.
Origin: Natural motion of shampooing hair.
Usage: I'm going for a *shampoo* and cut.

SCISSOR, CUT

Using the index and middle fingers of the right hand, imitate the cutting motion of a scissor.
Origin: As if using a scissor.
Usage: These *scissors* are sharp. The mayor *cut* the ribbon.

HAIRCUT

Use the index and middle fingers of both hands in a scissorlike motion at the hair.
Origin: Natural motion.
Usage: I need a *haircut* today.

TEAR, RIP

Use the modified "A" hands to grasp an imaginary piece of paper and then tear it, one hand moving toward you and the other away.
Origin: Natural motion of tearing.
Usage: She was upset and *tore up* the letter.
The sleeve was *ripped*.

SEW

With the right "F" holding an imaginary needle and the left "O" holding the cloth, go through the motion of sewing.
Origin: A natural sign.
Usage: *Sew* a button on the coat.

SEWING MACHINE

Pass the fingertips of the right "X" along the left index finger.
Origin: The sewing machine needle stitching rapidly across the fabric.
Usage: The *sewing machine* saves time.

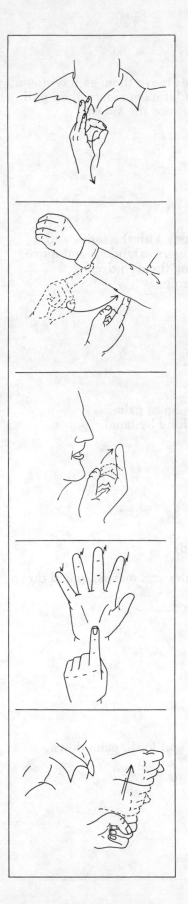

BUTTON

Place the "O" hand (with the other fingers open) against the chest, palm facing left; repeat several times, lower each time.
Origin: Indicating buttons on the shirt.
Usage: fancy new *buttons*.

BASKET

Place the right index finger under the wrist of the left arm, describe a semicircle and place it near the elbow.
Origin: Carrying a basket with the handle over your arm.
Usage: a green and yellow Easter *basket*.

LIGHT BULB, A SMALL LIGHT

Snap the index finger in front of the mouth (as in "ELEVEN"), palm side turned toward the face.
Usage: a 100-watt *light bulb*.

CANDLE

Place the tip of the left index finger, which is pointing up, against the heel of the right open hand, which is in an open position, palm facing left and fingers wiggling.
Origin: Representing the candle and flame.
Usage: dinner by *candlelight*.

UMBRELLA

Place the right "S" above the left "S," as if both hands are holding an umbrella; raise the right "S."
Origin: Holding and raising the umbrella.
Usage: No one had an *umbrella*.

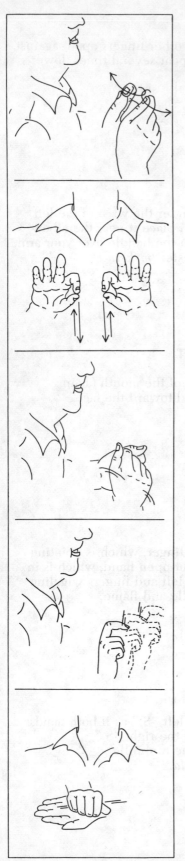

TIE (A knot)

Using both modified "A" hands move them as if typing a knot (make small forward circular movements, then pull hands away from each other toward the sides).
Origin: Natural movement.
Usage: *Tie* your shoes.

DYE

Hold an imaginary piece of cloth with the index and thumb of both hands (other fingers extended) and move them up and down as if dipping them in dye.
Usage: We *dyed* the curtains green.

WASH

Rub the "A" hands together palm to palm.
Origin: Natural motion of washing by hand.
Usage: Clothes need *washing*.

HANG UP CLOTHES (On a rod)

Using the right "X" position, the arm moves up and down slightly and toward the right.
Origin: Placing hangers on a rod.
Usage: *Hang up* your clothes.

IRONING

Slide the right "A" hand back and forth, palm down, across the left palm.
Origin: Natural motion of ironing.
Usage: *Ironing* is hard work.

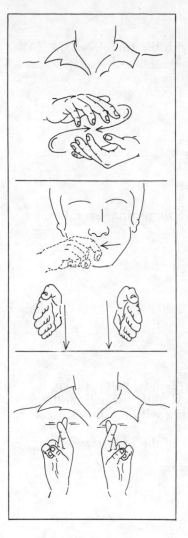

WASHING MACHINE

Move both open curved hands (facing each other) in a twisting motion.
Origin: Indicates the motion of the agitator.
Usage: The *washing machine* broke down.

DRYER

Sign "DRY"; then place both hands in front of you and away from the body (palms facing each other) and move them down a short distance. Note: This ending for objects is to be distinguished from the "PERSON" ending which is made closer to the body and which moves farther down.
Usage: We bought a new washer and *dryer*.

REFRIGERATOR

Shake both "R" hands.
Origin: The sign for "COLD" is initialed.
Usage: a new *refrigerator* in our kitchen.

ADDITIONAL HOME SIGNS

FREEZER—"FREEZE" + ending shown above for "dryer."
LIVING ROOM—"LIVE" + "ROOM."
DINING ROOM—"EAT" + "ROOM."
BEDROOM—"BED" + "ROOM."
RECREATION ROOM—"PLAY" + "ROOM."
  Or, "R," "E," "C" + "ROOM."
LAUNDRY—"WASH" + "ROOM."
FIREPLACE—"FIRE" + "PLACE."
APARTMENT—Spell "APT."
CONDOMINIUM—Spell "CONDO."
AIR CONDITIONING—Spell "A," "C."
PATIO—Spell.

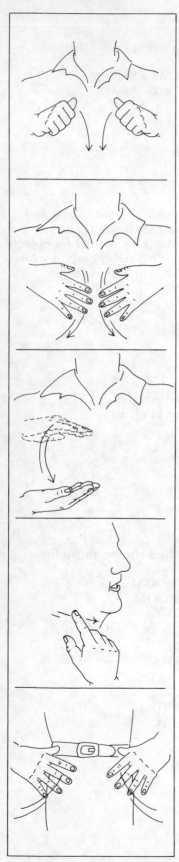

COAT

Trace the form of the lapels with the thumbs of the "A" hands.
Usage: Long *coats* are in style.

CLOTHING, CLOTHES, DRESS

Brush down the chest with the fingertips several times.
Usage: warm *clothing*.
many new *clothes*.
a fancy *dress*.

BLOUSE, JACKET

Place the slightly curved open hands, palms down, in front of the chest; move them slightly away from the body, down, and then in, ending with the little-finger side at the waist.
Origin: Indicating the fullness of the blouse.
Usage: a yellow *blouse*.
a heavy *jacket*.

COLLAR

Using the right index and thumb slightly separated, trace the collar from the side of the neck forward to the center.
Origin: Indicating the collar.
Usage: a blue-*collar* worker.

SKIRT

Brush the fingertips of both hands downward and slightly outward from the waist.
Origin: Indicating the skirt.
Usage: a short *skirt*.

GOWN

Move the fingertips of the open hands down the body beginning at the chest.
Origin: Indicating the long gown.
Usage: white wedding *gown*.

SLACKS, TROUSERS

Place the open hands just below the left side of the waist, palms facing each other and tips downward; give the hands a short upward movement from the wrist. Repeat at the right side.
Origin: Indicates both pant legs.
Usage: His *slacks* and shirt match.
new blue *trousers*.

PANTS

Draw the palms of the flat hands up against the body to the waist.
Origin: Pulling on the pants.
Usage: my old brown *pants*.

HAT

Pat the top of the head.
Origin: The hat is placed on the head.
Usage: He wears many *hats*.

GLOVES

Stroke down the back of the left "**FIVE**" hand slowly.
Origin: Pulling the gloves on the **hand**.
Usage: long white *gloves*.

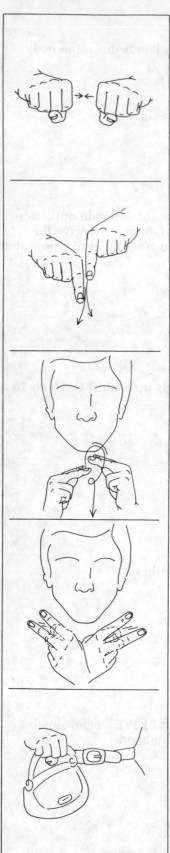

SHOES

Strike the sides of the "S" hands together several times.
Usage: Children like to go without *shoes*.

SOCKS, STOCKINGS, HOSE

Place the index fingers side by side, palms down, and rub them back and forth several times.
Origin: As if knitting socks.
Usage: plaid *socks;* black *stockings;* expensive *hose.*

NECKTIE

Using the "H" hands, tie an imaginary necktie and end with the right "H" being drawn straight down the chest.
Origin: Tying the necktie.
Usage: a Father's Day *necktie.*

BOW TIE

Crossing the hands, palms in, make the "12" sign with both hands at the throat.
Usage: He prefers *bow ties.*

POCKETBOOK, HANDBAG, PURSE

Using the "S" hand at the side of the body away from the chest, hold an imaginary purse by the handle.
Origin: Holding the purse.
Usage: I went to look for a new *pocketbook.*
    The *handbag* was large.
    A man snatched her *purse.*

20
Food and Related Words

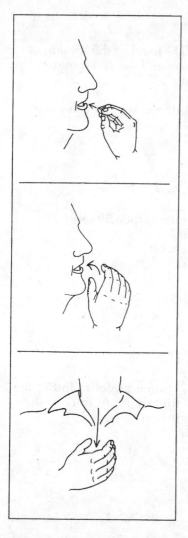

EAT, FOOD

The "AND" hand is thrown lightly toward the mouth several times.
Origin: Food is put to the mouth.
Usage: May I *eat* with you today?
The *food* is cold.

DRINK

Place the "C" hand in front of the mouth, palm facing left, and make a motion as if pouring a drink into the mouth.
Origin: Natural motion of drinking.
Usage: What would you like to *drink*?

HUNGRY, CRAVE, STARVED

Place the "C" hand just below the throat, palm facing in, and draw it down.
Origin: The passageway to the stomach.
Usage: *hungry* for a ham sandwich.
She had a *craving* for pickles.
starved for food and for attention.

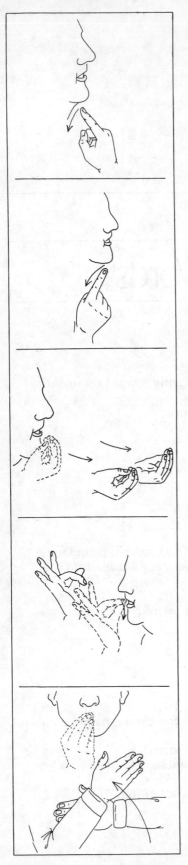

THIRSTY

Draw the tip of the index finger down the throat.
Origin: The throat is dry.
Usage: *thirsty* for cold water.

SWALLOW

Draw the index finger down the throat, palm facing left.
Origin: Indicating movement down the throat.
Usage: couldn't *swallow* solid food.

FEED

Place the tips of the right "AND" hand at the mouth; then move both "AND" hands away from the mouth, palms up, one behind the other.
Origin: Food is given.
Usage: We'll need lots of hamburgers to *feed* this crowd.

DELICIOUS

Snap the middle finger and thumb (other fingers extended) in front of the mouth.
Usage: Ellis prepares *delicious* food.

BREAKFAST

Sign "EAT" and "MORNING." Some prefer to initial the sign by placing the "B" (palm slightly in) in front of the mouth and moving it slightly upward.
Usage: What time is *breakfast?*

LUNCH

Sign "EAT" and "NOON." Some prefer to initial the sign by placing the "L" in front of the mouth, palm left.
Usage: Mrs. Kahl invited several people for *lunch*.

DINNER

Sign "EAT" and "NIGHT." Some prefer to initial the sign by placing the "D" in front of the mouth, palm in.
Usage: It will be a formal *dinner* at 8.

RESTAURANT

Place the right "R" at the mouth, once at each side.
Origin: The sign for "food" made with an "R."
Usage: a fancy *restaurant* in town.

FRY, COOK

Place the back of the right open hand in the left palm and turn the right over, ending palm to palm.
Origin: A pancake being turned over.
Usage: Would you like your eggs *fried*? *Cooking* can be fun.

BOIL, COOK

Place the right curved hand, palm up and fingers wiggling, under the left palm.
Origin: Fire under the kettle.
Usage: The water is *boiling*. The sauce should be *cooked* for 3 hours.

BAKE, OVEN

Slide the right upturned palm under the left downturned palm.
Origin: As if sliding a pan into the oven.
Usage: The pie is in the *oven*.
   baked, boiled, or fried chicken.

BREAD

Place the left hand in front of the body, fingers pointing right; draw the little-finger side of the right hand down the back of the left hand several times.
Origin: Slicing a loaf of bread that is in the arm.
Usage: Do you prefer white or dark *bread*?

SALT

Tap the back of the left "N" with the right index and middle fingers (both palms facing down).
Origin: The motion of salting food by tapping the knife on which it has been placed.
Usage: Pass the *salt*, please.

PEPPER

Use the right "O" position and imitate the motion of using the pepper shaker.
Origin: Shaking pepper over the food.
Usage: I'd like some *pepper* too.

SUGAR, SWEET

Draw the fingertips down across the mouth. (Some prefer to draw the fingertips across the chin for "sweet.")
Origin: As if licking candy.
Usage: *Sugar* provides energy.
   Sweet potatoes go with ham.

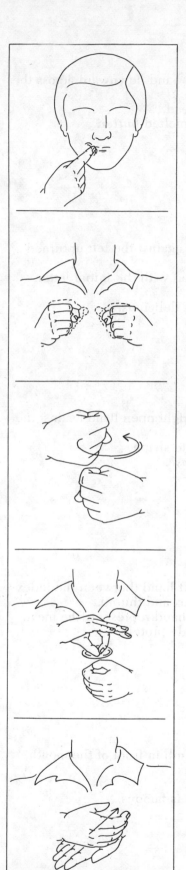

SOUR, BITTER

Place the right index fingertip in the corner of the mouth, and twist slightly, giving appropriate expression.
Origin: Slight puckering of the corner of the mouth and the facial expression indicate bitterness.
Usage: *sour* as a lemon; *bitter* medicine.

MILK

Squeeze the "S" hands.
Origin: Milking a cow.
Usage: lots of Vitamin D in *milk*.

COFFEE

Place the right "S" on the left "S" and make a circular motion with the right "S."
Origin: The motion of grinding a coffee mill.
Usage: *coffee* is ready.

TEA

Place the thumb and index tips of the right "F" into the left "O" and stir.
Origin: Stirring the tea.
Usage: Would you like some lemon for your *tea*?

CREAM

Draw the little-finger side of the right "C" hand across the left palm from the tips to the heel of the hand.
Origin: Skimming the cream off the milk.
Usage: Do you like *cream* in your coffee?

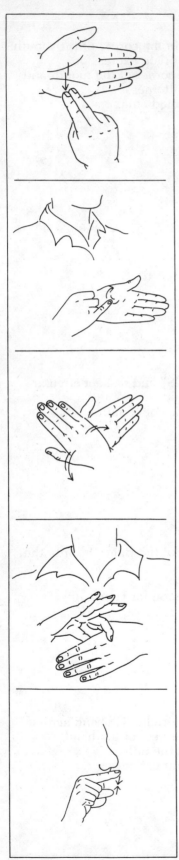

BUTTER

Draw the tips of the right "H" hand downward across the palm of the left hand.
Origin: Buttering a slide of bread.
Usage: Dip the lobster in hot melted *butter*.

JELLY, JAM

Scratch the tip of the right "J" against the left upturned palm.
Origin: Spreading jelly on bread with the initial letter.
Usage: peanut butter and *jelly*.
Stawberry *jam* is really delicious.

CHEESE

Rub and twist the heel of the right open hand against the heel of the left open hand.
Origin: Pressing the cheese into shape.
Usage: serve crackers and *cheese*.

MEAT

Grasp the fleshy part of the left hand (between the index and thumb) with the right index and thumb.
Origin: The fleshy part of the hand represents the meat.
Usage: *Meat* and cheese provide protein.

CHICKEN

Place the index finger and thumb in front of the mouth, opening and closing the fingers.
Origin: Representing the beak.
Usage: Southern-fried *chicken* is famous.

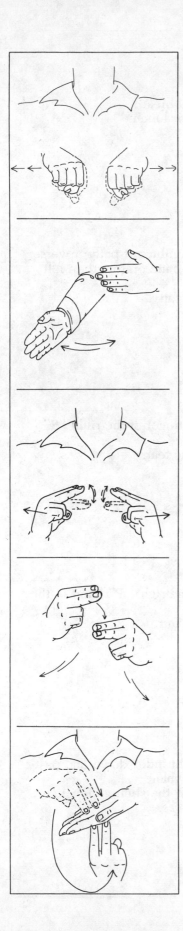

SAUSAGE, BOLOGNA

Move the "S" hands (palms down) apart while squeezing them several times.
Origin: Indicating a string of sausages.
Usage: *sausage* for breakfast.
bologna-and-cheese sandwich.

FISH

Point the right open hand forward, palm facing left (left fingertips touching the right arm near the elbow); move the right hand back and forth.
Origin: The movement of the fish's tail in the water.
Usage: The restaurant served all the *fish* we could eat.

BACON

Touch the tips of the "U" fingers of both hands, palms down; move the "U's" up and down while drawing the hands apart.
Origin: Indicating the crisp bacon.
Usage: a pound of *bacon*.

EGG

Strike the index finger of the left "H" with the middle finger of the right "H"; drop them and let them fall apart.
Origin: Breaking the shell of the egg.
Usage: How do you like your *eggs?*

TOAST

Place the tips of the right "V" first against the palm and then against the back of the left hand.
Origin: The old-fashioned method of toasting bread by using a fork to hold it over the fire, first one side, then the other.
Usage: *toast* and coffee every morning.

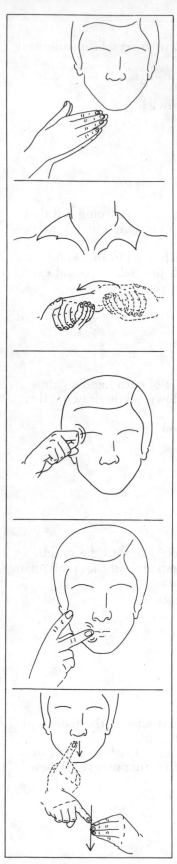

SANDWICH

Place the open hands together.
Origin: Represents two slices of bread.
Usage: a tuna-salad *sandwich* for lunch.

HAMBURGER

Cup the hands as if making a hamburger patty; reverse
the position of the hands (right hand on top, then left
hand on top).
Origin: Making the hamburger patty.
Usage: a *hamburger* and a Coke.

ONION

Twist the knuckle of the index finger of the right "S"
hand at the corner of the eye.
Origin: *Onions* cause the eyes to tear.
Usage: liver and *onions*.

PICKLE

Place the middle-finger tip of the right "P" hand in the
corner of the mouth.
Origin: Initialing the sign for "sour."
Usage: homemade *pickles*.

TOMATO

Sign "RED"; then draw the right index down and past
the fingertips of the left "AND" hand.
Origin: Represents the color and the slicing movement.
Usage: a vine full of ripe *tomatoes*.

MAYONNAISE

Draw the tips of the right "M" hand across the palm of the left hand.
Origin: The sign for "butter" initialed.
Usage: *mayonnaise* on your sandwich.

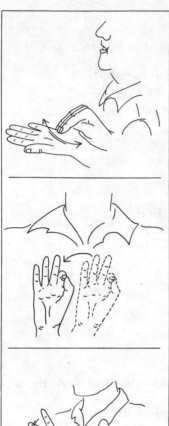

FRENCH FRIES

Make an "F" in front of you twice.
Usage: *French fries* are a favorite American food.

KETCHUP

Point the tips of the "K" forward and shake it up and down.
Origin: Using the initial letter and shaking ketchup out of a bottle.
Usage: He likes *ketchup* on everything!

VINEGAR

Place the index finger of the right "V" against the corner of the mouth.
Usage: apple-cider *vinegar*.

SAUCE, DRESSING

Using the thumbtip of the right "A" to represent the spout, make the motion of pouring sauce on food.
Usage: hot fudge *sauce*; salad *dressing*.

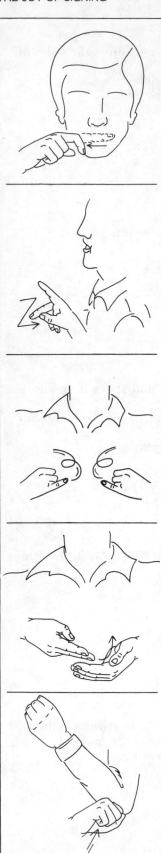

SYRUP

Draw the right index finger across the lips from left to right.
Origin: Wiping the syrup from the mouth.
Usage: Vermont maple *syrup* is my favorite.

PIZZA

Use the right "P" to draw a "Z" in the air.
Usage: We ordered a large cheese *pizza*.

SPAGHETTI

Place the tips of the "I" fingers together and draw them apart several times.
Origin: Showing the long thin spaghetti.
Usage: Italian *spaghetti*.

SOUP

Using the right "H" as a spoon, dip it in the left palm and up.
Origin: Bringing the spoon to the mouth.
Usage: Hot *soup* tastes good on a cold day.

CRACKER

Strike the index-finger side of the right "S" against the left arm near the elbow.
Origin: Striking the large old-fashioned cracker to break it in pieces.
Usage: many varieties of *crackers*.

POTATO

Tap the back of the left "S" hand with the tips of the slightly curved right "V."
Origin: Placing the fork in the potato.
Usage: I like hash-brown *potatoes*.

GRAVY, GREASY, OIL

Hold up the left hand, fingers pointing right; grasp the lower edge of the hand with the right index finger and thumb and draw down several times.
Origin: Gravy dripping from the meat.
Usage: potatoes and *gravy*.
       greasy food.
       vinegar and *oil*.

CABBAGE

Strike the sides of the head with the wrists of the "A" hands.
Origin: Showing the cabbage head.
Usage: You can have either white or red *cabbage*.

CORN

Place the right index in front of the mouth and twist it in and out.
Origin: Eating corn on the cob.
Usage: Do you prefer white or yellow *corn?*

FRUIT

Place the tips of the "F" into the right cheek and twist.
Origin: The sign for "apple" is used as a basis for this initial sign.
Usage: She ordered a *fruit* plate.

APPLE

Press the knuckle of the index finger of the right "S" hand into the right cheek and twist.
Origin: The cheek represents the apple and the knuckle pressing against it shows the indentation for the stem.
Usage: An *apple* a day keeps the doctor away.

BANANA

Go through the motion of peeling a banana, the left index representing the banana and the right fingertips used to pull off the skin.
Origin: Peeling the banana.
Usage: *Banana* splits are very fattening!

ORANGE

Squeeze the right "S" at the mouth.
Origin: Squeezing the juice.
Usage: Drink *orange* juice often.

LEMON

Place the thumbtip of the right "L" at the chin.
Usage: *lemon* meringue pie for dessert.

PEACH

Place the fingertips on the right cheek and draw them down into an "AND" position.
Origin: Showing the fuzz on the peach.
Usage: a bushel of Georgia *peaches*.

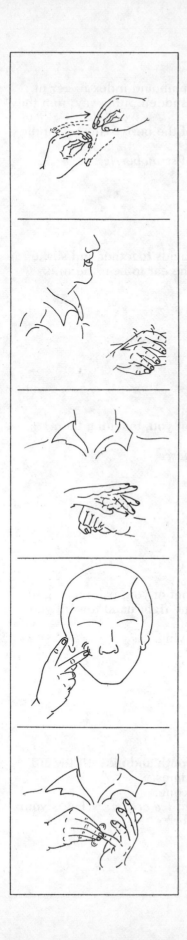

PEAR

Hold the left "AND" hand in front of you, fingertips pointing up; place the five fingers of the right hand over the left and draw up until the tips of both "AND" hands are touching.
Origin: Representing the shape of the pear.
Usage: *pear*-and-cottage-cheese salad.

GRAPES

Place the slightly curved right fingertips on the back of the left hand; repeat the motion several times, each time a little farther down on the left hand.
Origin: Representing a bunch of grapes.
Usage: purple or green *grapes*.

MELON, WATERMELON, PUMPKIN

Flip the middle finger off the thumb which is resting on the back of the left "S" hand.
Origin: Thumping a melon to test whether it is ripe.
Usage: a green *melon; pumpkin* pie with the
        Thanksgiving dinner; a large, heavy *watermelon*.
Note: "Watermelon" is often preceded by the sign for "WATER."

PINEAPPLE

Place the middle finger of the right "P" into the cheek and twist.
Origin: The sign for "apple" initialed.
Usage: *pineapple* and cheese make a good combination.

BERRIES

Grasp the tip of the left little finger with the right fingertips and twist the right several times.
Usage: picking *berries*.
Note: blueberries—sign "BLUE" + "BERRY."
blackberries—sign "BLACK" + "BERRY."
cherry—sign "RED" + "BERRY."

STRAWBERRY

Place the closed tips of the thumb and index finger in front of the mouth and give a sudden pull away from the mouth.
Origin: Pulling the stem out of the berry which is in the mouth.
Usage: I really enjoy a bowl of *strawberries*.

COCONUT

Touch the tips of the curved hands together and shake.
Origin: Shaking a coconut at the ear to hear the milk splashing inside.
Usage: a tall *coconut* tree.

DESSERT

Place the "D" hands in front of you, touching them together several times.
Usage: What is your favorite *dessert*?

PIE

Place the open left hand in front of you, palm facing up; draw the little-finger side of the right hand toward you twice as if cutting a piece of pie.
Origin: Cutting the pie for serving.
Usage: Who ate all the *pie*?

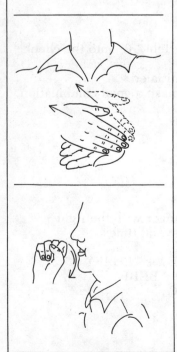

ICE CREAM

Place an "S" in front of the mouth and move it toward the mouth and down several times.
Origin: Licking an ice-cream cone.
Usage: Do you like soft or hard *ice cream*? What is your favorite *ice-cream* flavor?

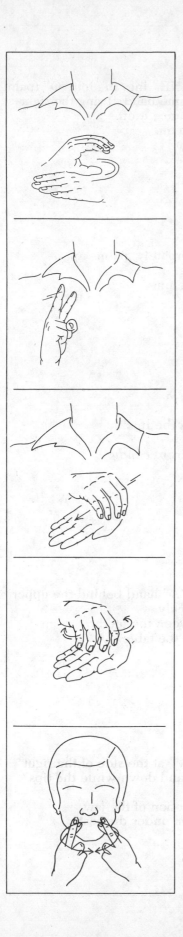

CHOCOLATE

Place the right "C" on the back of the left hand and circle it.
Usage: *chocolate* icing on the cake.

VANILLA

Shake the "V" in front of you. (Note: This will only be understood in context.)
Usage: *Vanilla* ice cream is America's favorite dessert.

CAKE

Place the tips of the right "C" on the left palm and move the "C" across the palm to the right.
Origin: Showing a slice of cake.
Usage: German chocolate *cake*.

COOKIE, BISCUIT

Place the tips of the right slightly curved fingers in the left palm, twist and repeat. (The sign for "BISCUIT" is not twisted.)
Origin: Using a cookie cutter.
Usage: chocolate-chip *cookies;* homemade *biscuits.*

DOUGHNUT

Place both "R" hands at the mouth and circle forward, touching the tips together.
Origin: Represents the twisted doughnut.
Usage: coffee and *doughnuts.*

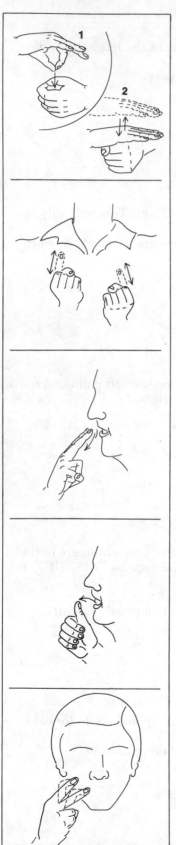

SODA, POP

Place the tips of the right "NINE" into the left "O" (palm right); lift the right out and immediately bring the right palm down on the left and bounce it off.
Origin: Pushing the bottle cap on.
Usage: Who will bring the *pop*?
a case of orange *soda*.

POPCORN

Snap the index fingers up alternately, palms up.
Origin: Showing corn popping.
Usage: We ate *popcorn* all evening.

CANDY

Rub the tips of the "U" across the lips.
Origin: Licking candy.
Usage: Don brought Beth a box of *candy*.

NUTS

Place the thumb of the right "A" hand behind the upper teeth and draw it forward quickly.
Origin: Cracking the nut between the teeth.
Usage: *Nuts* and mints are on the table.

CHEWING GUM

Place the tips of the curved "V" at the side of the right cheek and move the hand up and down while the tips stay on the cheek.
Origin: Shows the chewing motion of the jaw.
Usage: We found *chewing gum* under the seats.

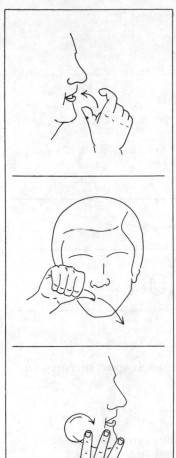

DRINK (Liquor)

Make a small "C" with the thumb and index finger, other fingers closed, and make a motion as if pouring a drink into the mouth.
Origin: Drinking from a small glass.
Usage: a choice of *drinks* at the bar.

DRUNK

Place the "A" hand at the mouth and make a motion as if pouring a drink past the mouth and down.
Origin: Pouring motion at the lips.
Usage: *drunk* every weekend.

WINE

Rub the right "W" in a circular motion against the cheek.
Usage: *wine* and cheese.

WHISKEY, LIQUOR

Extend the index and little fingers of the right hand; place right hand on back of left fist; move right up and down once or twice.
Origin: Indicating a drink so many fingers high.
Usage: opened a new *liquor* store.

BEER

Place the right "B" at the side of the mouth band draw down.
Usage: *beer* and pretzels.

21

Sports and Recreation

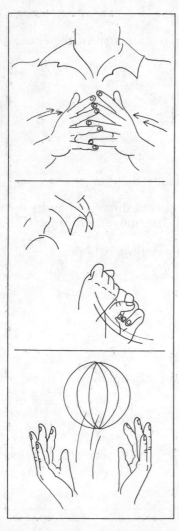

Generally speaking, the sign for each sport pictures an action that identifies it.

FOOTBALL

Bring the "FIVE" hands together, interlocking the fingers; repeat this motion several times.
Origin: Represents the teams clashing.
Usage: One of our seniors won a *football* scholarship.

BASEBALL, SOFTBALL

Hold an imaginary bat as if ready to hit the ball.
Usage: *Baseball* is a favorite American sport.
　　　　Our *softball* team is practicing today.

BASKETBALL

Hold an imaginary basketball with both hands and toss the ball.
Usage: The tall boy will be a real asset to the *basketball* team.

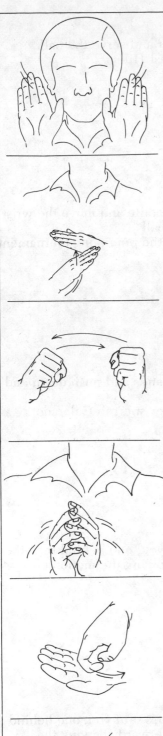

VOLLEYBALL

Hit an imaginary ball over the net with both hands.
Usage: Who wants to play *volleyball* today?

SOCCER

Strike the edge of the left open hand with the index-finger side of the right open hand.
Usage: The German *soccer* team won.

BOXING, FIGHTING

Using the "S" hands, go through the motions of boxing or fighting.
Usage: Joe Louis was a famous *boxer*.
Boys were *fighting* in the street.

WRESTLING

Clasp the hands, locking the fingers, and shake the hands back and forth from the wrist.
Usage: The *wrestlers* had powerful muscles. (Add the "PERSON" ending.)

HOCKEY

Place the right crooked index finger against the left palm; move the crooked right index several times toward you in short scraping motions on the palm.
Usage: Canadians made ice *hockey* famous.

GOLF

Hold an imaginary golf club with both hands as if ready to strike the ball.
Usage: It's a good day for *golfing*.

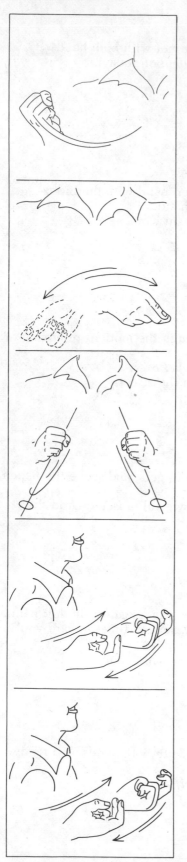

TENNIS

Hold an imaginary tennis racket and serve the ball.
Usage: *Tennis* is played at Forest Hills.

PING-PONG

Hold an imaginary ping-pong paddle and move the wrist back and forth as if hitting the ball.
Usage: The Chinese team won the *ping-pong* tournament.

SKIING

Hold imaginary poles in both hands and push down and back as skiers do.
Usage: *Skiing* is a popular winter sport in Colorado.

ICE SKATING

Hold the "X" hands in front of you, one behind the other, palms up, and move forward showing the motion of skating.
Usage: Dorothy is a smooth *skater*.

ROLLER SKATING

Hold the curved "V" fingers in front of you, one behind the other, palms up, and move forward showing the motion of skating.
Usage: We enjoyed *skating* to music.

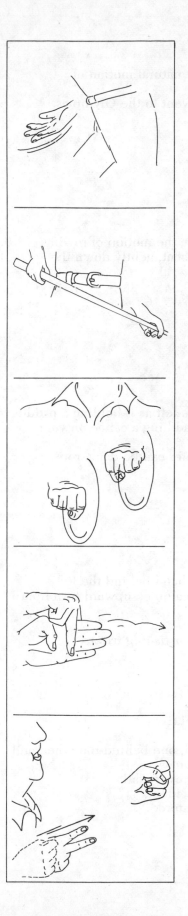

BOWLING

Hold an imaginary bowling ball with the right hand and roll it forward.
Usage: Our group *bowls* twice a week.

POOL, BILLIARDS

Hold an imaginary cue stick with the modified "A" hands and move the right one ahead as if striking the ball.
Usage: Let's play *pool* after a while.

BICYCLE

Using both "S" hands, palms down, circle them forward alternately as if pedaling.
Usage: *Biking* is good exercise. Have you seen my new 10-speed *bike?*

HORSEBACK RIDING

Straddle the index side of the left open hand with the index and middle fingers of the right hand, and move the hands up and down in this position.
Usage: *Horseback riding* is great fun.

ARCHERY

Imitate the motion of pulling back the string of the bow.
Usage: Our *archery* team is the best in the country.

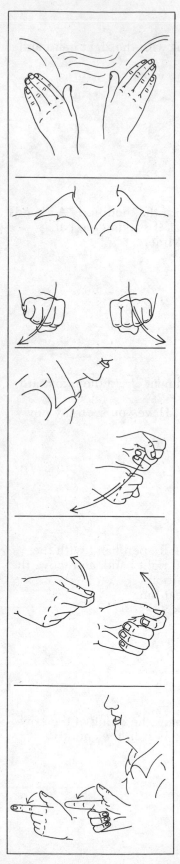

SWIMMING

Use the arms to represent the natural motion of swimming.
Usage: Our *swimming* team went to the Olympics.

ROWING

Hold imaginary oars and make the motion of rowing.
Usage: "*Row, row, row* your boat, gently down the stream . . . ."

CANOEING

With the right hand below the left as if holding a paddle, make the natural motion of paddling a canoe on your right side.
Usage: *Canoeing* in rough water can be dangerous.

FISHING

Place the right modified "A" hand behind the left modified "A" hand and make a quick upward turn from both wrists.
Origin: Pulling up on the line.
Usage: Let's leave early for our *fishing* trip.

HUNTING, SHOOT, GUN, RIFLE

Point both "L" hands forward, one behind the other, and move the thumbs up and down.
Usage: They go deer *hunting* every fall.
A man was *shot* by accident.
All *guns* must be registered.

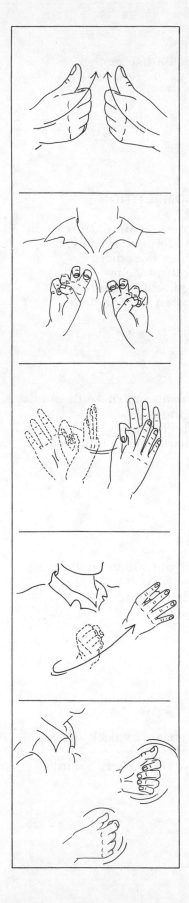

GAME, CHALLENGE

Bring the "A" hands toward each other (palms toward the body) in a slightly upward motion.
Origin: Two sides facing each other in competition.
Usage: The *game* starts at 2 o'clock.
　　　　Who wants to *challenge* our team?

TOURNAMENT

The bent "V" hands, facing each other, are moved up and down alternately.
Usage: The *tournament* lasted all day.

OLYMPICS

Lock the index and thumbs of both hands (other fingers extended) several times, facing in and out alternately.
Usage: Julie won a gold medal in the *Olympics*.

THROW

Throw the right "S" toward the left as the hand is opened.
Note: The hand position may change depending on the kind of object being thrown.
Usage: *Throw* the ball to me.

JOGGING

Both arms bent at the elbows move as if in the action of jogging.
Usage: Daily *jogging* keeps him well.

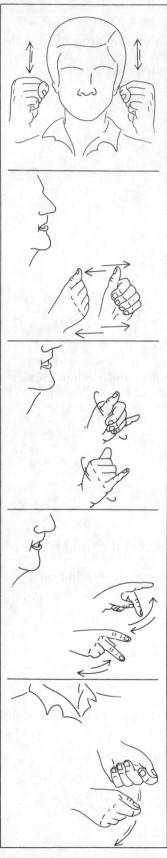

EXERCISE

Move the "S" hands in an exercise-like motion.
Usage: Doctors recommend regular *exercise*.

RACE, CONTEST, RIVALRY COMPETITION

Place the "A" hands in front of you, palms facing each other, and move them back and forth alternately.
Origin: First one gets ahead, then the other.
Usage: The *race* begins promptly at 9 a.m.
     Have you ever seen a pie-eating *contest*?
     There was *rivalry* between teams before *competition* began.

PLAY (Recreation)

Place the "Y" hands in front of you and shake them in and out from the wrist several times.
Origin: Activity indicated by the hands.
Usage: All work and no *play* makes Jack a dull boy.

PARTY

Place the "P" hands in front of you and swing them from side to side.
Origin: The above sign for "play" is initialed.
Usage: People enjoy a good *party*.

PLAYING CARDS

With the left hand holding an imaginary pack, use the right hand as if dealing out cards.
Usage: They sat around *playing cards* every Saturday night.

22

Countries, Cities, and States

NATION, NATIONAL

Circle the right "N" over the left hand and then place it on the back of the left hand.
Usage: A *nation* is no stronger than its people.

INTERNATIONAL

Revolve the right "I" hand around the left "I."
Origin: Circling the globe.
Usage: an *international* conference on deafness.

COUNTRY

Rub the inside of the right "Y" hand in a circular motion on the left arm, near the elbow.
Usage: This is my *country*.

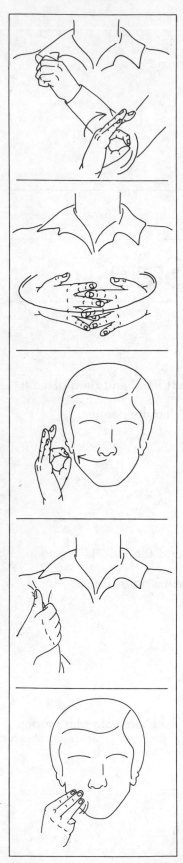

FOREIGN

Rub the side of the right "F" hand in a circular motion on the outside of the left arm, near the elbow.
Origin: The sign for "country" made with an "F."
Usage: Do you know any *foreign* languages?

AMERICA

Interlock the fingers of both "FIVE" hands, palms facing the body and tips pointing out, and move them in a semicircle from right to left.
Origin: The old American rail fence.
Usage: "God bless *America*, land that I love . . . ."

INDIAN (American)

Place the tips of the thumb and forefinger of the right "F" on the nose and then on the lobe of the ear.
Origin: Ring in the nose and ear.
Usage: *Indians* have a sign language of their own.

CANADA

Grasp the lapel with the right "A" hand.
Usage: Ottawa is the capital of *Canada*.

MEXICO

Rub the fingertips of the right "M" down the lower edge of the right cheek.
Usage: *Mexico* is our neighbor to the south.

EUROPE

Describe a small circle in front of you with the right "E."
Usage: Tourism is big business in *Europe*.

ENGLAND

Place the left hand in front of you, palm down; grasp the outside edge of the left hand with the right "Λ," palm down.
Origin: The English were known to be great handshakers.
Usage: The Queen of *England* visited Canada.

SCOTLAND

Draw the fingertips of the right "FIVE" hand down the left upper arm; then draw the backs of the fingers across the arm away from you.
Origin: Scottish plaid.
Usage: *Scotland* is famous for plaids, kilts, and bagpipes.

IRELAND

Circle the right "V" with the tips pointing down over the back of the left hand and place the tips on the left.
Origin: Similar to the sign for potato, referring to the Irish potato.
Usage: *Ireland* has had many problems because of religious differences.

FRANCE

Place the "F" in front of you, palm facing in; turn it so the palm faces forward, moving it slightly to the right and up.
Origin: Using the initial letter.
Usage: The Eiffel Tower is one of the attractions of *France*.

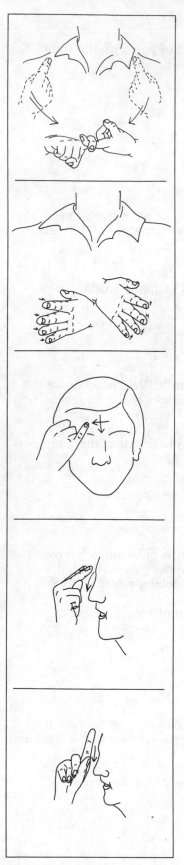

SPAIN

Draw the index fingers from the shoulders to the center, hooking one over the other.
Origin: The large scarf tied in front.
Usage: Would you like to see a bullfight in *Spain?*

GERMANY

Cross the hands at the wrists, palms facing the body, and wiggle the fingers.
Origin: Showing the double eagle.
Usage: East *Germany* and West *Germany* have separate governments.

ITALY

Draw a cross in front of the forehead with the right "I" hand, palm facing in.
Origin: The cross represents the religion of the country.
Usage: The Vatican is in *Italy*.

ROMAN

Place the tips of the "N" fingers on the bridge and then on the tip of the nose.
Origin: The Roman nose.
Usage: "Friends, *Romans*, countrymen...."

GREECE

Draw the right "G" down the nose, palm facing left.
Origin: The Grecian nose.
Usage: a vacation on the islands of *Greece*.

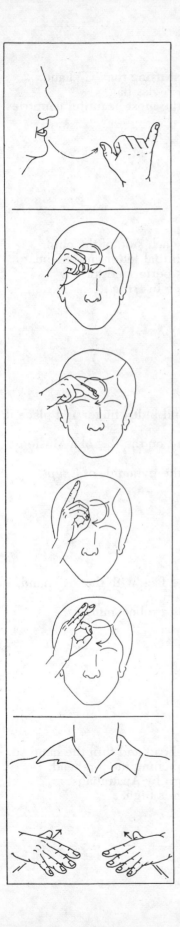

HOLLAND, DUTCH

Place the thumb of the right "Y" on the lips; then draw the hand down and out.
Origin: Indicating the pipe used by the Dutch.
Usage: *Holland* exports tulip bulbs.
The *Dutch* are known for their wooden shoes.

SWEDEN

Describe a circle in front of the forehead with the "S" hand.
Usage: *Sweden* is called the land of the midnight sun.

NORWAY

Describe a circle in front of the forehead with the "N" hand.
Usage: Oslo is the capital of *Norway*.

DENMARK

Describe a circle in front of the forehead with the "D" hand.
Usage: Copenhagen is the capital of *Denmark*.

FINLAND

Describe a circle in front of the forehead with the "F" hand.
Usage: *Finland* is in northern Europe.

RUSSIA

Place the thumbs of the "FIVE" hands on and off the waist several times.
Origin: Hands in position for the Russian dance.
Usage: Schools for the deaf in *Russia* support fingerspelling.

SWITZERLAND

Make a large cross on the chest using the "C" hand.
Origin: The white cross of the Swiss flag.
Usage: *Switzerland* is one of the most beautiful countries in the world.

ISRAEL

Draw the tip of the "I" down each side of the chin.
Origin: A combination of the initial letter and the beard.
Usage: The Gallaudet dancers performed for the international conference in *Israel*.

EGYPT

Make a "C" with the thumb and index finger and place it on the forehead, palm forward.
Origin: Represents the crescent on the flag of a Moslem country.
Usage: Tourists enjoy seeing the pyramids of *Egypt*.

AFRICA

Describe a circle in front of the face with the "A" hand, using a counterclockwise motion.
Usage: Many *African* countries are becoming independent.

AUSTRALIA

Place the fingertips at the forehead and turn the hand so the palm faces forward, tips touching the forehead.
Origin: Represents the hat worn by Australians.
Usage: Travel fare to *Australia* is high.

INDIA

Place the tip of the thumb of the "A" hand against the center of the forehead and twist slightly.
Origin: The red dot on the forehead of some Indian women.
Usage: *India* has a problem of overpopulation.

CHINA

Place the tip of the index finger at the corner of the right eye and push upward.
Origin: Representing the eye of the Oriental person.
Usage: Peking is the capital of *China*.

JAPAN

Place the tip of the little finger at the corner of the right eye and push upward.
Origin: An initialed sign representing the eye of the Oriental.
Usage: *Japanese* cherry trees were brought to America.

KOREA

Place the tip of the middle finger of the "K" hand at the side of the eye.
Origin: An initialed sign representing the eye of the Oriental.
Usage: Seoul is the capital of *Korea*.

PHILIPPINE ISLANDS

Circle the right "P" clockwise above the left downturned palm and then touch the left with the middle fingertip of the right "P."
Usage: Did you hear about the earthquake in the *Philippines?*
Note: "Filipino" is signed by circling the right "F" in front of the face, palm in.

Filipino

CITIES AND STATES

Many of the larger cities as well as some states have signs that are known and recognized throughout the country. However, signs used for some of the smaller cities are known only locally. States and cities having compound names are usually signed by describing small circles with the initial letters. This is the case with Los Angeles, St. Louis, San Francisco, New Hampshire, etc. States that have long names are usually abbreviated, for example: Mass. for Massachusetts and Pa. for Pennsylvania. Pictured below are signs generally known and used.

NEW YORK

Slide the right "Y" back and forth across the left palm.
Usage: *New York* City is an island.

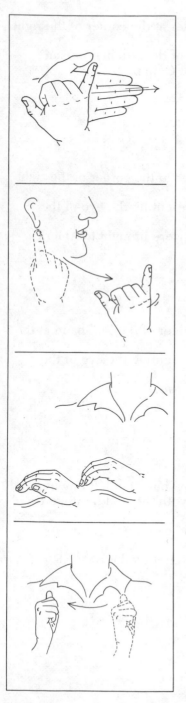

CALIFORNIA

Touch the ear with the index finger and bring the "Y" hand forward giving it a quick twist (as in "GOLD").
Origin: California is associated with the gold rush.
Usage: *California* is approximately 750 miles from north to south.

HAWAII

Place both hands open in front of you, palms down, fingertips pointing to the side; move the hands away in a wavy motion.
Origin: Hands are moved in hula fashion.
Usage: *Hawaii* is a favorite vacation area.

ATLANTA

Place the right "A" on the body just below the left shoulder, then at the right shoulder.
Usage: We always change planes in *Atlanta*.

BALTIMORE

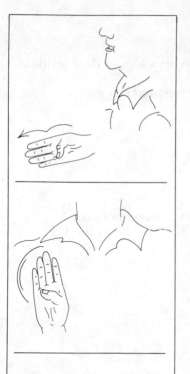

Move the right "B" hand forward twice (palm facing left and tips pointing forward).
Usage: *Baltimore* is known for its white steps and blue
       blinds.

BOSTON

Move the "B" in a slightly circular motion in front of you.
Usage: the famous *Boston* Tea Party.

CHICAGO

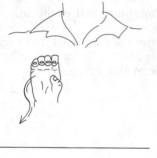

Draw the "C" hand down with a wavy motion.
Usage: *Chicago* is in northern Illinois.

DETROIT

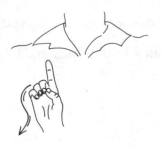

Draw the "D" hand down with a wavy motion.
Usage: *Detroit* is the home of the automobile makers.

MILWAUKEE

The right index finger, pointing left with palm down, is drawn back and forth just below the lips.
Origin: Beer is wiped from the lips.
Usage: *Milwaukee* is famous for beer.

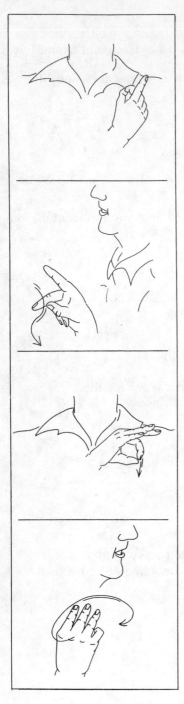

MINNEAPOLIS

Place a "D" at the left shoulder.
Origin: The "D" refers to David, a former deaf resident of Minneapolis.
Usage: *Minneapolis* and St. Paul are twin cities.

PHILADELPHIA

Draw the "P" downward with a wavy motion.
Usage: *Philadelphia* was the first capital of the U.S.

PITTSBURGH

The right "F" hand places an imaginary pin in the left lapel with a downward movement.
Origin: The pin represents the steel for which Pittsburgh is famous.
Usage: The *Pittsburgh* Pirates won the game.

WASHINGTON

Place the right "W" at the right shoulder, draw it up and forward.
Usage: Gallaudet College is located in *Washington*, D. C.

Note: The sign for a person from a particular location is made by adding the "PERSON" ending as in the following examples: America—American; Spain—Spaniard; New York—New Yorker.

23

Animals

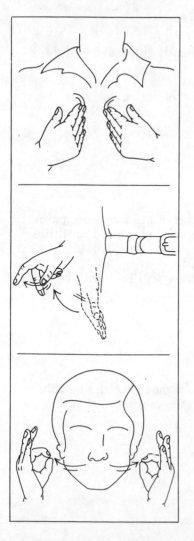

ANIMAL

Place the fingertips on the chest and rock the hands back and forth with the tips still resting on the chest.
Origin: Represents the breathing motion of an animal.
Usage: The children enjoyed the *animals* in the zoo.

DOG

Pat the leg and snap the fingers.
Origin: Imitating the natural motion of calling a dog.
Usage: a boy and his *dog*.

CAT

Place the "F" hands at the sides of the mouth and draw out to the sides.
Origin: Represents the cat's whiskers.
Usage: Siamese *cat*.

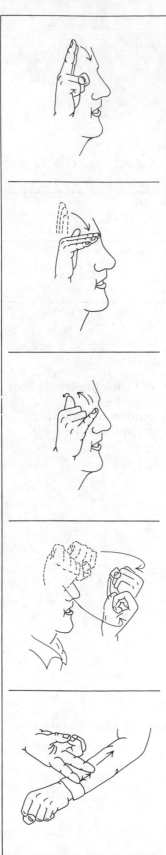

HORSE

Place the "H" hands at the sides of the head, palms facing forward, and move the "H" fingers up and down.
Origin: Represents the ears of the horse.
Usage: betting at the *horse* races.

MULE, DONKEY

Place the open hands at the sides of the head, palms facing forward, and bend them forward and backward several times.
Origin: Representing large ears.
Usage: an old *mule* on the farm.

COW

Place the thumbs of the "Y" hands at the sides of the head and twist hands up.
Origin: Representing the horns.
Usage: "The *cow* jumped over the moon."

BUFFALO, BISON

Place the "S" hands at the sides of the forehead, palm side forward; move them forward and around until the palm side faces to the back.
Origin: The horns of the buffalo.
Usage: Have you ever eaten a *buffalo* burger? The *bison* is found in North America.

SHEEP

Hold out the left arm; use the right index and middle fingers as scissors and imitate the motion of shearing on the back of the left arm.
Origin: Shearing the sheep.
Usage: one black *sheep.*

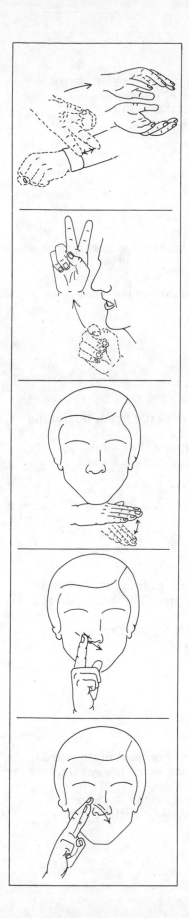

LAMB

Make the sign for "SHEEP"; then bring the open palms toward each other several times to indicate that the sheep is small.
Origin: Lambs are small sheep.
Usage: It was interesting to see the new *lambs*.

GOAT

Place the "S" hand at the chin, changing it to a "V" hand as it is placed at the forehead.
Origin: Showing the beard and the horns.
Usage: Here come Heidi and her *goat!*

PIG

Place the back of the right open hand under the chin and bend and unbend the hand several times.
Origin: Represents being full and having eaten to the chin; also, wallowing in mud up to the chin.
Usage: the story of the three little *pigs*.

MOUSE

Brush the tip of the nose several times with the tip of the right index finger.
Origin: The pointed nose of the mouse.
Usage: She was afraid of *mice*.

RAT

Brush the tip of the nose several times with the tips of the right "R."
Origin: The sign for "mouse" made with an "R."
Usage: *Rats* were used for testing.

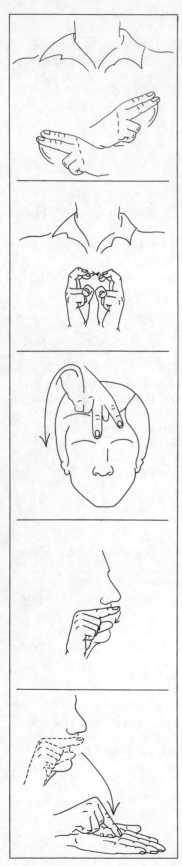

RABBIT

Place the right "H" on the left "H" crosswise; move the "H" fingers back and forth several times.
Origin: Representing the ears of the rabbit.
Usage: a white *rabbit* with pink eyes.

SQUIRREL

Strike the tips of the bent "V" hands together in front of you several times.
Origin: Indicates a sitting squirrel with front paws up.
Usage: *Squirrels* can do damage in the house.

SKUNK

Draw the right "K" hand back over the head, beginning at the forehead.
Origin: Indicates the white stripe of the skunk.
Usage: *Skunks* know how to keep people away.

BIRD

Place the index finger and thumb in front of the mouth, representing the bill; flap the arms. (The latter part is often omitted.)
Origin: The bird's bill and wings.
Usage: *Birds* fly south in the winter.

CHICKEN

Place the index finger and thumb in front of the mouth, representing the beak; then place these fingers into the palm.
Origin: Represents the chicken pecking at grain.
Usage: Which came first, the *chicken* or the egg?

DUCK

Make a bill in front of the mouth using two fingers and the thumb.
Origin: The wide bill of the duck.
Usage: Kim and Kay loved to play with the *ducks*.

ROOSTER

Place the thumb of the "THREE" hands at the forehead.
Origin: The rooster's comb.
Usage: Can you hear *roosters* crowing in the morning?

TURKEY

Place the right "Q" hand under the nose and shake it back and forth.
Origin: Represents the wattle of the turkey.
Usage: a *turkey* dinner with all the trimmings.

EAGLE

Hook the right "X" over the nose; flap the arms to represent wings.
Origin: The hooked beak and wings of an eagle.
Usage: The *eagle* flew above the mountains.

OWL

Place the "O" hands in front of the eyes so that the eyes see through the circle of the "O"; twist them toward the center several times.
Origin: The large eyes of the owl.
Usage: a wise old *owl*.

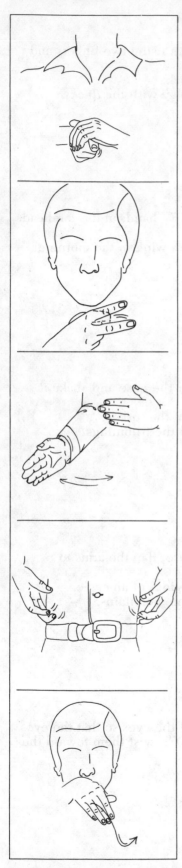

TURTLE

Place the left hand on the right "A," which has the palm facing left, and wiggle the right thumb.
Origin: Represents the head of the turtle protruding from under the shell.
Usage: Have you read the story of the *turtle* and the hare?

FROG

Place the "S" hand at the throat and then snap out the index and middle fingers, ending in a "V" position that is pointing left.
Origin: Showing both the croaking and the leaping of the frog.
Usage: The little green *frog* sat there looking at me.

FISH

Point the right open hand forward, palm facing left (left fingertips touching the right arm near the elbow); move the right hand back and forth from the wrist.
Origin: The movement of the fish's tail in the water.
Usage: many gold*fish* in the pond.

MONKEY

Scratch the sides of the body just above the waist.
Origin: Typical action of a monkey scratching.
Usage: playful *monkeys* in the cage.

ELEPHANT

Place the back of the right hand in front of the mouth, push up, forward, down.
Origin: The trunk of the elephant.
Usage: *Elephants* never forget.

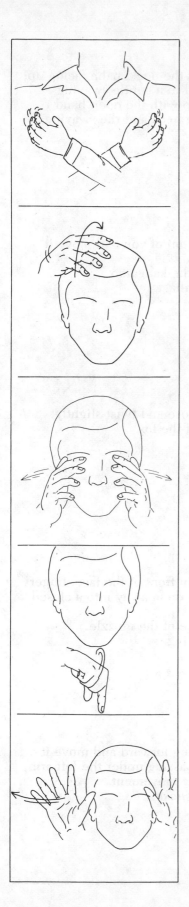

BEAR

Cross the arms, placing the right hand on the left upper arm and the left hand on the right upper arm; pull the hands across the arms towards the center.
Origin: Showing a bear hug.
Usage: a huge white polar *bear*.

LION

Place the slightly curved "FIVE" hand over the head, fingers slightly separated and pointing down; move the hand back over the head in a shaking motion.
Origin: Representing the lion's mane.
Usage: The *lion's* roar frightened everyone.

TIGER

Place the slightly curved "FIVE" hands in front of the face, palms in; draw hands apart several times and claw the hands.
Origin: Represents both the stripes and the clawing action.
Usage: a big yellow *tiger*.

GIRAFFE

Move the "G" hand upward at the neck.
Origin: Indicating the long neck of the giraffe.
Usage: a tall *giraffe* looking over the fence.

DEER, ANTLERS, REINDEER, MOOSE

Place the thumbs of the "FIVE" hands at the sides of the forehead and draw the hands away from the head.
Origin: Representing the antlers.
Usage: Santa and his *reindeer*.
  large *antlers*.
  Canadian *moose*.
  deer crossing.

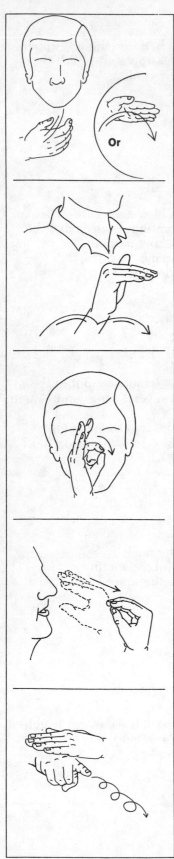

CAMEL

Place the "C" hand in front of the neck, palm facing up; move the hand up and forward in a gentle swaying motion. (Or, indicate the hump with the open hand.)
Origin: Showing both the long neck and the swaying motion.
Usage: traveled by *camel*.

KANGAROO

Place the right bent hand in front of you and move it forward in a hopping motion.
Origin: Natural movement of the kangaroo.
Usage: a *kangaroo* from Australia.

FOX

Place the right "F" over the nose and twist slightly.
Origin: The pointed muzzle of the fox.
Usage: a sly *fox*.

WOLF

Place the open "AND" hand in front of the face, fingers pointing to the face, and draw them away into a closed "AND" position.
Origin: Representing the shape of the muzzle.
Usage: a *wolf* in sheep's clothing.

SNAKE

Use the right "G" hand pointing forward and move it forward in a circular motion, passing under the left arm.
Origin: Indicating the crawling movement.
Usage: bitten by a poisonous *snake*.

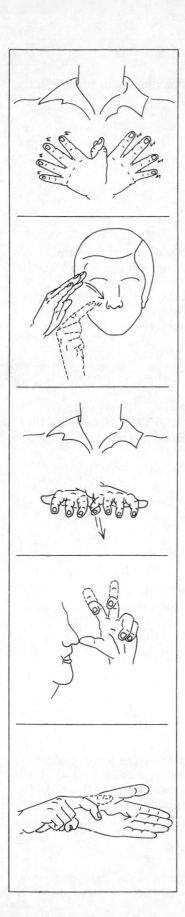

BUTTERFLY

Cross the "FIVE" hands in front of you, palms facing the body, and lock the thumbs; wiggle the fingers.
Origin: The fluttering wings of the butterfly.
Usage: a colorful *butterfly* among the flowers.

BEE

Place the tip of the right index finger against the cheek; then brush the open hand forward as if brushing off a bee.
Origin: Brushing a bee from the face.
Usage: a honey *bee.*

SPIDER

Cross the curved "FIVE" hands, palms facing down, and interlock the little fingers; wiggle the fingers to represent the legs of a spider.
Origin: Represents the spider legs crawling along.
Usage: "Along came a *spider* and sat down beside her."

BUGS, ANTS

Place the thumb of the "THREE" hand on the nose and crook the index and middle fingers.
Usage: afraid of *bugs;* millions of busy *ants.*

WORM

Place the right index finger on the left palm and wiggle it as it moves forward.
Origin: Represents the worm crawling.
Usage: a can of *worms.*

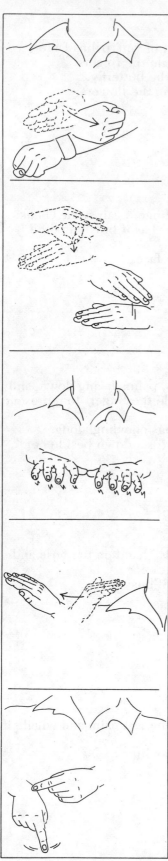

FLY

Use the right hand to catch an imaginary fly on the left forearm.
Usage: that awful *fly*.

MOSQUITO

Touch the back of the left hand with the tips of the thumb and index (in the "NINE" position); then slap the hand.
Origin: Indicating the bite and the killing of the mosquito.
Usage: many *mosquitoes* near the water.

INSECT

Touch the thumbtips of the bent "FIVE" hands together, palms down; wiggle the bent fingers, working them like a crawling insect.
Origin: The movement of the crawling insect.
Usage: afraid of all *insects*.

WINGS

Place the fingertips of the right hand on the right shoulder, draw them away and then turn the hands so the fingertips point away from the body.
Origin: Wings extending from the shoulder.
Usage: large *wings* of an eagle.

TAIL

Place the tip of the left index at the right wrist; right index swings below.
Origin: Showing the shape and movement of the tail.
Usage: The dog's *tail* was wagging.

24

Religion

Signs used in the religious context often vary in different churches. This is perfectly acceptable but it is important for the signer to know and to use those signs that are known to the congregation and accepted and understood by them. It should be noted that certain religious signs have theological implications associated with particular churches. An example is the word *baptize*, in which the choice of sign itself indicates whether immersion or sprinkling is meant. While Catholics and Protestants sign *Bible* as "JESUS" + "BOOK," Jews either spell the word or sign "GOD's" "BOOK" or "HOLY" "BOOK."

CATHOLIC

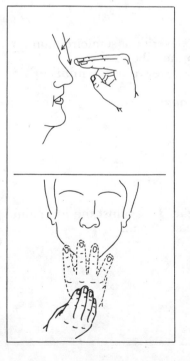

Using the "N" hand, palm toward the face, describe a cross in front of the face.
Origin: The cross made in front of the face, almost as if crossing oneself.
Usage: The *Catholic* Church has many priests who can sign.

JEWISH

Place all the fingers on the chin, palm facing you, and draw down, ending with all the fingertips together.
Origin: Representing the chin whiskers.
Usage: The *Jewish* family celebrated Passover.

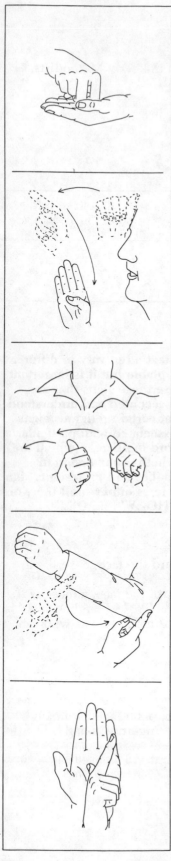

PROTESTANT

Make the sign for "KNEEL."
Origin: Representing the Protestant in the act of kneeling.
Usage: He attends one of the *Protestant* churches in our city.

ASSEMBLIES OF GOD

Place the right "A" on the forehead, palm facing left; then sign "GOD."
Usage: an *Assemblies of God* publication.

BAPTIST

Move both "A" hands to the right and down in the motion of baptism.
Origin: Baptism by immersion.
Usage: a good *Baptist* preacher.

EPISCOPAL

Using the right index finger, describe a semicircle under the left arm from the wrist to the elbow.
Origin: Represents the flowing sleeve of the minister's robe.
Usage: Rev. Berg is an *Episcopal* priest.

LUTHERAN

Place the thumbtip of the right "L" against the left palm.
Usage: *Lutheran* services are at 10 a.m.

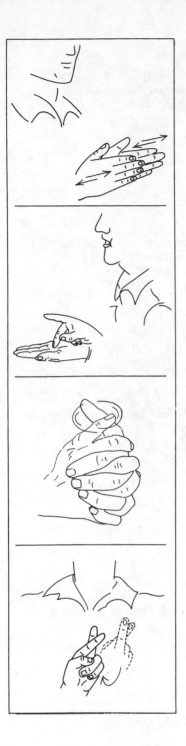

METHODIST

Rub the palms together, as in the sign for
"ENTHUSIASM."
Origin: Represents the fervor of the early Methodists.
Usage: an old *Methodist* hymnal.

PRESBYTERIAN

Place the middle fingertip of the right "P" in the left
palm.
Usage: a *Presbyterian* Sunday school class.

QUAKER

Clasp the hands, interlacing the fingers, and let the
thumbs revolve around each other.
Origin: Reputedly from the fact that the Quakers twiddle
their thumbs while waiting for the moving of the Spirit.
Usage: the gentle, friendly *Quaker* people.

RELIGION

Place the right "R" at the heart and draw it forward, palm
facing out.
Origin: Pointing to the heart where religious feelings
originate.
Usage: People sing about the old-time *religion*.

OTHER RELIGIOUS GROUPS

Some of the other religious groups use their initial letters
such as, S.D.A. for Seventh Day Adventists and L.D.S. for
Latter Day Saints. Other names of religious groups may
be signed literally, using the standard sign for each word.
Examples are: Church of Christ, Church of God.

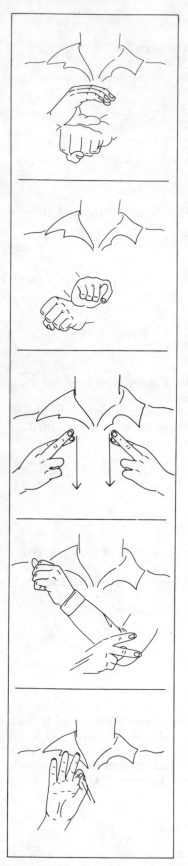

CHURCH

Place the right "C" on the back of the left "S" hand.
Origin: The church shown as being on a rock.
Usage: Europe has many old *churches*.

TEMPLE

Place the right "T" on the back of the left "S" hand.
Usage: The *temple* was in Jerusalem.

RABBI

Place the tips of the "R" hands just below the shoulder
and draw them down the chest.
Origin: Indicating the ecclesiastical stole.
Usage: A *rabbi* teaches the Jewish law.

PASSOVER

Strike the right "P" against the left arm near the elbow.
Origin: The sign for "cracker" made with the initial "P."
Usage: The *Passover* is an annual feast of the Jews.

PREACH, PREACHER, MINISTER, PASTOR

Hold the "F" hand in front of you and move it forward
and backward several times. For preacher, minister, and
pastor, add the "PERSON" ending.
Origin: "F" for "friars" combined with the sign for
lecturing.
Usage: practice what you *preach;* the *minister* of our
church; a famous *preacher;* our good *pastor*.

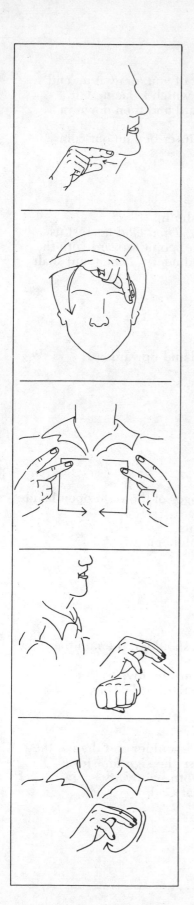

PRIEST, CLERGY, CHAPLAIN, MINISTER

Trace a collar from the center of the neck to the sides, using the right thumb and index fingers spread about an inch apart.
Origin: priestly collar.
Usage: the *priest* will perform the wedding; member of the *clergy*, our hospital *chaplain*; Episcopalian *minister*.

NUN

Use the right "N" to trace the outline of the face (up the left side, across the forehead, and down the right side).
Origin: Indicating the veil.
Usage: a *nun* in the Catholic school.

PRIEST (Old Testament)

Using the "P" fingers, trace the form of the breastplate worn by the priests of the Old Testament.
Usage: Melchizedek was called a *priest* of the Most High God. Old Testament *priests* offered sacrifices.

MINISTRY

Strike the wrist of the right "M" on the wrist of the left hand.
Origin: The sign for "work" made with an "M."
Usage: One of the *ministries* of the Church is to the elderly.

MISSION, MISSIONARY

Describe a circle over the heart with the right "M" hand, fingers pointing left. For "MISSIONARY" add the "PERSON" ending.
Usage: Is your church interested in overseas *missions?* The apostle Paul became a *missionary*.

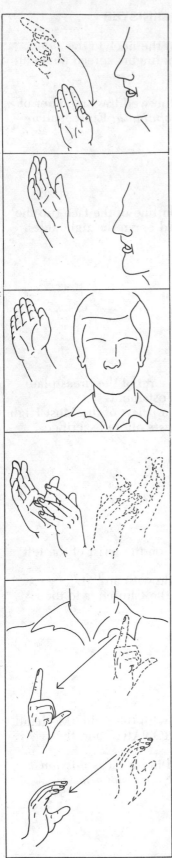

GOD

Point the "G" forward in front of you, draw it up and back down, opening the palm which is facing left.
Origin: Hand raised heavenward and then down in a reverent motion.
Usage: "In *God* We Trust" is inscribed on our coins.

THEE, THOU

Lift the open hand upward, palm in.
Usage: We give *Thee* the glory. *Thou* God hearest us.
Note: When referring to people, point forward with the index finger as in the commandment: "*Thou* [you] shalt not steal."

THINE (Deity)

Direct the open palm outward and upward.
Usage: "*Thine* is the kingdom."

JESUS

Place the tip of the middle finger of the right open hand into the left palm and reverse.
Origin: Indicating the nailprints.
Usage: *Jesus* was born in Bethlehem.

LORD

Place the right "L" at the left shoulder, then on the right waist.
Origin: Indicating the stole worn by royalty.
Usage: Sunday is often called the *Lord's* Day.

CHRIST

Place the right "C" at the left shoulder and then at the right waist. (Some prefer to use the sign for "Jesus.")
Origin: Indicating the stole worn by royalty.
Usage: Jesus *Christ*, the Son of God.

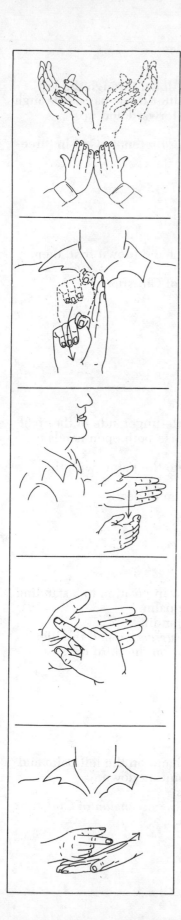

BIBLE

Sign "JESUS" + "BOOK." Alternatives are to fingerspell the word or to sign "GOD'S BOOK" or "HOLY BOOK."
Usage: The *Bible* contains words of wisdom.

TESTAMENT

Hold up the left open hand, palm facing right; place the side of the right "T" against the left palm twice, the second time slightly lower than the first.
Origin: The sign for "commandment" formed with a "T."
Usage: The Old and the New *Testaments*.

CHAPTER

Place the left hand in front of you, tips pointing forward; draw the right "C" down across the left palm.
Origin: Showing a lengthy passage.
Usage: He read several *chapters* in the Bible every day.

VERSE

With the thumb and index fingers about an inch apart (other fingers closed) draw them across the left open palm from left to right.
Origin: A short portion, as indicated by the space between the two fingers.
Usage: chapter 3, *verse* 16.

GOSPEL

Brush the little-finger side of the "G" hand across the heel of the left hand from right to left.
Origin: The gospel means good news and this sign represents the sign for "news" made with a "G."
Usage: He preached the *gospel*.

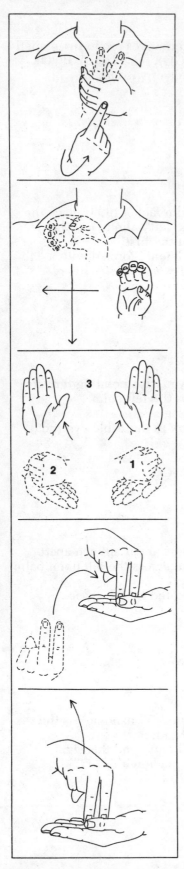

TRINITY

Draw the right "THREE" hand down through the left "C," changing it into a "ONE" after it has passed through the left hand; bring the "ONE" forward and up.
Origin: Three in one.
Usage: The doctrine of the *Trinity* refers to God in three Persons.

CROSS

Draw a cross with the right "C" hand (down first, then across).
Usage: The *cross* is the symbol of Christianity.

CRUCIFY

Strike the left palm with the little-finger side of the right "S"; repeat in the right hand; raise both open hands to the sides.
Origin: Hammering the nails into the palms with the hands raised as on a cross.
Usage: *Crucifixion* is a cruel form of death.

RESURRECTION

Raise the right "V" from a palm-up position to a standing position and place it on the left palm.
Origin: Lying down and then standing up.
Usage: Jesus said, "I am the *resurrection* and the life." Jesus *rose* from the dead on the third day.

ASCENSION

Place the tips of the right "V" hand on the left palm and raise the right "V," tips still pointing down.
Origin: Rising into the heavens.
Usage: The church celebrated the *ascension* of Christ. He *ascended* to heaven.

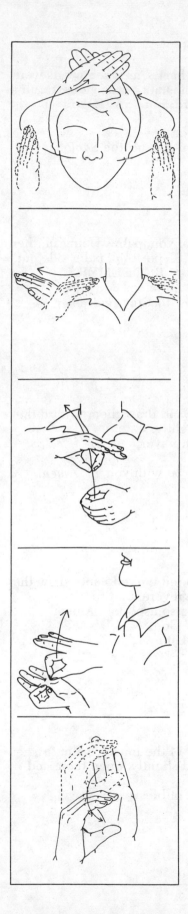

HEAVEN, CELESTIAL

Using both open hands, palms facing in, bring them around in a circle toward you and then pass the right open hand under the left and up. This sign is made slightly above eye level.

Usage: "Our Father, who art in *heaven* ...."
The choir sang about the *celestial* city.

ANGEL, CHERUBIM, SERAPHIM

Place the fingertips on the shoulders and draw the hands away so the fingertips point away from the body.

Origin: Indicating angel wings.

Usage: Isaiah saw a vision of *angels*.

SOUL

Place the thumb and index fingertips of the right "F" hand into the left "O," which is close to the body, and draw the right hand upward. Note: Some show no difference between the signs for "soul" and "spirit."

Usage: "Breathes there a man with *soul* so dead, who never to himself has said, 'This is my own, my native land'" (Scott).

SPIRIT, GHOST

The right palm is above and facing the left palm with fingers spread; as the right hand moves up, the index and thumbtips of both hands close.

Usage: "The *spirit* shall return unto God who gave it" (Ecclesiastes 12:7).
Believing in the Father, Son, and Holy *Ghost*.

COMMANDMENTS

Hold up the left open hand, palm facing right; place the side of the right "C" against the left palm twice, the second time slightly lower than the first.

Origin: The left hand represents the tablet on which the commandments were written.

Usage: The Ten *Commandments* are also called the Decalogue.

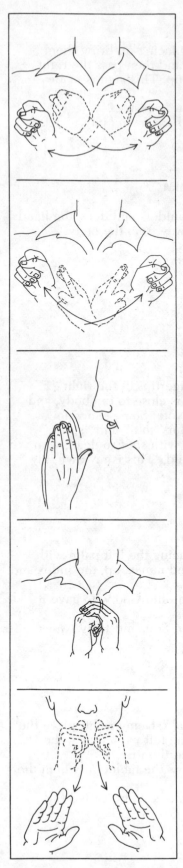

SALVATION, SAVE, SAVIOUR

Cross the wrists with the "S" hands, as if the wrists were bound; then bring the "S" hands out to the sides, turning them so they are facing forward. For "SAVIOUR" add the "PERSON" ending.
Origin: Bound and then set free.
Usage: the *salvation* of the soul; Jesus, the *Saviour*.

REDEEM

Cross the "R" hands in front of you, palms facing in; then draw them to the sides in an "S" position, palm side out. Add the "PERSON" ending for "REDEEMER."
Origin: The sign for "save" is initialed.
Usage: Our choir sang, "I know that my *Redeemer* liveth."

PRAY, AMEN

Place the hands palm to palm and draw them toward the body as the head is bowed slightly.
Origin: Hands in a position of prayer.
Usage: Let us *pray*.
May the God of peace be with you all. *Amen*.

WORSHIP, ADORE

Place the right "A" inside the left curved hand; draw the hands up and toward you in a reverent attitude.
Note: This sign is sometimes also used for "Amen."
Usage: The people *worshiped* God.
"O come let us *adore* Him . . . ."

BLESS

Place both "A" hands in front of the mouth, palm to palm; bring the hands forward slightly, open them and bring them down.
Origin: Hands move in an act of blessing.
Usage: God *bless* you.

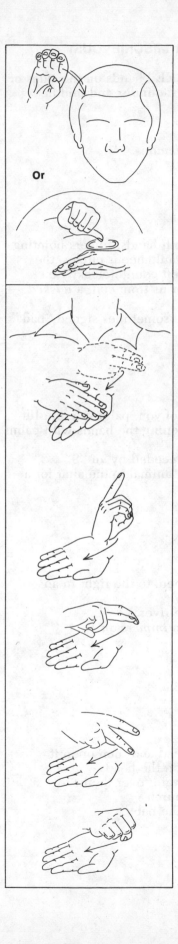

ANOINT

Using the right "C" hand, make a pouring motion over the head. Or, use the thumb of the right "A" hand, pointing downward, to make a counterclockwise circle above the back of the left to show a pouring motion.
Usage: "Thou *anointest* my head with oil . . . ." (Psalm 23:5).

HOLY, HALLOWED

Make an "H" and pass the right palm across the left palm.
Origin: "H" + "CLEAN."
Usage: We visited the *Holy* Land. "*Hallowed* be Thy name . . . ."
Note: With this group of words, some prefer to continue the initial letter across the palm instead of changing to the sign for clean.

DIVINE

Sign "D" + "CLEAN."
Usage: "To err is human, to forgive *divine*" (Alexander Pope).

RIGHTEOUS

Sign "R" + "CLEAN."
Usage: a truly *righteous* man.

PURE

Sign "P" + "CLEAN."
Usage: "Blessed are the *pure* in heart . . . ."

SANCTIFY

Sign "S" + "CLEAN."
Usage: "The very God of peace *sanctify* you" (1 Thessalonians 5:23).

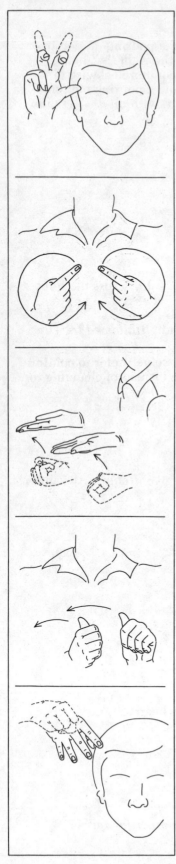

DEVIL, DEMON (Used also for MISCHIEVOUS)

Place the thumbs of the "THREE" hands on the sides of the temple; bend and unbend the index and middle fingers several times.
Origin: The horns of the devil.
Usage: a real *devil*.
      dreamed about green *demons*.
      a boy full of *mischief*.

SIN, EVIL, WICKED

Using the index position on both hands, fingers pointing toward each other, describe simultaneous circles, the right hand clockwise and the left counterclockwise.
Usage: forgive our *sins*; deliver us from *evil*; a *wicked* man.
Note: "Evil" and "wicked" are sometimes signed "bad."

SACRIFICE

Place both "S" hands in front of you, palm side up; lift both hands up and forward opening the hands with palms up.
Origin: The sign for "offer" preceded by an "S."
Usage: The people brought an animal to the altar for a *sacrifice*.

BAPTISM, IMMERSION

Using both "A" hands move them to the right in an imaginary motion of baptizing.
Usage: He was *baptized* in the river.
      This church believes in *immersion*.

BAPTIZE, CHRISTEN

Hold the "S" hand over the head and then open it quickly as if sprinkling water on the head.
Origin: The act of sprinkling water over the head.
Usage: *baptized* in a formal church.
      The priest *christened* the baby.

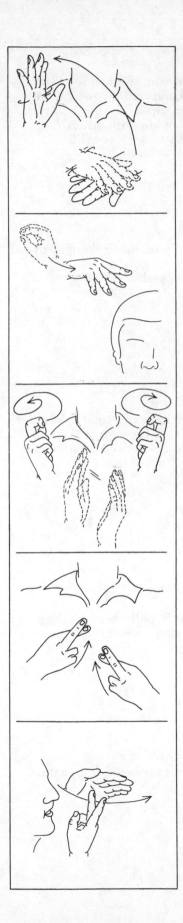

GLORY

Clap the right hand against the left, lift the right and describe a large arc in front of you with the right hand, shaking the hand as it moves.
Origin: Indicates shining splendor.
Usage: *"Glory* to God in the highest...." (Luke 2:14).

GRACE

Hold the "AND" hand over the head, bring it down and open it over the head, palm facing down. This sign is sometimes made over the heart.
Origin: Coming from above down to people.
Usage: May the *grace* of God be with you.

HALLELUJAH

Clap the hands once and then sign "CELEBRATION."
Usage: Our choir sang the *"Hallelujah* Chorus" from Handel's *Messiah.*

REVIVAL

Move the tips of the "R" hands alternately up the chest.
Origin: Feelings are stirred, as in "excite."
Usage: We are planning for some *revival* meetings.
Note: "Revive" may be signed "inspire," as in the song: *"Revive* us again, fill each heart with thy love...."

VISION

Make the sign for "SEE" and let it pass forward under the left hand which is in a palm-down position.
Origin: Seeing something not actually present; therefore, the sign is made under the left hand.
Usage: a *vision* of heaven.

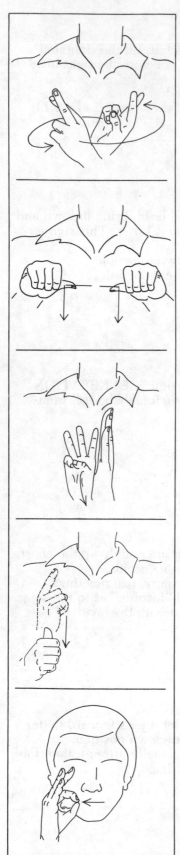

REPENT

Place the "R" hands in front of you, the inside of the wrists touching and the right hand on top; twist them around until the left hand is on top.
Origin: The sign for "change" made with an "R."
Usage: The man *repented* and started a new life.

ALTAR

Place the "A" hands in front of you, move them apart and down.
Origin: Indicates the shape of the altar.
Usage: the *altar* of the church.

WILL (God's)

Hold up the left open hand, palm facing right; place the side of the right "W" against the left palm.
Note: Some prefer to substitute desire, decision, or law for "will" in this context.
Usage: "Thy *will* be done."

TITHE

Sign "ONE"; lower the hand and sign "TEN."
Origin: A tithe is 1/10.
Usage: The people in this church believe in giving a *tithe* of their earnings every week.

FAST

Draw the right "F" across the lips.
Origin: The lips are sealed and prevented from eating.
Usage: a 3-day *fast*.

NAMES OF BIBLICAL CHARACTERS

For the most part, names of people in the Bible are fingerspelled. However, some of the more commonly known characters have been given sign names such as those listed below. If the name of a particular person is used repeatedly in a sermon, and no standard sign has been assigned, it is suggested that a sign name be created and used for that occasion. An example would be Nebuchadnezzar. This would be spelled out the first time it is used and after that the "KING" sign could be initialed with an "N," since he was a king and this is the first letter of his name. This principle is also followed for David.

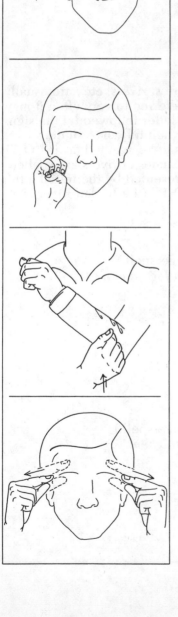

ADAM

Place the "A" hand at the side of the forehead.
Origin: An initial sign at the location of the "male" sign.
Usage: *Adam* was the first man.

EVE

Place the "E" hand at the side of the chin.
Origin: An initial sign at the chin indicating the female.
Usage: *Eve* was the first woman.

ABRAHAM

Hold the left arm up with the hand near the right shoulder; strike the arm near the elbow with the right "A" hand.
Usage: *Abraham* is called the father of the Jewish people.

MOSES

Place the thumb and index finger (slightly separated) at the sides of the temple, draw them away and close them.
Usage: *Moses* was the author of the first five Books of the Bible.

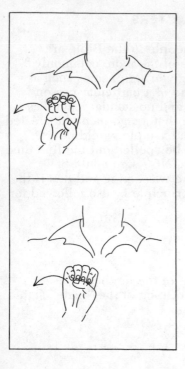

CHRISTMAS

Describe an arc in front of you, using the right "C" hand. Or, place the "C" at the chin (palm in) and move it out-down-in to show the beard of Santa Claus. This sign is also used for Santa Claus.
Usage: Everyone wished for a white *Christmas*.

EASTER

Describe an arc in front of you, using the right "E" hand. Other signs are used to represent Easter, such as: rabbit, egg, and resurrection.
Usage: *Easter* is an annual church celebration commemorating Christ's resurrection.

NAMES OF PLACES

Names of places (cities, countries, rivers, etc.) are usually fingerspelled, but if a city is referred to very often it may be signed by using the initial letter followed by the sign for "CITY." This is especially helpful when signing music, where fingerspelling is to be avoided (as in "O Little Town of Bethlehem"). Names of rivers are spelled but in music they may be represented by the initial letter followed by the sign for "RIVER" (the Jordan River is an example).

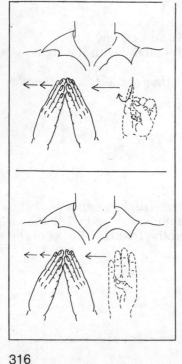

JERUSALEM

Sign "J" and "CITY." (Or, fingerspell.)
Usage: The Wailing Wall is in *Jerusalem*.

BETHLEHEM

Sign "B" and "CITY." (Or, fingerspell.)
Usage: Many tourists visit *Bethlehem*.

ADDITIONAL WORDS USED IN THE RELIGIOUS SETTING

The following words used in religious settings do not have specific signs but suggestions are made here for substitutions or combinations of standard signs.

Atonement. Use the "A" as in "anoint" (pouring over the left hand).

Calvary.
"MOUNTAIN"
+
"CROSS"

Christian.
"JESUS" or "CHRIST"
+
"PERSON" ending

Collection.
"MONEY"
+
"COLLECTION"

Communion (Lord's Supper).
"WINE"
+
"BREAD"

Condemn. Fingerspell or spell "JUDGE."

Consecrate. The sign most appropriate for the intended meaning should be used: 1) make holy; 2) presented; or, 3) offered to God.

Conviction. "CONSCIENCE."

Covenant. "AGREEMENT" or "PROMISE."

Create. "MAKE," or use the "C" hands to sign "MAKE."

Deacon. Sign "MEMBER" using "D" hands.

Dedicate. Sign "OFFER" or precede it with a "D."

Denomination. "CHURCH" or "RELIGION."

Disciple or Apostle. "FOLLOWER"; "12 FOLLOWERS"; or "FOLLOW" made with "D" hands.

Doctrine. "TEACH."

Father. The sign for "Heavenly Father" is made with two hands.

Flesh. "BODY."

Hail. "HONOR" or "CELEBRATE."

Hell. Spell or point downward and sign "FIRE."

Hymnal.
"SONG"
+
"BOOK"

Master.
"M"
+
"OVER"
+
"PERSON" ending.

Messiah. Spell or use the "M" as in the "KING" sign.

Miracle.
"WONDERFUL"
+
"WORK"

Nature (of a person). "N" over the heart.

Omnipotent.
"ALL"
+
"POWER"

Omnipresent.
"EVERY"
+
"WHERE"

Omniscient.
"ALL"
+
"KNOWLEDGE"
or
"KNOW"
+
"EVERYTHING"

Parable. "STORY."

Service (a church service). "MEETING" or "SERVE."

Supplication. Lift the sign for "BEG."

Thanksgiving.
"TURKEY" or "THANKS"
+
"GIVING"

Trespass.
"BREAK"
+
"LAW"

Verily. "TRULY" (sign "TRUE").

25
Numbers

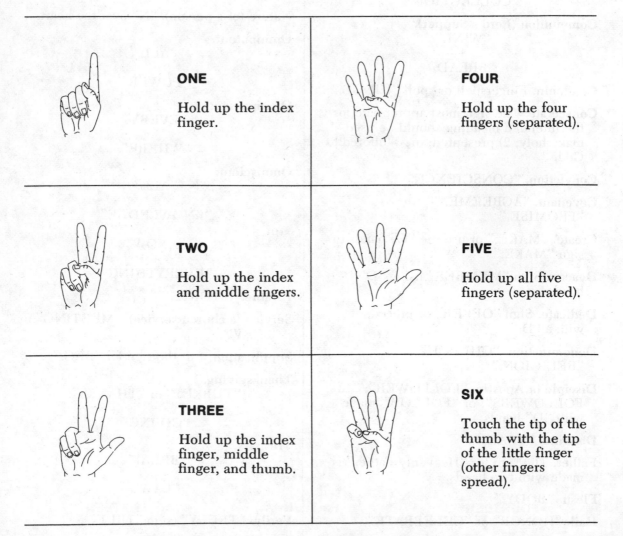

ONE

Hold up the index finger.

TWO

Hold up the index and middle fingers.

THREE

Hold up the index finger, middle finger, and thumb.

FOUR

Hold up the four fingers (separated).

FIVE

Hold up all five fingers (separated).

SIX

Touch the tip of the thumb with the tip of the little finger (other fingers spread).

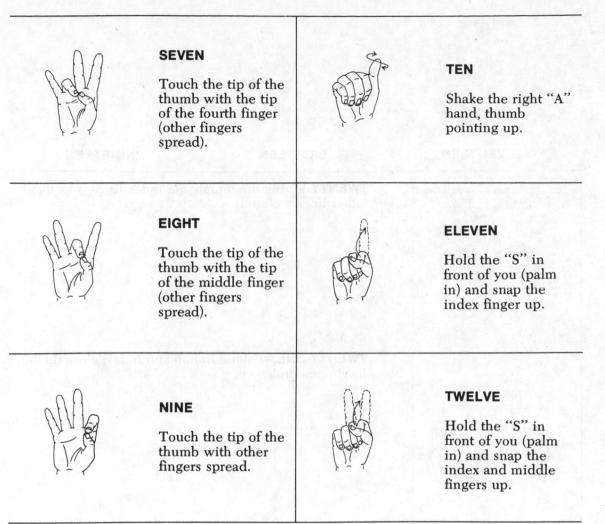

SEVEN

Touch the tip of the thumb with the tip of the fourth finger (other fingers spread).

TEN

Shake the right "A" hand, thumb pointing up.

EIGHT

Touch the tip of the thumb with the tip of the middle finger (other fingers spread).

ELEVEN

Hold the "S" in front of you (palm in) and snap the index finger up.

NINE

Touch the tip of the thumb with other fingers spread.

TWELVE

Hold the "S" in front of you (palm in) and snap the index and middle fingers up.

THIRTEEN—Sign "TEN" (palm in) and "THREE" (palm out).
Note: Follow this pattern for numbers 13 through 19.

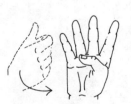

FOURTEEN

FIFTEEN

SIXTEEN

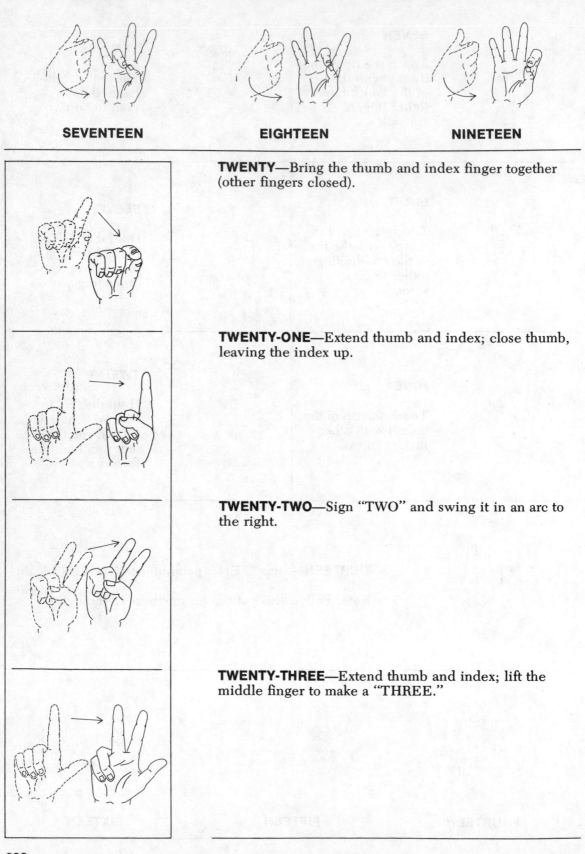

SEVENTEEN　　　**EIGHTEEN**　　　**NINETEEN**

TWENTY—Bring the thumb and index finger together (other fingers closed).

TWENTY-ONE—Extend thumb and index; close thumb, leaving the index up.

TWENTY-TWO—Sign "TWO" and swing it in an arc to the right.

TWENTY-THREE—Extend thumb and index; lift the middle finger to make a "THREE."

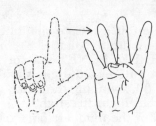 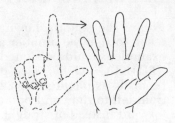 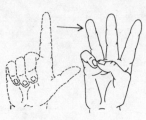

TWENTY-FOUR   **TWENTY-FIVE**   **TWENTY-SIX**

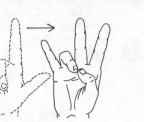 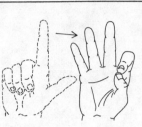

TWENTY-SEVEN   **TWENTY-EIGHT**   **TWENTY-NINE**

THIRTY

Sign "THREE"; then form an "O" with the three fingers.

THIRTY-THREE

Sign "THREE" and swing it in an arc to the right.

THIRTY-ONE

Sign "THREE"; move slightly to the right and sign "ONE."

THIRTY-FOUR

Sign "THREE"; move slightly to the right and sign "FOUR."

THIRTY-TWO

Sign "THREE"; move slightly to the right and sign "TWO."

THIRTY-FIVE

Sign "THREE"; move slightly to the right and sign "FIVE."

THIRTY-FIVE TO NINETY-NINE

Follow the pattern shown for the thirties. Care should be taken to sign the number as it is written. Number 31, for example, should be signed "THREE" "ONE" and not "THIRTY" "ONE," (see picture). Repeated digits should be made as pictured for 22 and 33, swinging the hand from left to right and pointing the fingertips slightly forward instead of straight up. For the numbers 66; 77; 88; and 99 the thumb separates slightly from the finger before making the second digit.

Special care should be taken with double digits that combine any two numbers between six and nine. When the smaller digit is first, the hand moves in a small arc to the left; when the larger digit is first, the hand moves in a small arc to the right. The following numbers move from right to left: 67; 68; 69; 78; 79; 89. Moving from left to right are: 76; 87; 96; 97; 98.

ONE HUNDRED

Sign "ONE" and "C." (Represents the Roman numeral.) Combine this with any of the preceding numbers to form any combination in the hundreds.
Try these numbers: 416; 897; 852; 639; 225; 712; 150; 365; 367; 296; 828; 911; 705; 113; 125.

THOUSAND

Place the "M" tips in the left palm. (Represents the Roman numeral.)
Try the following combinations: 1,723; 8,116; 3,578; 9,693; 5,500; 6,892; 2,319; 4,225; 7,309; 6,111; 17,300; 60,789.

MILLION

Strike the "M" tips into the left palm twice. (Represents 1,000 thousand.)
Try the following combinations: 1,500,000; 8,231,000; 2,670,000; 7,486,105; 50,625,000; 500,000,000.

MONEY

DOLLARS—The number may be followed by the sign for "DOLLAR," as described in a previous chapter.
However, there is a shortcut that is commonly used from $1 to $9. Hold up the number, palm forward, and turn it from the wrist, swinging downward and up to a palm-in position.
Examples of this shortcut are pictured here:

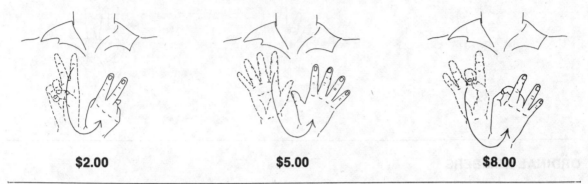

| $2.00 | $5.00 | $8.00 |

CENTS—Touch the forehead with the index finger and follow with the number.

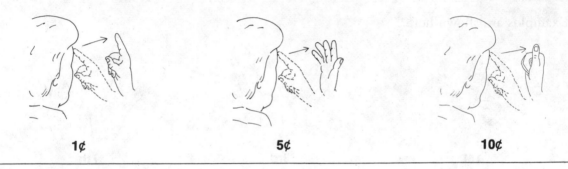

| 1¢ | 5¢ | 10¢ |

ADDRESSES

Addresses are signed as they are spoken:
145 Blair Road is signed 1-4-5 B-l-a-i-r R-o-a-d.
1600 Pennsylvania Ave. is signed "16" "C" P-a. A-v-e.

TELEPHONE NUMBERS

Phone numbers are signed as they are spoken, with seven separate digits.
Try a few. 447-0837; 524-8162; 352-9719; 624-9176; 621-8969.

YEARS

Years are signed as they are spoken. For instance, 1865 is signed: "18" "65."
Try a few: 1800 ("18" "C"); 1492; 1776; 1963; 1980.

FRACTIONS

Sign the numerator, then lower the hand slightly and sign the denominator.

Here are examples:

½   ¾   ⅔

ORDINAL NUMBERS

Signs for "FIRST" to "NINTH" are made by forming the cardinal number with the palm forward and then giving the hand a quick twist inward.

Examples are shown here.

1st   3rd   7th

In the case of TENTH and other higher numbers having a "TH" ending, the ordinal number is made first and the letters "T" and "H" are added.

Usage: *first* child; *second* row; *third* seat; 25*th* anniversary.

Suggested References

To provide the student of signs with a variety of background information related to deafness and the language of deaf people, the following publications have been selected from an extensive list of resource materials. Complete publication lists are available from organizations serving deaf people, and local libraries will also have references for the interested reader.

Deafness

Bender, Ruth E. *The Conquest of Deafness.* Cleveland: Western Reserve Univ., 1960.
The history of the education of the deaf from 1550 and on.

Crammatte, Alan B. *Deaf Persons in Professional Employment.* Washington, D.C.: Gallaudet College Press, 1968.
Interviews with 87 deaf professional workers regarding many aspects of their lives.

Fine, Peter J., ed. *Deafness in Infancy and Early Childhood.* New York: Medcom Press, 1974.
Information on the psychological, social, educational, and medical aspects of deafness in the young.

Furth, Hans G. *Deafness and Learning: A Psychosocial Approach.* Belmont, Calif.: Wadsworth Publishing Co., 1973.
Provides a solid theoretical foundation from which a more technical treatment of education of the deaf can follow.

Greenberg, Joanne. *In This Sign.* New York: Holt, Rinehart and Winston, 1970.
The story of a deaf couple's life and their hearing children at the turn of the century.

Jacobs, Leo M. *A Deaf Adult Speaks Out.* Washington, D.C.: Gallaudet College Press, 1974.
A deaf man's honest account of the world of deaf adults.

Katz, L.; Mathis, S. L.; and Merrill, E. C. *The Deaf Child in the Public Schools.* Danville, Ill.: The Interstate Printers and Publishers, Inc., 1974.
Questions on deafness and the deaf and educational planning for deaf children in public schools.

Levine, Edna S. *Lisa and Her Soundless World.* New York: Human Sciences Press, 1974.
The story of an 8-year-old deaf child, written to create understanding attitudes toward the deaf at the child's level.

Mindel, E. D., and Vernon, M. *They Grow in Silence.* Silver Spring, Maryland: National Assoc. of the Deaf, 1971.
An informative manual providing insights on the deaf child and his family.

Northern, J. L., and Downs, M. P. *Hearing in Children.* Baltimore, Md.: Williams and Wilkins Co., 1974.
A comprehensive text on the audiological problems of children providing information for the physician, audiologist, and educator.

O'Rourke, T. J., ed. *Psycholinguistics and Total Communication: The State of the Art.* Washington, D.C.: American Annals of the Deaf, 1972.

Parsons, Francis M. *Sound of the Stars.* New York: Vantage Press, 1971.
The diary of two teenage deaf girls' experiences growing up in Tahiti.

Schein, J. D., and Delk, M. T., Jr. *The Deaf Population in the United States.* Silver Spring, Maryland: National Assoc. of the Deaf, 1974.
The first national study of the numbers and characteristics of deaf people in 40 years (a census study).

Schlesinger, H. S., and Meadow, K. P. *Sound and Sign: Childhood Deafness and Mental Health.* Berkeley, Calif.: Univ. of California Press, 1972.
Covers the controversy over the "either-or" question and proposes a combination program.

Spradley, Thomas S., Spradley, James P. *Deaf Like Me.* New York: Random House, 1978.
A heartwarming, inspiring story of a family trying to reach across the barrier of silence.

Tidyman, Ernest. *Dummy.* Boston: Little, Brown & Co., 1974.
The true story of a young deaf black man who is without any means of communication and on trial for murder.

Illustrated Sign Language Dictionaries

(Depicting signs that are used by the adult deaf population.)

Fant, Lou J. *Say It With Hands.* Washington, D.C.: Gallaudet College Press, 1964.
A series of 46 lessons in signs containing line drawings.

O'Rourke, T. J. *A Basic Course in Manual Communication.* Silver Spring, Maryland: National Assoc. of the Deaf, 1970.
Line drawings of signs prepared for use by the Communicative Skills Program of the National Association of the Deaf.

O'Rourke, T. J. *A Basic Vocabulary of American Sign Language for Parents and Children.* Silver Spring, Maryland: National Association of the Deaf, 1977.
A basic vocabulary of signs prepared especially for parents and young children.

Riekehof, Lottie L. *Talk to the Deaf.* Springfield, Mo.: Gospel Publishing House, 1963.
Line drawings, full explanations of signs, and origins (arranged in categories according to meaning).

Watson, David O. *Talk With Your Hands*, Volumes I and II. Winneconne, Wisconsin: David O. Watson, 1973.
Line drawings with partial explanations of signs. Grouped in natural categories.

American Sign Language (Ameslan or ASL)

(Manuals describing ASL signs and word order.)

Fant, L. J. Ameslan, *An Introduction to American Sign Language.* Silver Spring, Maryland: National Assoc. of the Deaf, 1972.

Fant, L. J. *Sign Language.* Northridge, California: Joyce Motion Picture Co., 1977.
American Sign Language illustrated with large photographs with directions on communicating effectively in Ameslan.

Hoemann, H. W. *The American Sign Language:* Lexical and grammatical notes with translation exercises. Silver Spring, Maryland: National Association of the Deaf, 1975.

Madsen, W. J. *Conversational Sign Language II; An Intermediate-Advanced Manual.* Washington, D.C.: Gallaudet College Press, 1972.

Babbini, Barbara E. *Manual Communication; Fingerspelling and the Language of Signs.* Urbana, Ill.: Univ. of Illinois Press, 1974.
(Separate manuals for students and for instructors.) Contains a section on ASL usage.

Signed English for Educational Settings

Bornstein, Harry, et al. *The Signed English Dictionary.* Washington, D.C.: Gallaudet College Press, 1975.
A dictionary of signs to meet the language needs of elementary levels of education and preschool based on traditional American signs.

Gustason, G., et al. *Signing Exact English.* Rassmoor, Calif.: Modern Signs Press, 1975.
An alphabetically arranged listing of signs prepared for use in educational settings.

Kannapell, B. M., et al. *Signs for Instructional Purposes.* Washington, D.C.: Gallaudet College Press, 1969.
Depicts new signs for vocabulary used on the secondary and post-secondary levels of instruction. Arranged by subject.

Fingerspelling

Guillory, L. M. *Expressive and Receptive Fingerspelling for Hearing Adults.* Baton Rouge, La.: Claitor's Book Store, 1966.
Learning to fingerspell phonetic elements found in the English language instead of learning individual letters.

Interpreting

Quigley, S P., ed. *Interpreting for Deaf People.* Washington, D.C.: U.S. Dept. of Health, Education and Welfare, 1965.
Reprinted by National Association of the Deaf, Silver Spring, Maryland.

Signing in the Religious Setting

Bearden, Carter E. *A Handbook for Religious Interpreters for the Deaf.* Atlanta, Ga.: Home Mission Board of the Southern Baptist Convention, 1975.
A manual providing basic instructions for the worker in a church ministry. Helps for both the experienced and the inexperienced interpreter.

Bearden, Carter E., and Potter, Jerry F. *A Manual of Religious Signs.* Atlanta, Ga.: Home Missions Board of the Southern Baptist Convention, 1973.
An illustrated manual of religious signs including some innovations.

Lawrence, Edgar D. *Sign Language Made Simple.* Springfield, Mo.: Gospel Publishing House, 1975.
Illustrated sentences signed in English word order.

Yount, William R. *Be Opened!* Nashville, Tennessee: Broadman Press, 1976.
Designed for the minister to the deaf, both the volunteer and the full-time worker. A useful, practical text for those interested in ministry with deaf people.

Interpreting Music

Gadlin, D.; Pokorny, D.; and Riekehof, L. *Lift Up Your Hands.* Washington, D.C.: The National Grange, 1976.
A collection of songs prepared with notes, chords, words, and illustrations of suggested signs.

Organizations Serving the Deaf

National Association of the Deaf (NAD), 814 Thayer Ave., Silver Spring, MD 20910 Publication: *The Deaf American*. Complete publication list available.

Convention of American Instructors of the Deaf (CAID), 5034 Wisconsin Ave., N.W., Washington, D.C. 20016. Publication: *American Annals of the Deaf* (directory issued in April).

The American Deafness and Rehabilitation Association (ADARA), 814 Thayer Ave., Silver Spring, MD 20910. Publication: *Journal of Rehabilitation of the Deaf*.

Registry of Interpreters for the Deaf (RID), P.O. Box 1339, Washington, D.C. 20013.

National Fraternal Society of the Deaf, 1300 W. Northwest Highway, Mt. Prospect, Illinois 60056.

International Association of Parents of the Deaf (IAPD), 814 Thayer Ave., Silver Spring, MD 20910. Publication list available.

Alexander Graham Bell Association for the Deaf, Inc. (AGB), 3417 Volta Place, N.W., Washington, D.C. 20007. Publication: *Volta Review*. Publication list available.

Gallaudet College, 7th and Florida, N.E., Washington, D.C. 20002. Publication: *Gallaudet Today*. Publication list available from college bookstore.

National Technical Institute for the Deaf, 1 Lomb Memorial Drive, Rochester, NY 14623. Publication: *NTID Focus*.

National Center for the Law and the Deaf, Gallaudet College, 7th and Florida, N.E., Washington, D.C. 20002.

Index